OTHER BOOKS BY BARBARA MOON

Workbook for Handbook to Joy-Filled Parenting

Joy-Filled Relationships

The Lost Dome of Atron-Book One

The Genesis of Atron-Book Two

The Redemption of Atron-Book Three

Jewels for My Journey

Jesus Never Fails

Workbook and Guide for Hinds' Feet on High Places

Leader's Guide for Hinds' Feet on High Places'

Workbook and Guide for The Rest of the Gospel

Leader's Guide for The Rest of the Gospel

The Craziosity Twins

Handbook to

Joy-Filled

Parenting

by

Barbara Moon

Table of Contents

DEDICATION

To whom else but Jim, Bob, Greg and Jodi could I dedicate this book? They are such examples of God's grace and work, and they have forgiven me for all my mistakes and blunders. Their lives, along with their families' lives, glorify their Heavenly Father far above the dreams and goals I had for them. Each one loves and serves God along with their spouses, Elizabeth, Amy, Chris and Rick. "No greater joy do I have than that of seeing my children walking in the truth." (III John 1:4) I will occasionally speak of and tell stories here about these, my children—and their children—Jake, Erica, Elysia; Aaron, Josh; Tyler, Kayli, Kori, Brenna; Connor and Ryan. These are truly my greatest blessings.

Barbara's grandchildren (2010)

THANKS

Thanks first go to Dr. E. James Wilder for his work developing the *Life Model* upon which part of this book is based. Thanks, also, Jim, for making the new brain research easily understandable so that the rest of us could use and apply it. Without your foundation and input, I could never have put this book together. Most of us would have drowned in the technical language for the brain research before gleaning much good from it.

Dr. Wilder spent years wading through thick, technical works by the principle authors and researchers of neurobiology such as Alan Schore, Ph.D., Daniel J. Siegel, M.D., and Daniel G Amen, M.D. Dr. Wilder reworded their technical and scientific findings into everyday language, while at the same time bridging the gap between their research and the Scriptures. He gives us a fresh new way to look at God's handiwork—the human brain—and brings hope for the next generation to be reared through joy-filled parenting. I have learned much from Dr. Wilder and am very grateful for his work to condense these new ideas into understandable concepts while interposing them with the old concepts of the Scriptures.

I also want to thank the people that helped me get the technical information into an even less technical form. Debbie Sellmann poked and prodded me until I was able to break the first few chapters into much smaller bites. My daughters-in-law, Chris and Amy made countless suggestions and my daughter, Jodi, passed me her ideas after she perused the manuscript with her young-mother friends in mind. Anne Bierling from Shepherds House in California read for correctness and clarity. My son, Jim, made suggestions for the layout and Greg consented to tell his teen-age story. And I could never do any book without my son, Bob, who patiently does all the designing. Thanks to all of you!

INTRODUCTION

Are you passionate about being a good parent? I was and I still am. At this writing, I have been a parent for 42 years and a grandparent for 16. Throughout those years, I have spent time with countless other children through church, school, babysitting, counseling and being a nanny. For years I have wanted to write a book on parenting because of the love and passion God put in my heart for children of all ages. I am glad that I waited until now to begin this project, because in the last few years, technology has increased to a point that researchers can now observe what is going on inside a living and operating brain.

"So," you might ask, "what does new brain technology and new research have to do with parenting?" "And," you might also be thinking, "why another book on parenting? Aren't there countless titles already published?" And yet another question: "Why another Christian book on parenting? Aren't there countless Christian titles already published?"

In this book, I want to answer these questions while I am talking to you, the parent. I want to focus on the benefits that come with understanding the new brain research and its tremendous impact on early childhood parenting, and how joy is God's basis for all of it. Understanding the new technology that allows doctors and researchers to actually see and document what is going on in the human brain as it develops in the first two to three years can greatly impact the way we rear our children. But some of you readers may not be interested at all about the whys of what this book is about. You may only want answers to a problem or a question. If you are looking for practical tips and suggestions, you can find them throughout the chapters, often divided by age groupings. Chapter Three contains the new information about the brain that is a bit technical. I hope you won't skip over that chapter which is foundational to the "whys," about the brain and go straight to the chapters on discipline and tips. I have worked very hard to entice you to read all, giving you a list of definitions and many illustrations and pictures.

Other readers may like to go deeper in understanding why I am saying some of the things I say. It might take some study to learn different terminology, but I assure you that it will be worth the effort. It is my deep desire for this to be a handbook that you can refer to over and over throughout your parenting years.

In addition to the new brain research, I also want to work from a model that can help bring new life into families and communities. *The Life Model, Living From the Heart that Jesus Gave You* was written and compiled by Dr. Wilder, Dr. James Friesan, Anne Bierling, Rick Koepcke, and Maribeth Poole. These writers/counselors from Shepherd's House counseling clinic in Pasadena, California have put together a practical model for developing healthy maturity, recovery from trauma and good skills for relating. The *Life Model* can help us understand the brain research and why it is important. We can see how many aspects of life fit together.

The way the *Life Model*, the Scriptures and the brain research merge will help us answer our second question above, "Why another book on parenting?" Most current books on parenting of infants do not even take the physical development of the brain into account, especially in the light of the new research and how Dr. Wilder associates it with the Biblical principles of joy and peace. One of the brain researchers, Dr. Daniel Siegel, has written a great book called, *Parenting from the Inside Out.* I highly recommend it, as he emphasizes one of my passions--the need for us parents to get help and healing for our own lacks in order that we may better impact the children we are influencing. Dr. Siegel says that making sense of our own childhood frees us from recreating negatives that happened to us and passing them on to our children. He says that we can carry issues into parenting that make us the source of impatience and irritability and thus hinder our very own desire to be a great parent. (Paraphrased, pp.1 and 26, *Parenting from the Inside Out.*) Dr. Siegel's emphasis goes along with Shepherd House's desire to help people recover from their own traumas and grow in maturity. This handbook will help you personally as a parent while emphasizing the Christian view of parenting and giving you useful and everyday practical tips.

To further answer the question above, I also see the need for another parenting book because I know how some of my own parenting ideas changed drastically after I understood the new research and how God designed the emotional part of the brain to function. Some aspects of discipline changed and changes in daily relating brought more joy, peace and love into my life.

As I journeyed along this new path, I saw the extreme importance of what parents do the first two years in setting physical pathways and patterns in the developing brain. Dr. Siegel says, "How we treat our children changes who they are and how they will develop. Parents are active sculptors of their children's growing brains." (p. 34, *Parenting from the Inside Out.*) I have a passion to help parents understand that importance, especially the parents of pre-born or newborn babies. With that passion I hope to deter parents away from some books and philosophies that, not only do not take into account how the brain functions, but even go so far as to advocate means of parenting that go against the way the infant's brain develops through joy. The opportunity is here today through this new research to build a new generation of joy-filled children and it would be foolish to ignore that information.

The third reason I see for another parenting book is that the findings from the new brain research, even though the scientists and doctors do not acknowledge God in their writings, point to Him as the Creator and Designer of the brain. He is the one to whom we must look for the best ways of parenting and the new research fits too well with Scripture to be ignored. Down through the years, parents have often taken God's principles by faith, and now that researchers can "see" the brain while it is alive and working, we can affirm that there are not only Spiritual and emotional reasons for certain parenting activities, there is also <u>physical</u> evidence. It is my desire to take both the scientific literature that Dr. Wilder has put it into laymen's terms, and *The Life Model* with its Biblical principles for relating, and focus this book on parenting in such a way that parents can give the best start possible to their newborns and thus prevent many of the problems that can occur later in life. I am passionate about prevention.

When prevention fails, psychologists, counselors, Christian teachers and many others from related disciplines have to work long hours to help us understand how events from childhood are affecting the present we now live in as adults. My hope and desire is that joy-filled parenting will be a huge step in preventing future problems. My hope is that this book will become a "handbook," one that you pick up often and refer to throughout all the stages of your child's life.

If you are reading a parenting book, it is probably because you desire deeply to do the best job possible under God. None of us can be a perfect parent, but as we follow His design from the Bible, and continue to work on our own maturity while weaving the brain research into our parenting skills, there will be prevention. And when we accept that we cannot be perfect, that acceptance will take much of the burden from our shoulders. If we could be perfect parents, then our children would not need Jesus

So, let's put the burden of child rearing where it belongs—in God's hands and see if we can shed some new light on an old subject. Let's discover what our part is and what part is His. Let's look at how parenting affects a child's rapidly developing brain in the first two-three years of life and how that development affects the future emotional, mental and even physical health of the child. And along the way, we will look at many practical tips for everyday parenting.

SECTION I -- FOUNDATIONS

CHAPTER ONE: MORE IS CAUGHT THAN TAUGHT

Goal: To Build a Strong, Healthy Family

INTRODUCTION

As I have already said, I am passionate about prevention. Being a counselor since 1980 and listening to many, many stories of people's pain and the damage that brings havoc to their lives has convinced me that prevention of problems in child rearing would save the world a ton of trouble. It seems to me that parents in general do not realize that what they do at birth, two, three and five affects how their children will be at twelve, fifteen, twenty and adult.

I've heard it said that most parents do not think enough about how their children are progressing until around middle school age when it is almost too late to remedy problems that may have arisen. In talking with teachers of all grades, I hear the problems that are common today—from unruly children who can't be disciplined to teens having sex in the restrooms at school. It's easy to see that many of the problems are different than they were twenty-five years ago, and all of us who are old enough can think of ways that our world has changed since the 1960's. My purpose here is not to dissertate on these changes that greatly affect our society, but to remind us of age-old answers, proven by time to mold children, while adding answers from the new discoveries made possible by our current technology. Much of the new technology is simply proving what the age-old instructions already knew.

For those of us who believe in the Creator God who designed our brains, the new technology just confirms what we could not, up until now, see with our eyes. We took it by faith because His word said it is so, but now brain scans light up the very places that are functioning in a living brain. We must add this new information to our supply pack of parenting skills.

THE LIFE MODEL

But I have another passion about parenting. I am passionate about parents realizing that they cannot teach or model anything to their children that they do not already have (or are acquiring) in their own life. More is caught than taught. This will be an underlying theme throughout this book and presumes that you will want to grow and mature in your own life. What you wish for your child must be true in your life.

Dr. Wilder and his associates have put together a good model to help us mature as we live and grow in our communities. With a guide such as *The Life Model*, God and His people can help you find the places in your life where you are stuck emotionally, where you need healing from trauma, and/or where you need support and encouragement to be the best parent for your children.

In the introduction to *The Life Mode* it says, *"The Life Model* is not just a theory—it is a model. The *Life Model* does not just talk about growing—it gives you practical steps on how to mature."* (Intro to *The Life Model, Living From the Heart That Jesus Gave You.)* In the next chapter we will look at ways to assess maturity—both our own and our children's. This will be a good opportunity to take a look at places that you might be stuck or need healing. If you have experienced traumas in your life, you need healing from those traumas so that their effects will not get passed down to your children.

Along with healing, growing spiritually is a must to be the best parent possible. Since more is caught than taught, the Lord Jesus Christ must be the center of your life if you truly desire to bring your children up in the "nurture and admonition of the Lord." Growing mature and God-loving children are worthy goals that cannot be accomplished alone. You must have a support system of other Godly people, especially those who are parents. As the *Life Model* states, "People need people to recover . . . We grow in our faith in relationships, we find healing from our wounds in relationships, and we come to the Lord through relationships." (p. 5, LM)

So, no matter where you are in your Spiritual journey, you can quickly see that earthly relationships are necessary in life. Authentic relationships help us grow and mature. And they help us know how much God loves us and how much He wants a vital, living relationship with us so we can live abundantly. God has a plan for you and your family and He desires for you to know it. He loves your children more than you do and knows your limits and imperfections. As you join with other parents, grandparents and friends, God will use your community to help you raise your child.

Another reason for needing honest, open and vulnerable relationships is because we all have imperfections and thus none of us can be a perfect parent, though many of us will mistakenly strive for that goal. Striving for perfection itself can sometimes cause more problems than it prevents. Children have their own journey after a point and in order to need God, He has set us parents up to fail here and there, in spite of our desires for perfection. (I will speak to perfectionism in a later chapter.) Although we cannot do it perfectly, I do believe that learning and applying certain parenting practices will greatly increase the prevention of many problems. Where we have existing problems, either for ourselves as parents or with children that are out of control, we will have to look for help through counseling, church groups or helpful friends. Finding a place in our community to build earthly relationships will help us to have both a support base and way to get help to solve many existing problems.

As we take a look at the new brain science, understanding how God designed the brain to work will also enhance the deep desire many of us have to rear our children the best we can in spite of our limited energy and abilities. This material will add some good information and ideas to help you parent better. And as an added bonus, some of this new material will enhance all your other relationships at the same time it shows you new ways to parent.

I have already seen these ideas about the brain make a difference because I live with my third son, Greg, his wife, Chris, and their four girls—Tyler, Kayli, Kori and Brenna. (Their family is in red on the back cover) My material is fresh. I often say "we" when talking about rearing the girls since I have been involved all through their early years after moving in with them when Tyler was 3 ½ and Kayli and Kori were seven months. Brenna was born nine months later. I will speak of them often. What a privilege to help out with another generation and watch them grow. What a blessing to watch parents take advantage of every resource that will help them build a strong, healthy family.

I have also watched another family grow through the years. I've mentored the mother, Debbie, since she graduated from college and I've had the privilege of walking with her through many stages of her life. I count her as one of my closest friends. Because of her background she was very uneasy about becoming a parent. Knowing that "more is caught than taught" terrified her. I have had the privilege of watching Debbie face into her fears and diligently work on her own maturity in order to be the wonderful parent/person she is today. She wanted to share part of her story here.

DEBBIE'S STORY

When I first understood the concept "More is caught, than taught," I felt hopelessly inadequate to become a good mother.

I had read and studied what being a good parent is all about from God's perspective, and I had developed some of my own goals for what kind of adults I hoped to raise my children to be. Yet I knew that I had so many places in my own life where I wasn't equipped to handle the situations with my children.

One example that comes to mind is the time I was talking with my 4-year-old son, and before I knew it our discussion had escalated to a battle of wills between us and suddenly I was a 4-year-old talking with a four-year-old. I walked away feeling like something was really wrong, and feeling hopelessly trapped. I was the one who needed to act like an adult, yet I couldn't seem to pull it off.

Now my son is 17 years old, and I can look back and see that being a parent has been one of the greatest adventures I've had in my life. Having the courage to look inside myself and begin the sometimes painful process of healing and growth has been the path I needed to follow to grow into the parent I knew God was calling me to be and the parent my children deserved.

If you are like me, and look inside and find many places that need healing, I encourage you to grab hold of this chapter of Barbara's book, find someone who can help you (either a counselor or trusted friend) and begin to repair the damage that you've brought with you into adulthood. I believe it will be one of the most rewarding quests you will participate in as an adult.

I am so thankful for the relationships I have with my two children, and for God's faithfulness and grace that have not only allowed me to heal a little but have also equipped my children to be very forgiving of my shortcomings. I didn't realize that becoming a parent would be one of God's greatest gifts to me personally. Wanting to become a good parent has given me the courage and determination I've needed to tackle some difficult issues in the way I relate to others, making me not only a better parent, but also a better friend.

A BEGINNING STEP

Now that you've had a glimpse into Debbie's determination to allow God to work in her life as a parent, let's look at an important question that will help any parent begin the path of building a strong family: **"What do I want my child to be like when he or she leaves home?"** As time quickly flies, that day can come much sooner than we anticipate. One day your child may leave home for college or it may be that he moves out on his own. It will be helpful to consider what kind of person you want to send out into the world.

I like dividing our answers to this question into four categories in which I will give a spattering of possibilities to guide you. These are in no way intended to be all-inclusive or in any order of importance. Many of the desires we parents have for our children are common, while other goals may be family-specific. It would be helpful for you to write out *your own goals* at the end of this section, using these guidelines, while adding what pertains to your specific family. (I will elaborate more on parenting "how to tips" later.) The four categories that we want to consider are Character Qualities, Life Skills, Spirituality, and Miscellaneous.

CHARACTER QUALITIES

Honest: We want our children to tell the truth, to keep the laws of the land and not steal from others. We want adults who will be faithful in marriage and pay their taxes as required.

Respectful: Children must learn at an early age to respect authority. It is extremely difficult to learn later at school and even more so at work. Respect is a verbal issue, often a facial issue and many times a material issue. We want to teach them early how to speak respectfully and have a decent attitude on their face and in their hearts. Not bothering other people's property seems to be a lost value these days. Let's determine to renew that value.

Kind, loving, joyful, compassionate, and empathetic: Children are not naturally kind. They are born selfish and they reflect what is said and done to them. It takes much time and energy to model and teach these qualities. It is well worth the effort to persevere with it at a young age, but more importantly, remember: these qualities are more caught than taught. Along with these qualities, it is important to assure that our children know how to relate well, handle distress, and have emotional stability.

Giving: We want our children to share and give to others. It can take years full of opportunities to instill sharing, but again it is worth the effort. It isn't good to make them sacrifice too young, but they can learn to share and give to others as it's age appropriate. Children love to make and give cards and pictures and even babies share little bites of things with us. These are their ways of bringing life to others.

Forgiving: Years ago I learned in a seminar the importance of asking forgiveness in a specific way. Most of us were taught to say, "I'm sorry," even from an early age. When I learned this different way to seek forgiveness, it made sense and I have used and taught it ever since. When we hurt someone, it helps to say, "I was wrong about ____. Will you forgive me?" This helps in two ways: First, I have to put aside pride to say I was wrong. Second, the person can give a yes or no answer. When we just say, "I'm sorry," the other has no answer

14

other than perhaps, "Oh, that's okay." But it is not okay. When the offended one says, "yes" to the question, harmony is restored. If they are not ready to forgive, but they know the question was humbly asked, the offended one most always comes back later with a "yes." We have taught this as young as two and it becomes a habit. It's also interesting to watch the pride rise up occasionally when we remind the children (or ourselves) that they didn't ask the question.

LIFE SKILLS

Manage money: Helping children learn the value and management of money at a young age goes a long way in preventing future problems. This is another skill that is caught more than taught. I'll be giving you how-to's on this one later.

Manage time: Time management begins to be a big issue when a child starts to school. Kids today have homework as early as Kindergarten. They get busy with sports and lessons of all kinds. It is good to begin early saying, "After you have _____, then you can play." Time is one of our most valuable commodities and cannot be replaced when wasted.

Work on their education: Your child may not be college bound, but education is a must these days. If there are learning or emotional problems that hinder education, please find help that will keep the child from getting discouraged. Reading to children from an early age helps their natural love of learning.

Have a good work ethic: Even when very young, children can be praised for doing a good job on their level of accomplishment. As they move into older years, finishing activities they start like sports and lessons will help them with their future view of work. Quitting in the middle or not being dependable are attributes not well accepted in the business world and we can only help them by teaching them to "stick to it and not give up when the going gets hard." There is room for balance as well by not teaching them to be workaholics and, when appropriate, helping them see when it might be time to stop something.

Be a good citizen: Do you vote? Do you care about our country? Do you talk about why we keep laws and celebrate July 4th? These are things children observe and absorb.

SPIRITUALITY

Love, obey, follow, and share God: I will spend a whole chapter on this point at the end of the book, but for now, think about how you want your children to be in this area. When speaking to and about God is part of everyday life, young children easily accept that He is real, even though they cannot see Him. Focus on and emphasize the fact that Immanuel is always with us, every moment. Before the age of two, babies can understand the words, "Let's pray" and fold their hands and bow their heads. When Kayli was three she matter-of-factly told me one day, "Nana, God is real." I asked her, "How do you know God is real?" She answered, "I just know." And that was enough.

MISCELLANEOUS

Healthy, eat right: This is another issue that is very much more caught than taught. Today it is a big problem with all the food in the stores and the multiple restaurants from which we have to choose. Begin young to make good habits concerning food. We must be very careful never to use food as bribery or comfort. If your child is upset, don't give them food to calm them or tell them you will buy them something if they behave in the store.

Have fun: It is sad to me that I even have to speak to this issue. Many people experienced a childhood that was not fun. It is hard for some people to let loose and have fun. I'm talking about good fun, not chemically induced fun. Children were made for fun and for being children. Keep that in mind as they grow and are pulled more and more to be busy and not free to have fun. (Fun does not necessarily include TV and computer games). Children's favorite people with whom to have fun are their parents and/or other loving adults. Greg plays "Mean Pirate" with his girls as he chases them all over the house, their screams and squeals piercing the air. Children thrive on this kind of attention and such "predator" games teach aggression regulation.

Kori and Kayli play in the mud   ***Aaron & Erica clown around***

Free to be themselves: (I will speak more about this topic later as well.) We simply must observe, learn of, know and respect the person that God made our child to be. It is already there inside them when they arrive. We just help them discover it. It works best when we see them as an individual and not as what our dreams for them are or may have been. This is part of what Proverbs 22:6 is telling us: "Train up a child in the way *he* should go and when he is old he will not depart from it." Acceptance, unconditional acceptance, is one of the most valuable gifts we can give to anyone, especially those with whom we live and love the most.

Family Rules: As we look at all the ways we can work with our family to achieve these worthy goals, it will help to condense our family goals down to around three or four simple family rules that all ages can remember. They can be posted on the refrigerator as a reminder to everyone of the kind of family we want to have. A suggestion for these simple rules could be something like this: 1) Obey 2) Be kind   3) Respect others. You can add one or two others, but simplicity is the key. We can put just about any other quality or behavior under one of these three categories.

And Jesus kept increasing in wisdom and stature, and in favor with God and men. Luke 2:52

SET YOUR GOALS

Take a moment now and write here any other goals or dreams you have for your child. Add any family specific goals as well. Writing and referring to these long-range goals will guide your parenting.

_____

—

_____

—

_____

—

_____

—

Now that we have looked at possible goals and desires we want to instill in our child, let's ask two more important questions of ourselves: **"What am I doing to achieve the goals and desires I have for my child?" And, "What am I not doing?"** I hope by the end of the book you will have plenty of help in answering these two questions; that you will see areas in which you need to grow and mature and that you will see areas in which you are already strong. Again, keep in mind that what we want to pass on, we must have ourselves.

PARENTING AND MARRIAGE

The foundation for a strong, healthy family that pursues good parenting is a good marriage. Because I know that many today are parenting alone, I will occasionally speak to that, but principally I will be speaking to couples. But regardless of your marital status, this book is for any parent seeking information, help and support and wanting to follow God, I realize that I am presenting here somewhat of an "ideal" that begins pre-birth and continues throughout the lifetime, but nevertheless, that ideal is worthy of consideration. We never quit being parents and we never cease growing. So where the ideal is impossible, we will have to modify and do the best we can while trusting God who knows every situation. And, since I do not wish to re-invent the wheel, I will refer to other books now and then that can increase your database of information. There are plenty of good ones on both marriage and parenting.

Having a child can be very stressful and will bring forth into the light just about any existing problem in a marriage. The marriage foundation is best laid before the children arrive. A good marriage is one of the most important earthly treasures we can give our family and along with God's grace will bring blessings for many generations. As we consider the brain research in future chapters, the importance of that solid foundation between Mom and Dad will become evident. Children thrive under conditions that God has designed and being in a loving, joy-filled family is the first and foremost condition.

Jim and Elizabeth **Bob and Amy**

It is vital to work on your marriage so that the children will feel secure. It is a parent's job to unselfishly look out for the children and united parents send a very strong message that their children are important and valuable. Parents that are on the same page with each other wield a much mightier sword than those in constant conflict. They model the way God has designed the family. Children thrive in security, and nothing says security to the family like a dad and mom who are committed to each other.

If you are a single parent, I believe that the most valuable earthly treasure you can give your family is a non-stressful, conflict-free, joy-filled household. You probably have to work and much of your energy

21

will be given there, outside the home; so, it is important not to carry your work-stress home or to give so much of your energy away that the children suffer. You will need lots of help and a good support system from your community

In his book, *Living With Men (www.lifemodel.org)*, Dr. Wilder sums up the Scriptural instructions of a parent's job as serving, protecting and enjoying his family. Let's look at these three instructions separately and practically.

SERVING

A parent can serve his or her family in various ways. Having a helpful attitude around the house leaves chores up to everyone. If you cannot keep to a schedule of who does what, just do what needs to be done and be careful not to leave it all to one person. If the attitude is one of serving, there will be less arguing and blaming.

If each parent shares the regular household work, they will have more time for each other. If one goes out to work, let that one do a good job, be dependable and when at all possible leave the work at work. If one stays home, let that one not watch TV all day, but do their best to keep up with the household. "Whatever you do, do your work heartily, as unto the Lord rather than men." (Colossians 3:23)

Handling finances well and being content with one's place in life are another way to serve. Too much pressure can come on everyone if either one in the marriage wants to live above the means and is not wise about credit, debt and over spending.

Forgiveness is a prime ingredient in serving one another. Again I emphasize the importance of asking forgiveness instead of just saying, "I'm sorry." As you model and teach this way of repairing conflicts, you might find it more difficult at first and feel the pull of pride to skip over it. But give it a try if you never have and keep in mind that humility serves the family.

Giving grace is another great way to serve the family. I will talk more about grace-filled families in a later chapter. Grace acknowledges that there is a problem but does not condemn, put down or belittle the person. At the same time we give grace, we see the others in the family through God's eyes—that they are loved and accepted unconditionally. There is a great book all about this subject titled *Families Where Grace Is In Place,* by Jeff VanVonderen.

PROTECTING

I see protecting the family to be first and foremost about watching how we talk to one another. The opposite of a protected family is one full of anger, sarcasm, put-downs, yelling and strife. It seems to me that these are often overlooked as negatives in many families. But many parents are guilty of the verbal abuses listed above. We keep our children safe in the car, on their bicycles and in the house, but do not keep them safe from our tongues. If this is a problem, parents need to get help and deal with whatever is causing the anger. It can be changed. If these kinds of actions or any other kinds of abuse are happening in your family, or they happened to you growing up, it would be important to seek professional help when needed. I will mostly talk about issues that arise from abuse in a general way here in this book. Looking at these kinds of problems is a place where the *Life Model* can help. Finding help for a problem can involve counseling, community support and loving relationships. It is necessary to find the root of the anger and it takes a humble parent to admit the need and ask for help.

I see staying free of credit debt as another way to protect one's family. There are classes and books available to help us become debt free and manage money well. Money problems can be very undermining to any marriage.

Honesty is another way to protect family members. Most parents want their children to be honest, but the children are watching what we do more than what we say. There is no room for dishonesty between the parents. There is no room for family secrets or hiding life circumstances from children when age appropriate. Children feel more secure when they know what is going on, on the level they can handle and understand.

There is nothing like a praying father to bring God's protection over a family. When a father and mother pray and walk what they talk, children have added protection from the spiritually invisible world that wants to destroy us all. Let's cover our family with prayer.

Prayer warrior Dads – Bob and Greg

ENJOYING

As I said earlier, it surprises me how many families do not have lots of fun. There can be many reasons, most likely connected to parents who were not allowed to have fun as they were growing up. It could be because parents are too busy, too worried or just too tired. Fun should be fun and not associated with teasing and hurting. Tell stories about when your children were little, when you were young and good stories about the past. Know the love language of your spouse and each child and then treat them according to what says love to them. (You can check out the Love Language books by Gary Chapman. There are several, broken down into age groups.) Do things together that do not involve TV or computer. Parents, be sure to go on dates without the children. If money is a problem, get creative in ways to have dates that don't cost money. Laugh and have fun. Build lots of joy!

A pile of sibs and cousins having fun

SUMMARY

Since you are taking time to read a parenting book, it would be a good assumption that you desire to build a strong healthy family. You will most likely look at your marriage and work on long-range goals that you want for your children by asking yourself the questions we have asked here: **What do I want my child to be like when he leaves home? What am I doing or not doing to help achieve these goals?** You will have fun enjoying your family and learning creative ways to serve and protect. You will be open to input from your community to help you do your best in this lengthy endeavor. Your relationship with God will grow.

CHAPTER TWO: MATURITY

Goal: To act like myself and stay relational regardless of intense emotions

INTRODUCTION

In this chapter we are going take a detailed look at maturity—what it is, how to evaluate our own, and how to keep a watch on our children's progress in maturity. There will be comprehensive lists from the *Life Model Study Guide,* a guide for the book, *Life Model, Living from the Heart Jesus Gave You,* used with permission. These maturity lists come from years of study at Shepherd's House Ministry. They include five levels or stages of growth that we should ideally progress through over our lifetime. These stages are Infant, Child, Adult, Parent, and Elder. (www.lifemodel.org)

Before you begin to evaluate your maturity level, let's take a closer look at our goal statement above: ***to act like myself and stay relational regardless of intense emotions.*** We will be looking at this goal statement in various ways but for now, let's define it as "acting my age, coping maturely, when something distressful happens." Some questions might help us understand the goal. What kind of person do you want for your paramedic if you have a heart attack? Who do you want with you if your child has an accident or gets very sick? How do you act if your car gets scratched? The different reactions people have to distress can be a sign of their maturity. We all want a paramedic who will remain calm and knowledgeable when someone has a heart attack. If we've lost our child at the state fair, we want a calm and proficient policeman to help. We want these helpers to act like themselves and be able to communicate with us during the distress. We would be quite unhappy if they were indulging in an addiction or could not function at the time we needed help. In the same way, maturity can help us stay calm as a parent when daily stressors bombard us as we live in our families, our work places and communities. Maturity will keep us from attacking the person who scratched our new car, although we might have strong *feelings* about something we wish we could do about the scratched car.

Maturity is a central truth in the *Life Model*. In today's world and even in the Church, maturity is seldom discussed. All sorts of messages shouting "how-to" and "you should" bombard us, but we do not hear enough messages shouting, "Grow up!" I am personally on a mission to bring up the word "maturity" whenever I can. As I walk through life and interact with others about problems that they or their friends are having, when possible, I point out that maturity may be the issue. What I mean by maturity is not Spiritual maturity, but emotional maturity, the kind of maturity that helps us act like the age we are supposed to be. A person can have an adult body, know tons of Scripture, be a leader at work and at church and still be at Infant or Child maturity emotionally. Maturity is not necessarily about chronological age.

We all know adults (chronologically) who whine, blow up or attack when they don't get their way. The body may grow to adulthood while the person emotionally stays in a younger stage. To be at the maturity level that matches our chronological age, we must complete each task shown on the lists below. As we mature through the stages with all of their needs and tasks, those needs and tasks must carry forward to the next stage. We cannot skip a stage.

Now let's look at some questions that prepare you to evaluate your own maturity level as you look at the stages from the *Life Model*. Take a few minutes to answer them on a sheet of paper.

Do I know what satisfies the way God defines satisfaction?

Do I know how to do hard things or do I procrastinate?

Can I bring two or more people back to joy (reconnect after conflict) at the same time?

Do I know the characteristics of my own heart?

Am I able to regulate my own emotions?

Do I know how to ask for what I need?

Do I know how to give without expecting anything in return?

Do I protect others from myself so as not to hurt them?

What have I used to measure maturity?

As you look through the five maturity stages, keep your answers nearby and consider the answers you gave to these questions. You will see what stage these questions came from.

THE MATURITY STAGES

Below are the essential needs and tasks for maturity, used by permission, from the *Life Model Guide*. www.lifemodel.org Each stage builds on the previous stage: therefore each stage includes the needs and tasks of the previous stage. No stage can be skipped. The "ideal age" is the earliest age at which new tasks can be attempted. The end of that stage expects some degree of mastery. In no way does our maturity determine our value, but it does determine the level of responsibility we can handle.

Because the list of maturity stages is copyrighted, the levels will be listed as they are written, but underneath each need or task you will see questions that can help you better understand the need or task for both your children and for yourself as well. I thought it might help to first give you some definitions for the terms that are included in the list of needs and tasks. They will be in the order that they appear in the list of stages.

MATURITY: Completeness and wholeness at a given level.

EARNED MATURITY: The level of maturity at which one has completed the given needs and tasks, regardless of chronological age.

JOY: Someone is glad to be with me, I am the sparkle in someone's eye.

JOY BONDS: An attachment or bond with another person that is based on being glad to be together versus being based on fear.

THE EYES OF HEAVEN: The way God looks at our world and us.

RECEIVE & GIVE LIFE: Actions/attitudes that communicate love and caring and that build up another.

SYNCHRONIZE: To match energy and be on the 'same page' with another.

ORGANIZE SELF INTO A PERSON: Form one's unique personality

RETURN TO JOY: To be glad to be together in distress and/or reconnect with someone who hurt me.

REST: Calm oneself, experience peace.

WEANING: Leave mother's world and go out into the community.

NUCLEUS ACCUMBENS: An area of the brain that is commonly called the "pleasure center." It screams, "I must have _____ or I will die!"

RITE OF PASSAGE: An event or time when a young person is honored for becoming an adult.

INCLUSION IN SAME-SEX COMMUNITY: Men spend time with boys and women spend time with girls, helping pave the way into adulthood.

USING POWER FAIRLY: Not abusing those under us who have less power because of their age or position; allowing age appropriate choices without extreme penalties.

SHARE LIFE IN PARTNERSHIP: Learning to compromise for the good of all concerned; preparation for marriage, business, and/or living in a community.

PROCLAIM PERSONAL AND GROUP IDENTITY: Know where one fits in a group and be able to stand for that group if attacked.

BRING SELF & OTHERS BACK TO JOY: The ability to help oneself, and others, to reconnect after conflict so that all are satisfied.

PEER REVIEW: Finding and receiving accountability from peers.

GIVE WITHOUT RECEIVING IN RETURN: When one does not expect a reward of any kind for all that he or she has done for another.

GIVING LIFE TO THOSE WITHOUT FAMILY: Helping and showing hospitality, "adopting" those who for various reasons have no family.

ACT LIKE ONESELF DURING DIFFICULTY: To exhibit mature actions and attitudes without falling apart during distress.

THE STAGES

Dr. E. James Wilder/Questions by Barbara Moon

All rights reserved

THE INFANT STAGE   Ideal Age: Birth to Age 4

Infant Needs

1. Joy Bonds with both parents that are strong, loving, caring, secure

    (Did I (and my children) have a loving caring secure bond with each parent? What if my bonds were fear based? If so, do I **now** have a loving caring bond with a woman?   Do I have one with a man?)

2. Important needs are met without asking

    (Were my needs (and my children's) met in these first 3-4 years without me asking? One has to receive before giving. The adults met my needs instead of me being the "parent." If it was reversed, how have I dealt with that?)

3. Quiet together time

    (Do I (and my children) know how to quiet myself? Do I regularly have quiet together with   another person? With God? (This is quietness inside, not just sitting still.))

4. Help regulating distressing emotions

    (How am I (and my children) doing with the Big Six emotions? (See notes or Parenting book.))

5. Be seen through the "eyes of Heaven"

    (Do I (and my children) know I am accepted and loved outside of my behavior? Do I accept myself based on Heaven's eyes? Do I have at least one person who sees me this way?)

33

6.   Receive and give life

(Can I (and my children) receive without guilt or shame? Do I think I have to "give all the time?" Can I do good things for myself without feeling guilty?)

7.   Have others synchronize with him/her first

(Can I (and my children) allow another to help me, comfort me and synchronize with me without feeling guilt or shame? {Comforting a crying baby teaches hope.})

Infant Tasks

1.   Receive with joy

(Can I (and my children) receive with joy without feeling guilty or refusing the gesture? Do I try to keep others from serving me, helping me? Am I able to just say "thank you?")

2.   Learn to synchronize with others

(Am I (and my children) learning to synchronize (be in tune with) with others of all ages?)

3.   Organize self into a person through imitation

(Babies learn who they are by imitation, not instructions. Whoever pays attention to them is the one(s) they model after in these years. The attention can be positive or negative. They go by the face and what they see there to determine their worth and identity. Their cries are asking for help to feel better.)

(Do I (and my children) know who I am as a person? What is like me? Whom did I imitate growing up? What was my principle caretaker like? Have I had or do I have someone in my life now to help me form an identity or improve it?)

4. Learn to regulate emotion

    (Baby learns to regulate by being allowed to rest before she is overwhelmed. Mother synchronizes and knows when to allow rest during the joy building.)

5. Learn to return to joy from every emotion

    (Can I (and my children) be myself when upset in all the emotions? Which ones am I good at, which am I lacking? How do I handle disappointment and humiliation?)

6. Learn to be the same person over time

    (Am I (and my children) the same person when upset as when I am in joy? Would others say I am moody and different when angry or upset? Do I have someone to help me learn the missing skills?)

7. Learn self-care skills

    (Am I (and my children) able to take care of myself? At this stage, just myself is enough. As an adult that might mean saying "no" to things or asking for help when needed.)

8. Learn to rest

    (Can I (and my children) rest and not be hyper or intense all the time? This means inside rest as well as outside. Am I willing to learn this and do I have someone to help me with it?)

THE CHILD STAGE   Ideal Age: Ages 4-13

I have taken some of my comments here from *Living With Men*, by Dr. James Wilder. www.lifemodel.org At this age, the child will begin to branch out more into "daddy's world." She will begin to venture further from mom than before, growing into some independence, knowing mom is there for reassurance and help. Mom will no longer guess at the needs, the child will begin to ask and receive. If the child has had a close bond, he or she will know that when bad things happen it brings comfort. He doesn't have to fear adversity and pain. She knows there is a path back to joy. He does not have to control others to get needs met. She knows how to use her words.

Child Needs

1.   Weaning

(Weaning is the end of infancy and only done well by well-trained four year old brains. If the child was raised on fear, weaning will not go well. He or she will not know their needs and feelings.)

(Have I healthily separated from my mother? Do I expect people to read my mind? Can I take care of myself? What kind of relationship did I have with my father? Did he respond positively to my requests for needs? Did he show me how to increasingly take care of myself and broaden my world? Did I learn to go out on "adventures" and return home to rest?)

2.   Help to do what he does not feel like doing

(Can I (and my children) do things I do not feel like doing? Do I understand that others do not *only* do what they feel like doing? This skill learned around the age of five prepares us to be able to do hard things.)

3.   Help sorting feelings, imaginations and reality.

(Can I (and my children) separate feelings, imaginations and reality? Do I understand how the "real world" operates? Do I know how to judge if my feelings are real or not? Do I believe everything I feel? Do I have someone in my life that I can trust to tell me the truth and help me change my understanding when I have a misconception?)

4.   Feedback on guesses, attempts and failures

(Have I (and my children) been allowed to learn through my mistakes without being overly punished or rejected? Am I confident to take appropriate risks or am I overly performance based?)

5.   Be taught the family history

(Do I (and my children) know how my family came to be? This comes around the age of twelve. Was I taught how my actions would affect history? Did I hear stories of my family history? Was I taught how to avoid continuing the negative parts of my family history?)

6.   Be taught the history of God's family

(Do I (and my children) know the story of God's family? Was I taught how to truly live by knowing the stories and people of the One who gives life and knows how to do it? If not, am I learning that now?)

7.   Be taught the "big picture" of life

(Do I (and my children) understand the big picture of life? Do I understand consequences of my behavior can affect generations? Did I learn that I am not entitled to things without working? Was I prepared to become an adult by having a map that showed the path to maturity?

Child Tasks

1. Take care of self (one is enough right now)

   (Do I know how to take care of myself by saying, "No," when necessary? Did I receive love that I did not have to earn? Can I look back and notice any of the identity changes I have gone through? Did I have to take care of someone else when too young?)

2. Learn to ask for what he/she needs

   (Do I (and my children) know how to ask for what I need? I do not expect others to read my mind and guess what I need? I can ask without feeling guilty. (Unmet needs produce anger.))

3. Learn self-expression

   (Am I (and my children) able to enjoy myself without feeling guilty or inhibited? Can I express myself and not have to have someone else talk for me?)

4. Develop personal resources and talents

   (Am I (and my children) growing at what I am good at? Do I know my talents and spiritual gifts?)

5. Learn to make himself/herself understandable to others

   (If someone misunderstands me, do I (and my children)try in a calm way to help him or her understand me?)

6. Learn to do hard things

   (I (and my children) know how to do hard things. This is more than just getting up to go to work. It is also emotionally hard things—like facing pain and not avoiding it. I can actually choose to do hard things even if they hurt.)

7. Learn what satisfies

(I (and my children) know what satisfies. Satisfaction has a 24-hour shelf life, so it needs to be renewed each day. Some things that satisfy are sharing joy, doing hard things and getting through them, receiving and giving life, food, love, efforts. I know I am entitled to have my needs met. I receive joyfully, but also give cheerfully so as not to be only a consumer. I was not expected to sacrificially give before I was mature enough. (Ecclesiastes 8:15))

8. Tame the *nucleus accumbens*--our cravings

(Have I (and my children) tamed my cravings? (Genesis 25: 27-32) or I am working on that and have someone to help me and keep me accountable? If I have addictions, am I admitting and getting help?)

9. See self through the "eyes of Heaven"

(I (and my children) see myself through Heaven's eyes because someone else has seen or is seeing me that way. I am at least learning how God looks at me.)

THE ADULT STAGE   Ideal Age: Age 13-first child

(If your child is over age 13, insert his/her name also)

Adult Needs

1.   A rite of passage

(Do I remember any kind of "rite of passage" as I became a teen? What might we as a family like to do for our children as they become this age? Was I prepared well for becoming an adult?)

2.   Time to bond with peers and form a group identity

(How did I progress through my teen years? Was I allowed to form a group identity? Did I choose a group that was a good or a bad influence? Did my community help me with a group identity?)

3.   Inclusion by the same-sex community

(Did I have community with other men or women growing up? Do I have community with other men or women now? Do I feel included?)

4.   Observing the same sex using their power fairly

(Can I use my power fairly? Do I know how to negotiate and compromise? Have I seen this modeled by other men or women?)

5.   Being given important tasks by his/her community

(Was I given important tasks growing up? Do I feel I have an important place in my community now? (The Mormons do this with their young men who are required to serve 2 years. What is the main ingredient needed when we give young people an important task? We have to TRUST them. What if they fail? Jesus trusted the untrustworthy without condemning their failures.)

6.   Guidance for the personal imprint they will make on history

(Do I realize that because I am alive, life will not be the same for other people? Was I told how my behavior could affect history? Do I understand that now? *(The movie, It's a Wonderful Life is an example of this))*

7.   Opportunities to share life in partnership

(Have I had opportunities to share life in partnership? Have I practiced being in partnership with peers and older adults?)

Adult Tasks

1.   Take care of two of more at the same time

(Am I able to take emotional and physical care of two or more at the same time? Can I negotiate and compromise so that all are satisfied? Do I understand the real meaning of fairness? (A good analogy--A real estate agent's main job is to discover what everyone needs and bring all to satisfaction in the negotiations.))

2.   Discover the main characteristics of his/her heart

(Do I know the main characteristics of my heart? Do I know what hurts me and how that pain shows me the characteristics of my heart? Have I had or do I have someone who tells me the truth about my heart, encouraging me and supporting me as I live with a heart like mine and the pain it can bring? Do I know the spiritual disciplines that help me take care of my heart? *See Appendix B in workbook.*)

3.   Proclaim and defend personal and community(group)identity

(Can I tell others who I am and who my community is? Cults and gangs do this. Christianity calls it evangelism-- telling the Good News.)

4.   Bring self and others back to joy simultaneously

(Can I bring myself and others back to joy (reconnect) at the same time. Do I maintain who I am and act like myself when distress and conflict come? Adults realize, "We can do this together." Can I be glad to be with those in the shadows by being with them where they are? Are others glad to be with the "real me" or someone I want them to think I am? Do I have any relationships that are estranged and need repair? (This does not include unsafe relationships))

5.   Develop a personal style that reflects his/her heart

(Do I have personal style that reflects the uniqueness of my heart?)

6.   Learn to protect others from himself/herself

(Do I protect others from myself by removing myself when not able to stay calm and act like myself? Do I manipulate to get my own way? Am I able to interact without overwhelming another? Do I notice when someone says, "ouch!" Do I ask forgiveness when I hurt others? *(It is very important to recognize that something hurts. Many have avoided or repressed pain or been taught that it is not okay to know/admit that something hurts—for reasons such as, others may not care, no comfort, no support, codependency, etc. We have to say it hurts when it hurts.))*

7.   Learn to diversify and blend roles

(Can I function healthily and with balance in various roles that I am called to do?)

8.   Life-giving sexuality

(Do I know what it means to have life-giving sexuality? Have I had healing and/or redemption of any non life-giving sexuality from my past? Do I understand why God has instructions about this area of life?)

9.   Mutual satisfaction in a relationship

(Do I know how to find a compromise that will satisfy both people in a relationship? Do I have to always win? Do I know how to share and use my power wisely? *(Some ways to share power with children are things such as allowing them to have a say so about their rooms, helping them achieve goals, not being overly strict, allowing failures and mistakes, allowing age appropriate decisions.))*

10.   Partnership

(Partnership in marriage (and other relationships) is like buddy breathing on a deep-sea dive. It is like working out on many different machines at the gym in order to develop different muscles. (p. 116 LWM)

THE PARENT STAGE   Ideal age: From first child until the youngest child becomes an adult at 13

Parent Needs

1.   To give life

(Do I know what it means to "give life?" What is the opposite of giving life? Does one have to have a biological child to be a "life giver," and a "parent?")
(Have I looked at the kind of bond I had with my parents and how that can affect my parenting? Do I know my limitations as a parent? Bonds will be different with each child and bonds can change.)

2.   An encouraging partner

(Do I have an encouraging partner? If single, what does that mean? With my spouse, do I know that intimacy is not diminished when shared?)

3.   Guidance from elders

(Am I getting guidance from Elders? I need encouragement as I am stretched.}

4.   Peer review from other fathers and mothers

(Am I in a community with other fathers and mothers? Do I have someone to talk to about parenting? Am I open to input from other parents? Am I working to keep my marriage going well during the busyness of parenting? Will I have someone to help me with all the stages of parenting?)

5.   A secure and orderly environment

(Do I live in a secure and orderly environment or am I surrounded by chaos? What needs to change for my environment to be more secure? More orderly?)

Parent Tasks

1.   Giving without needing to receive in return

(Can I, or am I learning to give without receiving anything in return? This task is one of the most important tasks of the parent stage. It begins the day the first child is born and never ends. It will make or break you and highly determine what kind of person you will be and what kind of children you will rear. It is very difficult to learn if one has not gone through most of the parts of the previous stages. This stage costs you your life (time, energy, resources). The cost of something shows its value, how much it is loved. Can I rejoice in the call to unselfishness?))

2.　Building a home

(Am I building a home that reflects God's ways and His life? Am I taking advantage of opportunities to learn and grow in order to make a better home?)

3.　Protecting his/her family

(Do I know what it means to protect my family? Do I protect them from myself when necessary? Am I too overprotective? Am I too dismissive?) (See page 22 & 151 in *Handbook to Joy-Filled Parenting.*))

4.　Serving his/her family

(Am I serving my family? Do I expect a good balance for sharing household chores? Do I model a Biblical view of servant hood? This does not mean I do "everything." (See page 21 in *Handbook to Joy-Filled Parenting.*))

5.　Enjoying his/her family

(Do I know how to enjoy my family? Am I interested in my family members as individuals? Do I know how to have fun without being hurtful? Do I know how to include everyone? (See page 23 in the book.)

Look at Zephaniah 3:17, an example of a great parent

6.　Helping his/her children reach maturity

(Am I working on my own maturity and learning how to help my children reach their full potential? Do I look at my children as unique individuals and accept them as God has made them? Do I know where to go for help when needed? Do I take care of myself so I will be able to take care of others?)

(As one grows through the parenting of each child, each child and each stage the child goes through brings out different aspects of the parent's heart. Each brings out areas that need healing and growth. We will review and retrace ourselves with each child. In order to grow, I must face my pain. If I don't, the bond will break and the child will be crippled. This is all training for the Elder Stage, which is highly unselfish.)

7.   Synchronizing with the developing needs of: children, spouse, family, work and church

(Am I able to synchronize with all the people and the areas of life, being able to do more than one thing at a time when necessary? Do I have a working system for keeping track of all the family schedules? Do I remember the emotional needs that my family has and spend the necessary time it takes to help them? Am I able to satisfy more than one person at a time? Am I being careful not to do "Elder work" before my family is ready? Do I keep a balance of outside activities that might take too much time from my family?)

THE ELDER STAGE   Ideal age: Youngest child is an adult

From LWM—Elder is the longest developmental stage and the most slow-growing. It will last the longest. The Elder harmonizes many aspects of the community. A person who lived and motivated others through fear will not reach Elder maturity. They will be rigid, controlling and shriveled in their thinking. True Elders are known by how they can grasp complexity and respond with simple directness. Elders are at a place where their control is decreasing but their investment in people is increasing. Elders will make mistakes as they learn and they need community support during that time.

Elder Needs

1.   A community to call his/her own

2.   Recognition by his/her community

(Do I have a community to which I belong and where I am recognized as an elder?)

3.   A proper place in the community structure

(Am I building trust through warmth, authenticity and transparency? Am I good at telling stories?)

4.   Have others trust them

(Do others trust me because I have earned and proven my trustworthiness?)

5.   Be valued and protected by their community

(Does my community value me for who I am? Am I teaching my community how to recover from mistakes, both my own and others'? Do I stay involved when things get tough? Does the community protect me when that is necessary?)

Elder Tasks

1.   Hospitality

(Am I known as a welcoming person, warm and approachable? Am I easy to talk to? Am I willing to   use my resources to help those without?)

2. Giving life to those without families

    (Am I involved where possible in helping those who need a
    Spiritual family? One of the first aspects of the Elder stage is
    having a new son or daughter-in-law. This is part of
    welcoming new people into the family—both natural and
    spiritual. Then Elders bond with children they did not
    produce (grandchildren). As the bonds are extended, this
    forms the community. Elders become "parents" to those
    without a good family. They "adopt" adults to help them
    become parents, just as adults "adopt" children to help them
    become adults.)

3. Parent and mature his/her community

    (Can others look to me to do safe, parent-like things in my
    community such as love everyone, build joy, kiss all the
    babies, give resources to bad risks, hug and snuggle and give
    back rubs (p. 226 LWM)? Do I know how to build trust in a
    safe environment? I have to be known as a very safe person.)

4. Build and maintain a community identity

    (Am I helping my community build and maintain its identity?
    Do I help when changes come along that might threaten that
    identity?)

5. Act like him/herself in the midst of difficulty

    (Am I able to remain myself during distress and quiet myself
    and others? Do I bring stability and lessen anxiety? Can I
    bring myself and others back to joy? If I am in emotional
    pain myself, can I suffer well and remember what is
    important?)

6.   Enjoy what God puts in each person in the community
        (Seeing each of them through "eyes of Heaven")

        (Am I able to enjoy the value in all kinds of people and build
        joy as much as possible?)

7.   Building the trust of others through the elder's own
        transparency and spontaneity

        (Am I transparent, vulnerable, open and spontaneous? Do I
        understand the importance of not keeping secrets? Do I
        understand that these qualities are how trust is built and that
        others do not trust someone who is hiding things, even their
        responses? Can I be joyfully spontaneous, giving and fun?
        [In the brain, trust is built the same place that we learn to
        recognize and interpret faces. Trust is built over time, face to
        face, with honest authentic people who share our feelings. [p.
        237 LWM])

READ JOB 29:12-17

# # # #

I hope that you have now gone prayerfully through the stages,
comparing them to the list of questions you answered, and have at least
one or two areas that God has shown you that you could use help with.
Write one or two here:

_____

_____

If by chance you got overwhelmed by the list and found so many you felt hopeless, get in touch with a friend or other helping person and begin the process to work through your needs. Take no shame or condemnation for whatever level you may have. Your background greatly determines your maturity level and God loves to heal us and grow us. He desires to bring us to "earned maturity" that corresponds to our chronological age.

Earned maturity means that we have completed the needs and tasks for a certain stage of maturity. Chronological age does not necessarily correspond to earned maturity. When working through issues where earning maturity is taking place later than the ideal age, it takes perseverance and willingness to deal with pain from the past. It might involve counseling to discover where we got stuck in the process of growing up. We might have to explore the traumas that happened and arrested our emotional growth.

The *Life Model* describes two types of traumas—Type A traumas wounded us when there was an "**A**bsence of good things," when we did not receive the things in life that we were supposed to get. Type B traumas wounded us when "**B**ad things happened." Hard work, humility and willingness to admit needs are prerequisites to going back and completing needed tasks, while recovering from traumas. Traumas and neglect keep us from completing the maturity tasks and our emotional growth becomes stuck. In order to get unstuck we need relationships based on love bonds and to identify the needs and wounds from Type A and Type B traumas.

Let's look at some examples that describe maturity or "completeness and wholeness at a given level." For example, if one is old enough to have a car—there is a level at which that person should be complete and whole—the adult level. The law says we must have reached a certain chronological age. Emotionally to be at the adult level, we must have grown through all the previous stages on the list and carried them forward. Even though one is old enough to have a car, it's possible that one is not mature enough. So let's take one of my favorite tasks for evaluating the emotional maturity of the adult stage, "protecting others from himself or herself," and apply it to a person's reaction to a scratched car.

In a distressing, highly emotional moment such as this, we can quickly see if a person is protecting others from him or herself. Let's say the car gets scratched and anger rises. If I verbally attack someone is that an example of protecting that person from myself? Not at all. If I blow up, am I acting like myself and staying relational? Not really. At this moment I am not "giving life." I am giving death. This kind of situation and knowing how to assess maturity can act as a red flag to help me see where I need to grow and mature according to the unmet need or unmet task in that level.

Maybe a scratched car does not set you off. But an argument with your spouse does. Are you able to come to "mutual satisfaction in a relationship" or do you *have* to win and get your way. Do you see the conflict as my way/your way or a place to come to compromise where all are satisfied? An adult knows how to compromise for mutual satisfaction.

As a parent do you remind yourself that you are "giving without needing to receive in return?" When you get up for the third time in the middle of the night are you able to act like yourself? The same way you ask yourself questions, you can, as a parent looking at the stage that corresponds to your child's age, ask yourself questions from the lists to determine if he or she is on level. For example: Is my three to four year old doing fairly well at regulating his emotions? Is she beginning to take care of herself at her level? Is my thirteen year old able to ask for what he needs and make himself understandable to others? Does my teenager understand how his actions will make an imprint on history?

Dr. Wilder has a great illustration to help assess whether a teenager is a "child" or an "adult." He points out that if a young person understands his affect on history, he will not be as prone to behave "unseemly" in the back seat of a car. Pre-marital sex and pregnancies cause shock waves through more than one generation. A man realizes the consequences of sex outside of marriage and a boy does not. When young people understand that their actions can have ramifications for generations, they will be less likely to make choices that might bring disaster on their family both now and in the future. A young person in the adult stage will better understand that a sexual relationship is for bringing life to others, not "death."

These kinds of questions make it easier to assess where we are. And just as our maturity level could be lower than our chronological age, we can also try to do a higher stage before we are ready. Parents of young families must be careful not to be doing Elder stage work to an extent that the young family suffers. It's possible to become so involved in helping our churches and our communities that we are not at home to help our own families. We would not expect our two year old to babysit her new brother, nor do we want our fifteen year old to become a parent.

Working on our own maturity is absolutely vital in light of family, marriage and parenting, as is monitoring the growth of our children. Since more is caught than taught and we cannot pass on to our children that which we don't have ourselves, how can we ignore this issue of maturity? The list of stages can help us see more easily what we need to work on. Let your community help you mature so that your children and your family will benefit. Let God show you where you are lacking and have the courage to admit it and get help.

Where you may be lacking in maturity does not in any way diminish your value. As we work through maturity issues, it is extremely important to remember that maturity is not about value nor is it a place to take shame. Instead of determining value by maturity or immaturity, we can look at a person's level of maturity the way Dr. Wilder says it in *Living With Men*: "I am just not ready for that yet." When we look at infants, we know that they are valuable even though they can *do* nothing that seems valuable. Babies are right where they are supposed to be while growing through the needs and tasks pertaining to their first four years of life. Babies can smile and bring joy to us, but they are not ready for kindergarten. Six year olds are not ready to date and fourteen year olds are not ready for marriage. We can only mature as we journey through each need and task, even if that means going back and picking up where we might be stuck. Just because a person is not ready for something does not diminish his or her value. So as an adult, don't get down on yourself if you need to grow in an area. Keep in mind that it is all right to say, "I am not ready for that yet, but I am working, or want to work, on getting there."

How do we as adults work on growing through that level where we may be stuck? What is God's part and what is our part? From the Scripture, Dr. Wilder has separated these responsibilities quite well, although they overlap with each other as to cooperation. He says that salvation, deliverance, healing and redemption are God's responsibility. Maturing is a human's responsibility; it is not a spiritual gift (James 1:4). Maturing was not automatic during our childhood years and it won't be automatic now. Working on the unmet needs and unmet tasks requires courage and co-operation with God's guidance and leading, as we do our part with support from loving relationships. We do the hard work that it takes to grow up--to ask for help, to talk about and feel our unresolved pain, to get accountability from others who are willing to speak truth to us.

As you think about this short list of hard things that it takes to grow up it is easy to see that maturing is a job for the community. *It is not the job for a spouse,* though spouses will be supportive and encouraging. It will take authentic relationships with people who are trustworthy to tell us where the lacks are and to support us while we go back through a missed task, while we look at the Absence of good things that were supposed to happen (Type A traumas) and any Bad things that happened (Type B traumas). Small groups at church and close friends are good places for finding the community support we need. Keep in mind that maturing can be a *very long and slow process* and give yourself and others plenty of grace to move along.

SUMMARY

As a parent we want to keep in mind that our own maturity greatly affects our children's growth. Keep the maturity lists handy as you watch your child grow through the years. Find a place for yourself to get healing from any traumas that might have arrested your growth. Go to a good counselor and/or get into a church or small group that can encourage you and support your marriage and parenting. Remember that you are very valuable no matter the level of maturity you may have earned.

SECTION II -- THE TECHNICAL WHYS

INTRODUCTION

In the next chapter we will look briefly at the new brain research. You will remember at the beginning I mentioned that I hope you will not skip this chapter. My hope is that you will take the time to read through this information even though it can seem a bit technical. It is my goal to walk you through the technical whys one piece at a time. In Chapters Four and Five we will look at the importance of synchronization, the importance of building joy and quiet and returning to joy. These chapters are vital for you to understand the importance of this new research and how using it affects the newborn's emotional and relational development through the first two years. Knowing and using synchronization and joy affect all relationships throughout life.

In order to make this section easier to understand, below you will find definitions for some of the new terms that will appear in this section. They are in alphabetical order and a few are repetitive. Referring to these definitions may help you as you go through this section, looking at material that is probably new to most of us. I will speak more within the chapters about each topic.

ACTING LIKE MYSELF: Behaving in a manner that fits my maturity level, my unique personhood and the characteristics of my heart.

ATTACHMENT: Another word for bonding, connecting or belonging with another person. Sharing a state of mind.

BUILDING JOY: The interaction with another person that results in true emotional joy between the two (or more). This interaction happens non- verbally through joy smiles, eyes that light up, voice tone and proper touch. It means we are glad to be together.

DESYNCHRONIZATION: Not tuning in to what another person is feeling when interacting with them, causing disharmony both emotionally and within the brain.

FLESH (*SARK*): The condition of believing false ideas (lies) about oneself that do not coincide with what God says. Leaning on my own understanding. (Proverbs 3:5-6)

HEART: The human spirit, the essence of a person, where Jesus lives and guides when one is a Christian

JOY BUCKET: A part of our emotional brain, our emotional make-up that, when filled with joy enables us to thrive, relate well and endure hardships, disappointments and trials.

JOY CAMP: The state of being where God designed us to live.

JOY: Someone is glad to be with me and I am the sparkle in someone's eyes. (It takes at least two)

MINDSIGHT: A function of the brain that enables us to focus on ("see") another person's mind and know what they and we are feeling, perceiving, believing, intending. (Siegel)

MOTHER CORE: The part of the brain that enables us to match energy (synchronize) with another person. It is the place where true joy smiles originate, the place that enables us to dance, to have empathy and know there is anther mind behind the face we are interacting with.

QUIET TOGETHER: During joy building, the more mature person synchronizes with the other's need to rest and backs off the intensity, allows the other to rest, but does not leave.

RETURN TO JOY: Being glad to be with someone during distressful emotions and helping him or her stay stable or become stable until the distress passes. Also, reconnecting with someone who distressed me.

STAYING RELATIONAL: Being able to interact in a stable and mature way with others, in spite of distressing emotions in or around us.

SUFFERING WELL: Having enough joy strength to prevent us from "falling apart" when distress comes, and to enable us to stay relational and act like who we are during that time of distress.

SYNCHRONIZATION: The state of being on the same wavelength with another person and sharing energy levels. Synchronizing takes place both emotionally with self and others, as well as physically in the brain.

THE EMOTIONAL CONTROL CENTER: The places in the emotional brain that need to be synchronized in order to function well and thrive.

THRIVING: Developing healthily, having a stable and fully developed life, reaching one's potential.

Because I want you to see how significant this new research is to the first two years of life, maybe it will be helpful if we can compare the "brain stuff" to a computer. In Chapter One, we talked about what we want our children to be like when they grow up and leave home. We began to set some goals for parenting. I would like to compare those goals you set to the software in a computer. Those "software" goals are like computer software programs that we want instilled in our children's hearts that will empower them to do and be all that God wants them to be.

But computers need hardware before they can run the software. The hardware is a level below the software that enables the computer to run the software efficiently. This hardware below those goals we set for our children is the brain. So before we go on to talk more in-depth about the "software" of parenting, in the next few chapters we can take a look at what makes that software run most efficiently. How do we make sure that all of the hardware is wired up the way the Designer designed it?

Another pertinent question comes to my mind from our last chapter where we talked about the type of person we all want to have around us in a crisis: What causes one person to be able to function "like a hero" in a crisis while others around them are falling apart? I believe that part of the answer to both of these questions is the same. Much of the hardware and the capacity to function in a crisis are wired inside of a child during the first two years of his or her life.

During the first two years of your baby's life, critical windows of development open and shut in the brain. In those two years you can build neurological pathways that will affect the way your child lives and relates as an adult. Why is this so important? What happens in a child's brain through interaction with caregivers affects how he or she will learn to rightly handle the situations and events in their lives that involve pain and distress. How they are wired will determine how they manage what is hard for them to do. If children don't receive what they need most during this period of their lives, it is likely that they will not develop as well as they could. They can learn unhealthy ways of relating that may block them from progressing through the stages of maturity in a natural way. Depending on the input from you, the interaction with your infant and young child can even strengthen or weaken the child's immune system and how it is going to operate the rest of his life. These first two to three years are crucial as the most ideal time to take advantage of knowing this brain science.

Although we can use the analogy of a computer to look at how our brains work, humans are much more complex and varied than any machine. I'm in no way meaning to diminish other aspects of a person's upbringing or negate that the way God has made each of us is unique and individual. I simply want to get this information out so that we can do as much prevention as possible and do our best to give our babies what they need. Babies and the care they receive early in life have always been important to me, and now this research confirms how important the primary caregiver is in the process of helping a baby thrive.

In the next three chapters, I want to help you see how baby and caregiver can build a secure bond, gain the ability to handle distress, and strengthen the capacity to relate to others in healthy ways. I also hope to show you how important it will be for you to build your child's capacity to experience joy, because children will only be able to deal with the painful situations in their lives if they have enough joy in their hearts to make it through difficult times.

Although some of the information may be a bit technical, I am excited to share with you that there is great evidence from these new brain studies to help confirm our part as parents in helping hardwire our little bundles of joy as we integrate this information with what we know from the Scriptures and what has been passed down through the generations. I want you to have all that's possible to give your child the best start.

If your child is past this early infant stage, don't worry. There are plenty of steps you can take at whatever stage your child is in to help them receive what they need in order to better their chances of becoming what God has in mind for them. And of course, there are situations in parenting that are beyond the scope of this book, such as ones where a child's "hardware" is faulty in some way, and all the correct wiring in the world will not help that hardware do what it was meant to do. If you are in this situation, I pray that you will find the in-depth help you need in parenting your child. But read on and find that joy will always be a contributing factor to anyone's life.

As you will see in Chapter Three, what we already know and have in our own brain as a parent is pretty much what we will pass on to our newborn, unless someone helps us learn new ways of relating. Mothers actually download part of their brain into their babies' brains. As I began learning this, I realized how good of a mother I had had myself, because I could look back and see how I had done many things well in those early years with my own four. In no way had I done all perfectly, but for the basics those first two years, I was thankful for the good mothering (good wiring) that had been passed on to me. As I learned the new research, I passed it along to Chris, my daughter-in-law. At that time I was not living with them and Tyler, Chris and Greg's oldest daughter, was eighteen months old. We realized (and thanked God) that Chris had already been doing very well building joy and quiet with Tyler.

So what changed after I learned the brain research? How do I interact differently with my grandchildren and other children that I am with now? What do I do and/or tell a young parent differently since learning what is in these next three chapters? The answers to these questions are contained in some of those definitions we just looked at, along with some insight into their meanings. In a nutshell, I learned what happens when we interact face to face with each other. I learned the reason why I always hated seeing someone tickle a child until they cried. I learned how important it is to build joy and have quietness with a baby. I changed the way to do Time Out. I found out why it does little good to try to convince someone to change their mind about an issue. I learned why words and lectures were not helpful at certain times. I learned why comfort was such an important gift to another. And much of what I learned was a better way to say things that I already knew intuitively from my passion for children and experiences with them.

In 2000, God blessed me with another outlet for my passion about kids. I moved in with Greg and Chris and lived with them until 2010. As Tyler grew and Kayli, Kori and Brenna were quickly added to the family, Chris and I continued to dialogue about things we could do differently and better. We now had words for what we had already done well, (build joy and quiet) but there were new things to consider that we had never heard anyone talk about before. As the twins hit the "return to joy" age from twelve to eighteen months, we observed and noted when they were in the Big Six emotions (more on that topic) as we helped them learn to return to joy from those emotions. You will see pictures of these very events in Chapter Five where the Big Six emotions are defined and illustrated.

As Chris and I enjoyed trying out new ideas with her little ones we decided to do Time Out differently. I will share that in detail in the chapter on discipline. We also began to fine-tune how we were relating on a daily basis with the girls and each other. If you could ask Chris what is the one thing about the brain information that has changed her parenting (and relating) the most, I know she would answer, "Synchronizing!" Chris would tell you that understanding joy, quiet, returning to joy and synchronization are crucial to her parenting and so far her girls show the results of being reared by joy-filled parenting.

"Synchronizing," defined above as "being on the same page as another and sharing energy levels," is one of the new terms that I will use in Chapters Three and Four. I highly encourage you to make this word part of your vocabulary, to come to understand it and to *do* it, not only with your child but also with everyone. Again I encourage you to attack these chapters with gusto. The terms may be new, but synchronizing, joy, quiet and bonding are four basic ingredients you need to know in order to set your child on a path of thriving. If you are a reader who wants to know "whys" you will be likely to dig through the new terms. If you are not, try to hang in there until you "get it," and don't give up because it is new. Go ahead and look up the answers to your practical needs, but go over the technicals until they, too, are part of your parenting arsenal.

CHAPTER THREE: THE NEW BRAIN STUDIES

Goal: to understand thriving, synchronization and the Emotional Control Center

INTRODUCTION

Now we are almost ready to look at an overview of the new brain research. Keep in mind that this research has to do with the *emotional* aspects of the brain, not the intellectual. It is about relationships. Thanks again to Dr. Wilder for getting it into everyday language. I have his permission to use some of his material from a conference he does on thriving. My interpretations and suggestions will be intermingled. Dr. Wilder has skillfully combined the *Life Model* principles, (based on Scripture) and the brain research to give us a good picture of what it takes to thrive, to fully develop. He correlates the ingredients needed for thriving, or lack of it, to a specific part of the brain. For this book, I feel that most parents won't care about the particular brain part, its name (though I will name them) or location, but can be satisfied knowing what it does and why it is important. That is my objective in sharing it at all. Knowing its importance will change, if we allow it to, the way we parent and relate. So hang in there with me through the little bit of definitions and other technical stuff while you look at the whats and whys and hows.

But before we look at the chart that I have modified from Dr. Wilder's conference on thriving, let me ask you some questions like I did in the chapter on maturity. Hopefully wanting answers to these questions will tickle your curiosity enough to go through this chapter.

Do you know what it takes for us as humans to develop healthily?

What happens to a person's ability to cope when frightened?

What kind of bond did you have with your parents, especially Mother?

Are you a joy-filled person?

How do you feel when someone is not on the same wavelength you are?

What do you do with emotional pain (like missing someone or hurt feelings)-feel it or medicate it?

Do you know how to calm yourself and others?

Are you open to receive love and connection, or closed and avoidant?

If some of these questions were difficult for you and you're feeling uneasy about being the kind of mother (or father) that you would like to be, I would encourage you to look around in your church, your family or your community and find a mother (or father) who seems to possess some of the qualities you want. Observe how they interact with their children and if the children are basically joyful and obedient. Ask that other parent to help you. They can "download" some of their brain to yours. And stick with me here. You will find good information and clues to help you with some of the answers to the questions above. Now let's begin learning what it takes for a person to truly thrive as they grow from baby to child and even on through adulthood.

Dr. Wilder's thriving chart illustrates what it takes to thrive, what the opposite of thriving is and the area of the brain that is involved in thriving. This chart is an overview to which I will speak more specifically as we go. The first four areas of the brain involved are on the right side, the side for emotions and relationships. The last area brings in the left side of the brain where words and logic reside. These five centers are designed to work together, to be synchronized, for thriving.

WHAT DOES IT TAKE TO THRIVE?

THRIVING	(opposite) DEATH	BRAIN LEVEL
1) Belonging	Insecure Attachment	The Attachment Center (Thalamus) **Who or what is important to me?**
2) Receiving & giving life.	Self-centered	The Evaluation Center (Amygdala) **What is Good, Bad, Scary?**
3) Synchronizing, Return-to-joy, Forgiveness	Loss of Synchronization	The "Mother Core" (Cingulate) **Peace, Joy, Distress**
4) Maturity	Immaturity	The Joy Center (Pre-frontal-cortex) **My identity and attention to the World**
5) Knowing My Heart	Living by the Flesh	The Logic Center (Left and Right Hemispheres together) **My explanations of my life**

I want to take a moment and look briefly at the "Thriving" versus "Death" sections of each component of this chart in order to get a better understanding of each part. I've included a little scenario with each one to help you get a better handle on their meanings:

BELONGING VERSUS INSECURE ATTACHMENTS

As most of us know, the basis for life is a place to belong. It is universal and desired by every human, bringing much emotional pain when not a part of life. In our deepest being we know "who is important to us," and who we want to be important to. As we go through our study here, we will see the benefits of a secure attachment from birth and the pain and destruction that come from feeling that we don't belong.

At birth and immediately after, infants want to bond with their parents. These are the most important bonds. But belonging is so important that all of us need many loving bonds at every age and stage of life. Dr. Wilder talks about both. "In the bonds we form with parents we see who we are as if looking in a mirror. Because those mirrors are imperfect, we need a loving community of bonds to fill in the gaps." (p. 56 *Life Model*) This means that our children need lots of people in their lives who will love, cherish and care for them. None of us can have too many loving attachments. And the principle loving attachment we all need is God's family, because without Him there is no true life. When we receive His Son, the Lord Jesus, God adopts us into His family with a secure and loving bond. (If you are not certain that you have a personal relationship with Jesus, talk to a trusted friend for help.)

Baby Daniel

Baby Daniel's mother and all the other nursery workers at church could not understand why Baby Daniel cried the whole time he was there. The other babies, if they cried at all, stopped crying and played happily within just a few minutes of being left. Baby Daniel was clingy with his mother. *She thought that was a good sign of his security, but it was, in fact, the opposite—it was a sign that he did not have a secure bond with his mother. Baby Daniel felt scared when his mother left him because her attention was very often sporadic and distracted by her own problems. Baby Daniel was only quiet when his mother was holding him.*

RECEIVING AND GIVING LIFE VERSUS SELF-CENTERED

As I hope you noted in this second heading from the Thrive chart, it is reversed from the way we usually think about it. We must receive (emotionally or physically) *before* we can give. We are dependent on God for each and every breath. If we try to give before we receive, whether it is emotional support, leading at work or helping others, we will burn out. There will not be a good foundation from which to give. It might look like we are interested in others when, in reality, we may be looking to feel important and valuable because of the giving. On the other hand, if we only receive and seldom give, we will consume everything for ourselves. Both of these extremes turn the focus to self instead of others.

God demonstrates every moment the opposite of self-centeredness as He constantly pours out His grace and mercy upon us. Receiving life first from Him and having strong relationships with others build a good foundation for giving. God's perfect love casts out fear; one of the principle factors in self-centeredness, and replaces fear with His deep, need-meeting love. We must connect with God and look to Him to fill us with those characteristics we need to teach our children in order for them to live in love instead of fear.

Little Jessica

Little Jessica was very unhappy and worried most of the time, though few people could see it, because Little Jessica tried to be" invisible" wherever she was. Little Jessica's father hit her mother when he was upset. Little Jessica had to be the parent at home, a task that she was not built to carry. This made it very difficult for Jessica to live life, as she was not receiving enough herself. Having to give without receiving enough first was forming Little Jessica into a person with lots of fear and worry. The foundation for her self-image was very shaky. As Little Jessica grew up, it was going to get more and more difficult for her to relate authentically, because of growing up in an environment full of addictions and abuse.

SYNCHRONIZING/RECOVERY VERSUS LOSS OF SYNCHRONIZATION

Because synchronization is so important to what I desire to get across here, we will take more than one chapter to look at it. We will look at how synchronizing affects bonding, peace, joy and distress. Understanding synchronization maximizes thriving, whether we are speaking of synchronizing in our hearts with God, within ourselves, within the brain, or with others. Synchronizing—matching energy and being in tune with, on the same page with another—is vital in parenting and all relating. When we synchronize with another, they feel valuable, special and loved.

The opposite happens with long-term or early loss of synchronization. That kind of de-synchronization can be traumatic and the person then must find recovery from traumas in order to reach maximum growth. Recovery involves embracing all the pain in our lives and allowing God to heal us. We work through our own pain and help others with theirs. As we build joy strength from those who are glad to be with us, we find peace in the healing and learn how to handle distress. (p. 36 TLM) Parenting through a model of synchronizing joy, peace and distress can prevent traumas and build strength into our children that will under gird them in times of distress.

Toddler Kaleb

Toddler Kaleb never knew how Mommy was going to respond to him. Sometimes she paid attention and sometimes she ignored him. This made him feel sad so he pretended not to care. After a while he mostly played by himself and tried not to bother anyone. Now and then he heard people say what a good little boy he was. Toddler Kaleb's mommy didn't synchronize very well and later in his life Toddler Kaleb would find it difficult to handle distress and connect with others.

MATURITY VERSUS IMMATURITY

We have already looked at maturity in the last chapter as a vital part of healthy development. We defined maturity as "reaching one's God given potential." Maturity grows best in real joy-filled relationships. In the following chapters we will look closer at the importance of joy strength as the basis for reaching maturity. Joy strength means to have enough joy in one's life to offset distressing circumstances. Handling distress well is one sign of maturity.

There is an area of the brain that interacts and functions through joy. Although many places in a baby's brain reach an end to their growth during the first few months, the Joy Center in the brain never stops growing as we interact in loving bonds. As we said in Chapter Two, the community of loving relationships helps us reach our full capabilities. (pp. 15, 16 TLM) Having maturity as one of our parenting goals can help us with periodic check-ups as we determine how our children are progressing. Knowing how joy fits into the equation will insure a strong foundation.

Teenager Veronica

Teenager Veronica almost never does anything except what she wants to do. She expects everyone to know what she wants and gets upset when they don't. She thinks being popular and wearing the right clothes will make her happy, so she spends every penny she gets in her hands. If anyone crosses Teenager Veronica, she pouts or whines or blows up. It is very hard for her to calm down if she doesn't get her way. She did not have very much joy built into her life as a baby. Teenager Veronica is still in the Child stage.

Teenager Vanessa

On the other hand, Teenager Vanessa is progressing well at home and school and church. She is a stable influence with her peers. Teenager Vanessa knows what she likes and somewhat who she is, and thus she is free to be different than the crowd when necessary and to discuss issues with those around her, including her parents. She is willing to do her part and feels free to speak her mind even though someone might disagree with her. At the same time, Teenager Vanessa is also able to compromise. She understands some of the consequences that come with not living God's way and is willing to adjust her choices accordingly. Teenager Vanessa's parents gave her a foundation for thriving by building lots of joy into her life (and brain) during the early years of her life. Teenager Vanessa is not perfect, but her stability and commitment to growing up are taking her in the right direction. Teenager Vanessa has entered the Adult stage.

KNOWING MY HEART VERSUS LIVING BY THE FLESH

In a later chapter we will look more closely at this point about thriving. We get to know our heart from input of those around us who truly know us and see us through Heaven's eyes, those who see us the way God sees us. If we have not been told correctly who we are, we will not be able to walk out what we talk. We will have faulty explanations of life and live from lies instead of truth. We will try to get our love and acceptance from the wrong places. When we receive Jesus into our hearts, we can learn to live from His guidance and see life as He does, and we will know the truth that our love and acceptance come from Him. As we grow with Jesus, we will be less likely to listen to old beliefs that were part of our past that do not fit us. As we live from God's perspective we can walk what we talk.

Young Man Will

Young Man Will is a leader in his church's college and career group. Most of the church members think Young Man Will is the model Christian. But they do not see Young Man Will when he is out and about with his buddies. Young Man Will's walk does not match his talk because he is looking for acceptance in the wrong places. One of the reasons is because Young Man Will's parents always expected him to be perfect and put him down when he was not. They did not do a good job of providing a safe place to make mistakes and fail. Their focus was on what Little Will did instead of who God had made him to be. Living with perfectionism instead of acceptance has influenced Young Man Will to act like a different person depending on whom he is with. Young Man Will lives out many lies that he believes in his heart about who he really is.

##

SYNCHRONIZATION

After looking at the five ingredients for thriving and some scenarios to illustrate each one, let's go a step further and look at how healthy development in a baby's life fits with the way God has designed our brains to synchronize with Him, with each other and with ourselves. Synchronization is one of the most important foundations for thriving because it is the basis for a secure attachment. The mother's ability to "read the baby" insures that she will build good hardwiring into her infant as they interact in joy and quiet. The mother's ability to synchronize actually affects the growing brain and the child's emotional stability.

As you will see shortly, the Joy Center (where joy building takes place in the brain) eventually becomes 35% of the adult brain. Like our computers, we want the hardware (the brain) to run efficiently so that the software will work. The software, the goals we want for our children from Chapter One, all have to do with relationships in some form or another. Relating healthily is the basis of all that software. A mother who does not synchronize well will, over time, set her baby up for emotional and mental problems that will hinder him or her from relating well with others. Remember Toddler Kaleb and his mother who met his needs too sporadically? In Chapter Four you will see more clearly how the lack of synchronization affects bonding, which affects how we relate to others, God and ourselves.

If I could only talk about synchronization (and the other three ingredients for thriving—joy, peace and bonding) I feel that it would be worth our time to do so. Synchronization means to be on the same wavelength with, to be on the same page with, and/or to have the same energy levels as another person. As we begin to truly synchronize with others, whether it is with our children, spouses, or friends, relating changes in a very positive way. We communicate unconditional love and acceptance, we communicate caring, we communicate that the other person is important, all basics for our child to build a good self-image. Synchronizing and being glad to be together are how they "get it." There is a message sent that says something like, "I can put myself aside here and focus on you and where you are at this moment. You are so important." Anytime I am feeling low, the person I want to talk to is someone who knows how to synchronize. I might want to hear some truth, but usually after I've first had some empathy in the form of synchronizing. I like it when another person meets me in my distress right where I am and does not try to "fix" me quickly so he or she will feel better.

In *Living With Men*, Dr. Wilder compares synchronization to good music. He calls it "the emotional equivalent of good music: timing, intensity and tone." We all know how beautiful a guitar sounds when it is played with good timing, correct intensity and right tone. We recognize a familiar song and enjoy its harmony. Not only does harmony sound good, it feels good to our whole body. We feel quite the opposite when we hear an instrument out of synchronization, with bad timing, intensity and tone. We feel our skin crawl and our teeth grate.

After learning about the importance of synchronizing, I realized that sometimes an easy time to de-synchronize would be when we feel that surge of love for our precious child and then swoop down upon him to give a big hug when he is playing quietly. This would not really be synchronizing, because the timing is not good. The motive and desire were great, but the timing was jarring.

Like making good music, one of the main functions of a good mother is to teach her baby how to synchronize--by synchronizing with him or her. Synchronizing will help the baby learn how to deal with distress and her brain itself will grow correctly. The good mother uses proper timing, intensity and tone by matching the baby's timing, intensity and tone. It is vital and good only when *the mother synchronizes with the baby, watching to see when baby needs to rest.*

The mother, as the older brain, "leads" in the sense of knowing when to allow rest. It is not good, and is in fact damaging, if the mother tries to get the baby to match her needs when wanting connection.

The synchronizing process begins as soon as the baby can focus his eyes. Good synchronization needs to take place the whole lifetime and the foundation is laid early between mother and baby as they interact face to face. Most everyone enjoys playing joyful "goo-goo," getting the baby to smile and then laugh as we smile and speak that silly language. Brenna, Chris and Greg's fourth daughter, was so good at playing joy that we nicknamed her, "Grinna." When playing joy with its accompanying baby talk, what we don't consciously realize is that we are communicating back and forth eye to eye. Although it is not really noticeable, this communication is taking place left eye to left eye. It is going on between the mother's right brain and the baby's right brain at a subconscious level. They are synchronizing joy, which is affecting the brain very positively when done correctly.

Brenna in high joy—three months old

So where do timing, intensity and tone come in? When done correctly, the mother and baby are synchronizing joy and quietness. In a good situation, the mother matches the baby's intensity of joy, watching for when he has reached his peak of joy so that she can let him quiet (rest) at that proper timing. The mother synchronizes the tone (joy) of the encounter according to how much joy and quiet the *baby* desires. In good synchronization, and in good parenting, the baby's needs are monitored in this process and a good mother stays "in tune" with her baby's needs. The mother leads in the sense that she watches the baby's need to connect or rest, but the baby's needs are the determining factor. This dance of synchronization is all about building joy and allowing the baby to rest in between and is the basis for wiring up the hardware (brain) the whole first year of life.

Connor and Jodi synchronize joy, left eye to left eye

As the mother and baby smile at each other, the joy increases and they climb higher in intensity, until the mother senses that the baby is at his peak, and she backs off to let him rest. Then when he is ready, they build joy again. Whatever is going on in the right side of the brain (joy) of each shows up in each one's left eye. *Six complete cycles* of interaction pass back and forth between both the mother and the baby in one second, too quickly for conscious thought, but the interactions through their eyes are having an effect. These cycles take place below conscious level and cannot be faked. If some other emotion besides joy is going on in the mother, this is what will show up in her left eye. Because this joy and quiet (or other emotions) cannot be faked, baby is affected by what she sees on the other face. What baby sees will be the mirror in which she builds her self- image. The best self-image building and brain hardwiring are done with joy!

Erica (15) synchronizes perfectly with Ryan (8 months)

So what if the mother is not synchronizing, being on the same page and matching energy with her baby? This is de-synchronizing. De-synchronization, the opposite of good synchronization is like bad timing, intensity and tone in music. Upon hearing a musical discord, we can hardly bear more than a few seconds of the noise. De-synchronization feels the same way on an emotional level. De-synchronization happens when an encounter between an adult and baby or child is about the adult's needs instead of the baby or child's. A stranger, or even an unfamiliar relative, might approach a baby with a big smile, wanting to "play joy." Quite often the baby does not respond with a smile and maybe draws back. Bad synchronization increases the intensity by perhaps reaching out to touch the baby and get her to play, pressing her to perform. In de-synchronization, the baby's needs are not monitored and he feels the discord that we feel upon hearing the out-of-tune guitar. A bad "mother/adult" tries to get the baby to meet "her" needs. The following picture of Kori (age 1) and a stranger cousin is an example of this de-synchronization.

Cousin Bronzie "presses" Kori to respond

Although Bronzie is a cousin, Kori did not know him and she was not sure about playing joy with a stranger. A temporary press from a stranger is not damaging, as it would be from a caretaker who relates in a desynchronized manner day in and day out. De-synchronization is not good mothering and when we look at bonding we will see what results can happen from not synchronizing.

As a good mother interacts and synchronizes with her baby, over time the baby learns what to do with emotional distress, those moments when he is stretched to the limit and needs to rest. He learns how to stay synchronized in the relationship while mother helps him calm because she does not overwhelm him. As the pair practices building joy and quiet together, the emotional control center in the brain learns how to get back to peace and joy from uneasy emotions, and very soon the baby knows how to self-calm. When the baby is older, around twelve months, mother will teach him to return to joy from more distressing emotions than he is equipped to handle the first year.

It is important to note that good or bad mothering is passed down physically through this right-brain to right-brain synchronization or de-synchronization. We download what we have. We received what our mothers had unless we have downloaded from someone else along the way. We either know how to do the joy building and backing off to rest or we don't. It depends on the bond we had with our mother and the training we practiced that first year with her. But please continue if that frightens you, because these techniques can be learned. Adults can "download" to other adults; it just takes more time and practice. And that is why I am passionate about giving you this somewhat technical information—first because we can prevent problems when done early, and secondly, it's possible to do remedial work later on.

Now let's look at how the emotional areas of the brain fit into the thriving chart. These five centers of the brain need to stay synchronized with each other in order for us to thrive, to be able to synchronize with others, and to be able to handle distress. Let's consider the five centers again as being somewhat like our computers. Most of us know how windows work in a computer, how more than one can be opened at a time. We also understand how frustrating it is when something on the computer is not functioning properly. Let's suppose we are working on a project where we need five windows open at the same time. One window is central for the top two and the bottom two to function. A problem arises in the middle window that causes the top two to shut down. Now the project is on hold and cannot operate properly just with the two bottom windows. All these windows are de-synchronized. This is a very simple analogy of the five centers and how they need to be synchronized for the person to thrive. We will look at them separately and then together.

Again, though you may not be interested in the whys here, I highly encourage you to go ahead with this section. I have interspersed pictures and stories to illustrate the points and make them easier to grasp. But you do not have to know the names of the brain parts or where they are located in order to be able to bond, build joy and quiet and synchronize. The information will simply give some detail and clarity to reasons why we have relationship problems when our brain de-synchronizes if we are overwhelmed. This chapter, along with Chapters Four and Five are foundational and will detail bonding, joy and returning to joy, all of which are relationship skills that we need to understand regardless of our age.

THE EMOTIONAL CONTROL CENTER

We can begin our more detailed look at the emotional control center of the brain with **The Attachment Center (Level 1),** the deepest level in the control center where bonding takes place, beginning at birth. (We will look closely at bonding in a later section.) You may remember this center as part of the thriving chart where Baby Daniel got so upset when left in the nursery because he did not have a secure bond. This center tells us who or what is important to us. The thalamus is in a deep, sub conscious area of the brain and actually lights up on the scans that the brain researchers are now using. The "attachment light" comes on when we want to draw close and goes off when we want to be alone. When there is a certain person that we want to be with, only that one person will do. We can notice when a baby is feeling this when Daddy is holding him and he wants Mommy. As we will see later, this is Daddy's first opportunity to help the baby calm when he cannot have something he wants.

Our deepest joys and pains are felt in the brain's Attachment Center. Attachment pain is the worst kind of pain we can feel; the kind of horrendous pain we feel when someone dies or a divorce happens. We experience a milder form when someone is on a long trip and we miss him or her. We feel attachment pain whenever we want to connect with someone and can't, regardless of the circumstances that may be preventing the connection. We feel very alone. Later we will look at how *avoiding* attachment pain is very detrimental to mental health and thriving.

This Attachment Center is where we build relationships. Here the baby develops what is called an "internal interpreter" (the ability to know what the person he is bonded with is thinking). We carry this ability with us into adulthood and it will continue to function even after the bonded person is dead. We all know what our mother would think about certain things whether she is living or not. I know my mother is proud of me for working so hard on this book. I know she would be disappointed in me if I did not persevere to finish it.

The capacity we have to synchronize with others and the ability to repair broken attachments are in the Attachment Center. When we look at the section on bonding, we will see how these two fit together. When we know how to repair ruptures (disconnects that result from conflict) in our relationships, we do not fear having a rupture. This makes disconnects easier because we know we will get back together (return to joy).

Because the Attachment Center in the brain is below consciousness level, it is always on and does not shut down during distress, as do some of the higher levels of the brain. That function makes it very important for this area to be strong and have steady, loving bonds with others. There will never be any human who does not need other people even if they pretend not to need others or seem to be self-sufficient. Secure attachments are foundational for healthy emotions.

The Evaluation Center (Level 2), the next deepest level of the control center, is technically called the amygdala. Dr. Wilder affectionately calls it our "guard shack," because it warns us when to fight or to flee. This area develops from pre-birth to two months. It responds all through life to the training it receives about what is good, bad, and/or scary, telling us what to approach or avoid, what is life-giving or not life-giving. You will remember the story for the thriving chart of Little Jessica who was afraid of her daddy, who worried all the time and tried to be invisible. Jessica felt afraid and disconnected.

As this area is programmed with what is good, bad, or scary, that is what the person will believe about that event, object, or person.

© 2007 Barbara Moon

Although what we believe about an event, object or person being good, bad or scary may not be the truth, whatever the Evaluation Center believes about it, that's what it will operate when it is in control if the higher levels shut down. This is another reason for keeping the five centers of the brain synchronized. When the Evaluation Center is in control, all of life is about fear and the person lives from that fear base, tracking his or her environment with fear. A child in school who is living from a fear base will have a difficult time focusing on class work. He will subconsciously be watching his environment for things that are bad and scary. His attention will not be on the teacher, as it needs to be and his classroom performance will show it.

The Evaluation Center functions non-verbally, getting programmed by responses from the body. What it believes about good, bad, and scary cannot be overcome by the will and it never changes its opinions. (There is a way to overcome what it has learned, but we will see that later.) The guard shack is not logical and can never be reasoned with. It never forgets what it has learned, and like the Attachment Center, it is always on, never shut down, ready to take over automatically when distress overwhelms the brain and shuts down the three upper levels (listed below).

Because of these attributes often based on fears, the Evaluation Center is Satan's favorite place to program, since it will continuously broadcast to the rest of the brain what is bad and scary, thus shutting down the upper levels and causing de-synchronization to occur. It uses fear to motivate others and tracks in fear if so trained. So parents who know how to avoid traumas that cause fears (or how to quickly repair them) can equip their child with a strong sense of security and set up building blocks for faith that will handle distress.

My earliest memory of bad and scary happened when I was about four years old. My mother took me to the dentist. In those days, the dentists did not give painkillers when they drilled. I experienced great pain more than once as a dentist drilled and filled my decayed teeth. To this day, I hate going to the dentist and I feel great anxiety even when my mouth is full of Novocain. I cannot choose for this fear to go away. But thanks to God who designed the brain, there is a way to calm the Evaluation Center and after many years of practicing that calming, I can now go somewhat adult-like to the dentist.

An incident happened with Kayli and Kori, the twins with whom I now live, which can illustrate how dealing quickly with a fear avoids a trauma. One evening when they were almost two, the twins and I were in the bathroom getting ready for their bath. Tyler, who was in Kindergarten, opened the door to proudly show off a little paper mask that she had made at school that day. When the twins saw an odd-looking bear's face peeking and growling at them through the now opened door, they immediately and loudly screamed in terror. They had never seen a mask and had no idea what was growling at them right there in the bathroom. I quickly told Tyler to remove the mask so they could see it was she and after a few minutes I was able to calm both twins. Then we took time to look at the mask while I held them and helped them to face this new thing that had caused so much terror. As we synchronized, calmed and observed the mask, we quickly repaired the "trauma." I did not want them to be afraid of masks the rest of their life.

The **Mother Core (Level 3),** the cingulate is the third center of the emotional brain. It is in the middle of the control center. I am calling it the "Mother Core," since this is what much of the scientific literature calls it. From this part of the brain, mothers literally download their Mother Core into that part of their new baby's brain. This takes place during the second to ninth months and is associated with all the time spent synchronizing and building joy and quiet, as the two interact left eye to left eye while building their bond. The Mother Core enables the two brains to match energy states (synchronize). Dr. Wilder says in *Living With Men*, "The mother's older brain duplicates itself in her baby, including what mother knows and how her brain is built." The Mother Core synchronizes the different lobes of the brain, the upper and lower levels of the control center, and baby and mommy's Mother Cores with each other. (pp. 39-40 *LWM*) When the Mother Core functions as it was designed, synchronizing the lower and higher places in the control center, the person thrives. Feeling overwhelmed will shut it off.

The Mother Core is also the part of the brain that understands personal space, tracks eye movements, enables us to dance, and knows empathy. It is the place that produces a true joy smile, not a smile that says "cheese" for a camera.

Brenna has a joy smile   ***Brenna and Aaron say 'cheese'***

At about five months of age, babies' brains are able to discern that there is another mind behind the face they are looking at. This is called "mind-sight." Babies become like the faces with which they are synchronizing, copying the mother's brain (or principle caretaker's). They learn who they are from the reflection of that other face and whether their world is bounded by joy or fear. The caretakers pass on what they have in their Mother Core. They cannot pretend to have something they don't have nor try to pass on something they wish they had. Toddler Kaleb knew his mother's limitations and resigned himself to not having her synchronize well with him.

But there is good news—*the Mother Core can be improved!* Synchronizing with a person who has a stronger Mother Core than you have will grow that part of your brain. But it will take tons more time and energy than when done at the proper time at the age of two to nine months. Although it can take many years of counseling or mentoring, one on one, to grow a better Mother Core, it can be done. My daughter in law, Chris, believes that I helped her Mother Core improve before she had children because she lived with me for some years as a teenager. We built a strong bond and she worked through some difficult issues as she asked questions and trusted God for healing and growth in her life. Chris wanted desperately to improve her children's chances of what they would "catch" from her. It took much courage to work on these issues and improve her Mother Core.

The Mother Core is the emotional bond for *two* faces. It can synchronize with only *one other* at a time. It can think about others, but can only synch with one at a time. The two people synchronize joy, quiet or distress. In a later chapter we will look closely at joy, quiet and calming distress.

Which one is synchronizing real joy?

Learning that we can only synchronize with one person at a time was very helpful living with a family of four girls under the age of four, with two of them twins. The twins were usually doing the same things, having the same distress and needing something at the same time. It was a blessing to have both Mommy and Nana available most of the day so that we could truly synchronize with each instead of feeling like a ping-pong ball bouncing back and forth between the two, or the four.

A few years ago, when Tyler, the oldest was about six, I had an exceptionally colorful lesson about only being able to synchronize with one other at a time. The girls and I were in the van on a hot summer day, hooking car seats and belts, in preparation for a trip to the grocery store. Have you ever been in a van with four little girls under the age of six, when a bee buzzed into the van? I don't think I have ever heard so much screaming, yelling and crying in my life. It was very difficult to calm this ocean of distress by myself as I frantically shooed at the bee while trying to use my voice to calm the girls. It felt like an hour went by before I got the bee out of the van and could one by one, back and forth, calm the screaming girls enough to continue our trip to the store. Interacting in a large family will always feel like a ping-pong match, but it became easier as I realized that going back and forth will work— it just takes a little longer to get to calm.

Intense distress, such as bees in a van or conflict between two or more people, can be overwhelming to any of us. When distress overwhelms our joy capacity to handle distress, the brain de-synchronizes. I call it a "melt down." As mother and baby train in synchronization, baby learns what he needs during overwhelming distress. That need is the same throughout our lifetime. We need, and look for, one brain that is greater (more mature) than ours to help us calm in the midst of the overwhelm. Children look to parents, other caretakers, or even older siblings. This is not always a conscious search, depending on the height of the intensity. It's important that children know they can find the needed help when distressed. Not only do we need to find peace before we can solve a problem, we *will* bond with those who calm us.

As adults (and as older children) the greater mind we turn to during overwhelming distress can be God's. His mind is always greater and always available. Wise is the person who knows when his/her capacity is overwhelmed and can ask someone for help. In a mature and strongly bonded relationship, adults can even be each other's "greater mind" during intense emotions, when one is able to synchronize with the other and both have not "melted down" at the same time.

Besides searching for a "greater mind" to help in need, another function of the Mother Core is the ability to detect when someone is lying to us. This is because the interchanges going back and forth in the eyes are six times per second, below conscious thought. When looking eye-to-eye and synchronizing we cannot fake what is going on inside our minds. This is why people who are lying look down. Perhaps a trained CIA agent or a hardened criminal might be able to hide their true feelings eye to eye, but most of us cannot.

All of the Mother Core's brain-synchronizing functions are done by joy between the two bonded faces. Remember that the Mother Core synchronizes the upper and lower levels of the control center and when the Mother Core becomes overwhelmed by distress, it causes a "melt down." It shuts down the top two layers that we have not looked at yet--the **Logic Center** and the **Joy Center**. Now the Attachment Center and the Evaluation Center, those below consciousness, will run the brain, or person, automatically. Relational circuits are off and this is not good, as we looked at before, because now *fear* will be the motivator of all that is going on with the person since the Evaluation Center is running the show. What is supposed to be motivating us? Joy, peace and love--*not fear*. As we look at what functions occur in the Logic and Joy Centers, we will see that very important life and relational skills are missing when these Centers are shut down. We want to keep the Mother Core running because it determines how the brain stays synchronized. How it runs and stays running is determined by the level of joy the person has.

The Joy Center (Level 4), the fourth center that we want to consider, is called the Right Pre-fontal cortex and is located in the upper front part of the brain in the Right Hemisphere. It develops in the first 24 months of life, becoming 35% of the adult brain. The Joy Center is the place where joy is built. Joy is so important to thriving that I will spend a whole chapter on it. We want to build and maintain lots of joy in order to train and keep this part of the brain running, because lack of joy capacity in this area will greatly affect moral and social behavior. When it goes off, we lose our maturity, become non-relational and do not act like ourselves.

Here in the Joy Center we also have our impulse control and goal directed behavior, functions that are vital to relating well and living life. Remember Teenagers Veronica and Vanessa? Their different foundations of joy strength and capacity to handle distress greatly affected their maturity and how they responded to the complexities in their world.

The Joy Center also carries our personal preferences, gives us creativity and personal identity, does emotional regulation and determines what we will pay attention to in the world around us. The

Joy Center enables us to switch the focus of our attention. If you stop to think about it, our attention is one of our most priceless commodities. Everyone wants our attention. This ability to focus and switch attention, as well as all the other functions of the Joy Center, are lost when there is not enough joy to keep it synchronized and functioning. We don't know what to do nor do we know what satisfies.

In the Joy Center, babies also carry an image of their mother's face that interprets the meaning of the baby's life. This message that the baby carries about life revolves around either joy or fear. The baby learns this message from non-verbal images and memories, not from words. In the chapter on joy, we will look at how joy is built non-verbally and re-emphasize the importance of lots of joy.

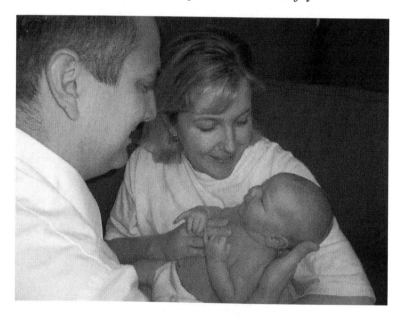

Three faces--Rick, Jodi and Connor (five days old)

Unlike the Mother Core, which is a two-way focus, the Joy Center has room for a *third* face. It carries a three-way mental image of two people looking at each other while the third face watches. Ideally in the formation months, the three faces are baby, mother and father. To work as this part of the brain is designed, these three faces must be in joy. The child sees from his or her perspective. He knows nothing about circumstances or problems going on in the adults. He simply records joy or fear. One reason this is important is that it affects the baby's view of God. If for example mother and baby are in joy and the baby looks to the third face (Daddy) and he is scowling, the brain can be programmed to think this is the way God is. When baby looks at daddy and his face is enjoying baby and mother's joy, the baby feels secure. He will get a realistic "picture" of God. (See Workbook, Appendix C for a re-training exercise.)

Throughout life, we are able to continue three-way bonds when the Joy Center is functioning. The three in the bond might be two friends and God, three friends, three family members, etc. In addition, when the Joy Center is running well, we can have three points of view. Having three points of view is very useful because the three-way focus in the Joy Center provides the means to calm the Evaluation Center and override it opinions of bad and scary. *Validation of emotions* and *comfort* are two necessary ingredients.

The Father's patience—Greg and Tyler—three-way focus

Here is how it works: Viewpoint one, the child's, sees or feels something scary. Viewpoint two, the adult's, decides how they will react to the scary situation. When the situation is not overwhelming to the adult, the adult synchronizes with the child, gives comfort and calms the distress. Now they can look at the scary and bad situation, object or feeling together while validating the feelings. Remember when I calmed everyone after the growling bear mask and then we looked at the mask? The older brain helps calm the distress in the younger brain and overrides the fear, bringing peace and quiet. Now the child will not experience a trauma because he or she has received comfort, synchronization and a different perspective on the fear. The bond will deepen between the two people, as we want to be with those who calm us. The three-way focus for calming works in all relationships regardless of age.

As your child gets older, you can add to this use of the three-way focus for calming by doing the Immanuel Process described in Chapter Eight under *Tips for Ages 5-10*. Be sure to look also at the body exercises in Chapter Six under *Calming the Brain* for additional help. A summary of the two is at the end of the book.

Another way to look at the three-way focus is through imagining a classroom, a seminar, or even job training. I cannot teach you anything until I get your attention. In the Joy Center we are able to direct attention and bring the focus onto the lesson at hand when all is functioning correctly. In the later chapter on joy we will talk more about the importance of this in discipline and training our children. When I am directing a child's attention to an important issue or important instructions, I usually say, "Look at my eyes." Now we are able to focus on the instructions or task. I have her attention.

It is vital to understand how important it is to build joy and quiet in these early years. How joy is built during the first two years of life affects the coping abilities that the adult will have and greatly determines how the person will walk through life, how he will handle distress, and whether he or she will shut down during intense emotions. When all is synchronized and well trained, the baby or person will not shut down easily under distress, but will, as Dr. Wilder calls it, "suffer well." Suffering well means that we can continue to be relational and remember who we are (at whatever maturity level we have) during the distress. Below is a picture of Brenna, around the age of three, after I had just pierced one of her ears. Although she knows there is about to be some pain, she suffers well in Mommy's arms and keeps acting like herself.

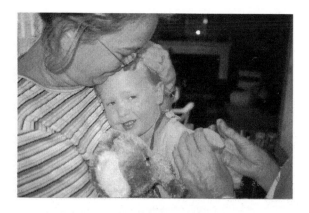

Brenna suffers well

The best example of suffering well is how Jesus behaved while on the Cross. Though His suffering was horrendous, both physically and emotionally, He continued to relate to those around Him and act like Himself. In Chapter Two we mentioned this ability also in emergency responders and others who act heroically, as they remain calm when many people would panic.

Suffering well happens when our joy capacity, a.k.a. our Joy Bucket, is at its fullest in the Joy Center. This joy capacity grows best at the times that the brain is most receptive, between the second and ninth months of age, but the Joy Center is one of the few places in the emotional brain where growth continues throughout life. This makes the Joy Center vital to helping those who did not receive the joy they needed as babies. Joy capacity can be built throughout the lifetime, but it will take much longer when not done the first two years of life.

While remembering that building joy is important enough to have its own chapter, let's briefly recap some of the importance of building this Joy Center in our children. When running well, the Joy Center directs our attention to the world and joy keeps the whole brain synchronized with access to all functions. If overwhelmed by intense emotions, this part shuts down, we lose our maturity and we cannot maintain our identity or act like ourselves. We've lost ourselves. We lose the ability to live from goal directed thinking, to maintain impulse control, to focus on tasks at hand, or remain calm during alarming situations. When the Joy Center shuts down we cannot calm the Evaluation Center and regulate distressing, fearful emotions. This affects moral and social behavior. We can no longer hear instructions. We need help from someone who is not overwhelmed by the distress, who can synchronize and bring us back to peace.

The Logic Center (Level 4+) is what I call the fifth area of the emotional control center. It is the left side of the pre-frontal cortex located in the Left Hemisphere, or left side, of the brain. When it is up and running, the Logic Center is the place for language and telling autobiographical stories. It is the place for explaining our lives. Like its name, it is the place for logic, reasoning and words. The Logic Center works best at school, seminars and listening to sermons and is not interested in helping us out much where negative emotions are concerned.

The Logic Center is the first level to be shut down (de-synchronized) when distress overwhelms the person's capacity for joy in the Joy Center. We will feel confused and not be able to walk what we talk. When it is not functioning because of a shut-down, counseling, preaching, teaching, exhorting and admonishing fall on deaf ears (or a deaf brain). Words do not help a person who has a non-functioning Logic Center, so it is useless to lecture and instruct at that time.

Someone has to sit with the overwhelmed person, synchronize with the distress and calm the distress before the person can hear instructions. The problem cannot be fixed by words. In the chapter on discipline I will explain the importance of realizing this when dealing with children.

As the brain stays synchronized from the **Attachment Center (Level 1)** all the way to the **Logic Center (Level 4+)**, we live from a coherent identity that is the same over time. We understand that we are the same person through the years and we act the same and have the same values regardless of distress. Remember Young Man Will who lived a dual life? He was not able to walk what he talked and did not have a consistent identity. This young man did not live from his heart, but rather lived from the lies that others had told him.

When all levels of the control center are up and running, we live by our heart. We Christians call this our spirit, which is the "eyes and ears" of the real us. After receiving Christ, the Holy Spirit lives in our spirit and leads us through our heart as we listen and obey His guidance. Living from the heart is the opposite of living by the "flesh," (*sark* in the Greek) the "old programming and lies" we received growing up. (Galatians 5:16) We will look more closely at this later in the book.

The Logic Center does not change its opinions or beliefs that it has formed through the years. It will resist changes even in the face of *evidence* to the contrary—unless things get upset inside. Think about when a person goes to war. Before going, he or she may not believe in God or want God to be part of their life. Upon facing the dangers of war, upset occurs and not wanting anything to do with God may quickly change. Similarly, when a child gets sick or someone has a car wreck, people often turn to God whom they have not acknowledged before the upset. Being upset allows the right side of the brain to decide that the Logic Center can change its opinion. Knowing this principle dealt a blow to my fear of "upsetness". I used to believe that "peace at all costs" was better than upset. Now I feel less threatened if upset occurs because I know that it will be easier for me or the other person to change something we believe that is not the truth. Knowing this fact also changed my opinion of giving lots of evidence to someone with whom I disagreed. I could save my breath by not trying to talk them into something their Logic Center could not hear.

When the Logic Center shuts down from de-synchronization, we lose the ability to explain ourselves and make sense of our circumstances. We feel confused and experience an incoherent identity. We aren't able to focus as well. This creates internal conflict and we need help finding the truth about the situation. According to Dr. Daniel Siegel, author of *The Developing Mind*, when the Logic Center is down, we also cannot tell a good concise story about our past. His research has shown that the ability to tell a concise story about our past will reveal which of the four attachment styles we have. (p. 112 TDM) We will be looking at those in a later chapter also, but for now let's look at why being able to tell stories is important to us as parents.

Stories help children make sense of their world as they talk about events and receive comfort and validation. As parents, we want to get good at telling stories—stories from our own past, stories about our people, stories about the current family, stories about God, and stories about the children when they were young. This is how we pass down our heritage. Story telling also helps the brain because we use both the left side of the brain (language and logic) and the right side (emotions and synchronizing).

A good way to begin telling stories is with picture albums and videos. But use words to tell the stories, not just the videos. As they listen, children will learn what it is like "us and our people" (their heritage) to do under various circumstances. Children love stories and they love to ask questions. As we tell our own stories to illustrate a value or resolution to a problem, or as we use Bible stories, parables, and fables, the children will absorb the lessons we want to instill in them. If you feel that you do not have a good heritage, tell stories that illustrate how *not* to do things. Use those stories; age appropriately, as examples of how you want your child to grow up differently than you or your ancestors did.

Another reason for telling stories is that when bad things happen, telling a story about it helps prevent trauma. This is one of the ways that children make sense of what happened. Children need to process both the event and the emotions involved. (Siegel, *Parenting from the Inside Out*) Their processing often takes the form of talking about the event and/or emotions over and over for a while, but it can also be helpful to act out what happened or use props to tell the story. Older children and adults as well, can tell stories about past experiences that they have never made sense of in order to process the emotions connected to the event. Unresolved traumas, grief and loss interfere with thriving and good parenting. (Siegel) As we talk about the event and the emotions that were bad or scary, it is important to give comfort and to tell the truth about all of it. It will not help prevent a trauma if we untruthfully tell them that something is "no big deal" when it may be a big deal to the child.

A while back my son, Greg, and his friend, Mike, had an occasion to practice comforting and telling the truth about an emotional event. They took Greg's four girls and Mike's son to see the movie *Eight Below*. The dads had not previewed the movie and did not know there was a part that was shockingly scary to little kids. Kori and Brenna nearly jumped out of their seats when, in one scene, a large leopard seal suddenly leapt out of a whale carcass, loudly roaring to the accompaniment of blaring music. Quickly each daddy took one of the girls onto his lap, held them closely and comforted them until the scene changed. For two days afterwards, Brenna, wanted to tell her mommy all about the scene in the movie, especially at bedtime. Mommy (Chris) allowed her to process it as long as she needed; while at the same time synchronizing and helping her to peace as she did so. If the parents had scoffed at or ignored the fear and said it was no big deal, they would not have been telling the truth. If they had called the girls, "baby" for feeling scared, or hurried them through the process, there would not have been any validation about the feelings of terror they'd had.

SUMMARY

I hope the brain stuff did not sound too confusing and technical to you, and I encourage you to study enough to get the gist of its importance. If you are pregnant, have a newborn, will one day have a newborn or know a newborn, spread the information as much as you can about synchronizing, building joy, allowing quiet together and bonding. These building blocks work best to make a good foundation when they are done at God's designed window of opportunity from pre-birth to around the age of two. But if that window of opportunity has passed, we can do remedial work, though it will take much longer than at the designated time. Keep in mind that you can't do everything perfectly, so when you blow it, seek forgiveness and stay glad to be together. Talk about scary things that happen so traumas won't settle into your child's emotions. Use the Immanuel Process and Shalom body exercises age appropriately for further healing as needed. And keep in mind that prevention takes much less energy than recovery.

(See Appendix A for information on the Immanuel Process and body exercises.)

CHAPTER FOUR: BONDING, SYNCHRONIZATION, JOY AND QUIET

Goal: to understand bonding and the synchronization of joy and quiet together

INTRODUCTION

As we looked at Dr. Wilder's chart for thriving along with the scenarios after each section, it was easier to see that healthy development requires synchronization, joy, peace and rest, and truth. We looked at the maturity stages that humans grow through in order for us to observe the responsibility of maturing. We have looked at the levels of the emotional control center in the brain and how these five centers need to be synchronized in order for a baby (or person) to be healthy. Now I would like to take a brief journey through the Infant Stage in order to illustrate how bonding, synchronization, joy and quiet contribute to children thriving through joy. Remember—I am passionate about prevention. (I will speak again about each of these years in **Chapter Eight**—practical tips for all age groups.)

When we build the ideal foundation, at the ideal time the brain is prepared for it, our task is much easier. As I have said, remedial work can be done, but it takes more time and energy than when done during the first two years. Dr. Wilder tells us that secure bonding, full joy capacity, synchronization, and God's truth are essential to a healthy life and with the topics at which we have already looked; we can now co-ordinate how the first three essentials fit with how God designed the brain. We will bring Dr. Wilder's fourth requirement for healthy development—truth—into a later chapter.

BONDING

Bonding securely is the very cornerstone of your baby's new life. Some kind of bond affected your little one even before he was born, as you carried him or her close to your heart.   Your attitude about being pregnant, your state of mind and emotions, and your physical and emotional health all contributed to the cornerstone you two would lay. Babies already "know" something of their world before they leave that warm and snug environment inside. The first hours and days outside the womb are vital to his health and well-being, setting the foundation upon which he will grow. All of us continue to bond one way or another throughout life.

The foundational bond that your baby needs in order to be healthy in all respects is a secure bond. Bonding takes place in the brain within what we called the Attachment Center when we looked at the emotional side of the brain in Chapter Three. But all bonds that people build are not secure bonds. According to Dr. Daniel Siegel and other researchers, there are four styles of bonds, only one of which is a secure bond. I want to describe each of these bonds and what determines which kind of bond it is; that is, whether it is based on love or based on fear. As we look closer at these types of bonds, I will use Dr. Wilder's interpretation of Dr. Daniel Siegel's book, *The Developing Mind*. He has "renamed" three of the attachment styles so that they are easier to remember. As we look at them, we will again see why synchronizing is so important to good development. We shall call the four types of bonds (1) Secure, (2) Dismissive, (3) Distracted, and (4) Disorganized.

As you read through the information on the four bonds, here are some questions to consider and answer:

Which of the four bonds do I think I had as a child?

What kinds of bonds have I seen modeled around me?

How do I want to bond differently with my own children?

Do I know a person who bonds/relates well who might mentor me?

What strengths for bonding do I have?

What weaknesses do I bring to bonding with my child?

Where might I need to seek help or repair for existing bonds?

What do I turn to for comfort?

Keep these questions and your answers handy as you read. We will look at them again.

SECURE

A secure bond is one that is based on love and desire and is not based on fear. Bonding begins at birth, at first by smell, even before the infant can see. Keeping the infant warm and giving him or her food adds to positive early bonding. At about the sixth week touch helps the bonding process. When the infant can see better around three to twelve weeks, he begins to interact more and build joy. Around twelve weeks bonding continues with voice tone and facial expressions. In a secure bond, the parent synchronizes with the baby and watches closely how the baby is feeling, matching his timing, intensity and tone as they interact building joy and quiet. Through the bonding process, by three months of age, baby has a picture in his mind of what his mother feels about him. We want that picture to be framed in joy.

During a joy-filled bonding process, the parents are attentive to the baby's needs for comfort, food, and protection, meeting those needs in a timely manner. A secure bond is built with lots of cuddling and holding. The baby feels safe and loved. He or she does not encounter angry faces or negative voice tones. The atmosphere around her may be calm or filled with "happy noise," but in either case, fear is not part of her world.

Baby is not looking for fear. He is looking for someone who is glad to be with him. As the new brain technology evolved that enabled researchers to observe the living brain, scans of what we are calling the Attachment Center of the brain showed an actual "light" that comes on in the brain when a person wants to bond or draw close to another. This desire is communicated by the brain in non-verbal communication—through eyes, through sounds, through body movements. Baby looks for a face and eyes that will sparkle with joy at seeing him. He is looking for joyful faces. When he wants to disconnect he will look away and up towards the left.

This little light is the key to bonding and how it progresses. In a secure bond the light goes off and on according to the desire of the child to be engaged with another. A good parent knows when to engage (draw close) and disengage (back off), following the pattern of the child. A secure bond is about the baby and his desire, not about the parent. This is synchronization, when mother follows the baby's need for attachment or quiet and both of their attachments lights go off and on together. Baby learns that connecting is "good." (p. 39 Living With Men)

One aspect of knowing (at any age) that connecting and relating is a good thing comes from each person in the relationship having the freedom to "come and go." What that means is that in the relationship neither person clinches, controls or holds on to the other in any way that would hinder the other's growth and uniqueness. In infancy and childhood, we symbolically express this freedom to "come and go" in the dance of synchronization where the caretaker stays aware of the child's need to connect (build joy and bond) and disconnect to rest. Children are not actually free to come and go from the home at a young age, but synchronization is an emotional interaction that will later become an actual physical event. As a child grows into greater maturity the *symbol* of freedom will remain as we allow a teenager to try his or her unique wings at the same time he or she is coming and going *physically* from the home. For the infant we are aiming towards an authentic, healthy relationship where one person does not try to control the other person by telling them what to do, think, feel and become. One does not punish the other for having desires and interests that may be different than the other's desires and interests. Being free to "come and go" without fear of retribution is part of synchronization and one sign of a secure bond. Teenager Vanessa from Chapter Three has a secure bond. Like Vanessa, adults with a secure bond thrive, are relational and are a joy to be around.

DISMISSIVE

In a dismissive bond the baby's little "light" in the Attachment Center stays off most of the time because his need for closeness has been dismissed or gone unnoticed. Unlike the secure bond, which is based on love, this bond is based on fear, as are the other two we will look at. When baby's emotional needs go unmet or are not synchronized with well, the child fears that no one will dependably synchronize with him, so he "gives up." The parent ignores the child's desire to connect by being rejecting or emotionally unavailable and eventually the child pretends that this is all right. (A child can portray a false self as early as eighteen months of age. Remember Toddler Kaleb from Chapter Three?)

Nothing will ever hurt more than having one's attachment light ignored. (Wilder) The pain from being dismissed and ignored will cause the child to decide that wanting to connect is "bad" and she will try to hide her need for it. Since the child is "pretending" that all is well, in the family there may be an appearance that the child is a very good child, when in truth, the child has resigned himself to not having his needs met when they arise. The damage from this type of bond may not show until it is time to bond with his/her spouse and children. (p. 40 LWM) A dismissive bond is about the parent and his or her needs, not about the child. Adults with a dismissive bond find it difficult to connect with others and may appear independent, unemotional and aloof.

In order to avoid forming a dismissive bond, a baby's needs must be met immediately and joyfully up to about the twelfth month. Doing so builds hope. Around the twelfth month, as we will look at later, things change, but a crying infant needs attention and we must do all we can to figure out how to help. There are on the market right now a few parenting books that teach parents the dismissive type of parenting. They advocate letting a newborn cry himself to sleep in the crib whenever the parent decides it is time. The infant eats when the mother decides. Everything is scheduled firmly by the parent, even at a very young age. Babies need a schedule, but not too early. They eventually come to one on their own around three to four months but should never be left to cry it out the first year. Some of these books speak against "attachment theories" but after we understand how God designed the brain, we cannot agree with such a form of parenting. Using these methods, one might have an infant that gives no sleep problems, but we must ask ourselves what might be the reason? Did the baby give up on getting his needs met or did she healthily learn to self-comfort? I would not want to risk the former for any amount of sleep or time to myself. The only reason to leave an infant crying in a crib is if the parent is so upset that being with the child would endanger the child. The parent should leave and get calm, then return as soon as possible— or call for help. Being ignored is very painful.

DISTRACTED

Like the dismissive bond, the distracted bond is also based on fear instead of love. Again because of inconsistent synchronizing, in a distracted bond, the child fears he might miss getting his needs met because they get met so sporadically. His little "light" stays on all the time. This child is needy and clingy and gets very upset when caregivers are out of sight. Remember Baby Daniel when he was left in the nursery? This bond is also about the parent instead of about the child. The mother wants the baby to synchronize with her. She looks for the baby to meet her needs for closeness when *her* "light" is on, regardless of the baby's desire at the moment. (p. 40 LWM) A mother distracted by her own neediness, with intrusions of unresolved issues from her past, often approaches the baby for closeness when she needs it. Not being in tune with the child's state of mind, and ignoring the baby's desire and signals for closeness, her interruption will distract him and then he will cling to her. Sometimes a needy mother gets pregnant thinking that having a baby to love her will bring her happiness. Adults who have a distracted bond will seem to have emotions that are too intense and will often seem needy and clingy.

DISORGANIZED

The most harmful type of bond is a disorganized bond, when the attachment light comes on and the desire to draw close produces unpredictable or scary reactions from those around the baby. Fear is the cement in all parts of a disorganized bond. The baby is trying or wanting to bond with either someone who is angry at him, someone he fears, or the one with which he wants to bond is afraid of someone else.

This leaves the baby with no one who can soothe him as the caretakers are caught up in their own unresolved pain. This is the kind of bond that Little Jessica has. Babies cannot thrive in this kind of fear-filled environment. They desire closeness based on joy, on someone being glad to be with them. When desiring closeness brings anger, fear or too much intensity, the baby becomes disorganized. He will have difficulty coping, setting the stage for future mental illness and poor relationships. (p. 41 LWM) It is very difficult to relate to adults who have a disorganized attachment from living with too much anger and fear. A life filled with fear and anger is very painful.

Before we continue, I want to add one tip about bonding from Dr. Wilder. Because smell is such an important part of bonding, Dr. Wilder recommends keeping artificial smells to a minimum during the first six weeks. "Bonding with cigarette smoke or alcohol on the parents' breath, the smell of fresh paint in the baby's room or perfumes may include these smells among those which will say comfort, love and belonging for the baby's whole life. Under stress they will seek these for comfort." (p. 14 LWM) This recommendation seems to make sense and at the least would be wise to consider. I don't think we want alcohol or tobacco to be what our children turn to for comfort. What we do want our children to turn to for comfort is people with whom they are joyfully bonded.

Now that you have looked more closely at each of the bonds, let's review the questions, along with your answers, that you considered at the beginning of this section:

Which of the four bonds do I think I had as a child?

What kinds of bonds have I seen modeled around me?

Do I know a person who bonds/relates well who might mentor me?

How do I want to bond differently with my own children?

What strengths for bonding do I have?

What weaknesses do I bring to bonding with my child?

Where might I need to seek help or repair for existing bonds?

What do I turn to for comfort?

If after looking at your answers, you feel ill-equipped to bond securely with your child, or you just want to do a better job than your own parents did, here's what you might want to consider. The basis of professional counseling is exploring one's childhood. Depending on your need, a Christ-centered counselor could be a great help. As I said in the maturity chapter, small groups at church, conferences, regular church attendance, and being mentored all help us to grow. The very fact that you are reading a parenting book says that you want to do your best, so don't be shy to ask for help.

I had a counselee several years back who longed to improve her chances of building a good bond with her children. Her childhood bonds had principally been based on fear. It seemed growing up that she never knew what was going to come her way—nurture or rejection.

She was not allowed to express any negative emotions except sadness. She spent most of her life pretending to be okay. Two things she wanted to do differently when she became a mother were to build loving, secure bonds with her children and to allow them to express their emotions, thoughts and desires. I still know this person today and, because she faced her needs and lacks and grew in her relationship with Jesus, I can tell you, that with God's grace, she has accomplished both of her longings. Her children are secure and loving, able to show negative emotions and to voice their opinions respectfully without fear.

SYNCHRONIZING JOY—THE FIRST YEAR

We have just looked at the importance of bonding and how tuning in to our newborn's needs and meeting them timely are important aspects of secure bonding. We have seen how important synchronizing joy and quiet is in helping babies feel loved and wanted. Babies thrive and bond best with whoever brings them joy. Love (secure) bonds grow through shared joy and those strong joyful bonds help minimize stress as joy keeps our brains functioning the way God designed them. I believe that joy and what it means is important enough for a closer look.

Joy means that someone is glad to be with me—no matter what. They are glad to be with me at whatever level of maturity I am and my emotions do not frighten them away. Joy means that I am the sparkle in someone's eye and they light up when they see me. We are creatures of joy by our Creator's design; it's our natural state. (Wilder) The Scriptures are full of verses about joy. Joy seems to be extremely important to God. In one concordance, I counted over 160 verses just with the word "joy." Here are a few examples:

Joy and Strength: Do not be grieved, for the joy of the Lord is your strength. (Nehemiah 8:10)

Fullness of Joy: In Thy presence is fullness of joy. (Psalm 16:11)

Joy is the Youngest Emotion: For when the sound of your greeting reached my ears, the baby leaped in my womb for joy. (Luke 1:44)

Joy Gave Jesus His Strength: . . . who for the joy set before Him, endured the cross. (Hebrews 12: 2)

Joy is Why Jesus Spoke to Us: These things have I spoken unto you. . . that your joy may be made full. (John 15:11)

Joy Brings Us Through Trials: Consider it all joy, my brethren, when you encounter various trials. (James 1:2)

Why Jesus Said We Should Pray: . . . ask and you will receive that your joy may be made full. (John 16:24)

Joy is Why Scripture Was Written: And these things we write that your joy may be made complete. (1 John 1:4)

Joy is Why We Fellowship: . . . I hope to come to you and speak face to face, that your joy may be made full. (2 John 1:12)

We Are Each Other's Joy: For you are our glory and joy. (1 Thessalonians 2:20)

Joy Characterizes Disciples: And the disciples were continually filled with joy and with the Holy Spirit. (Acts 13:52)

Joy comes from Godly parenting: And he who has a wise son will joy in him. (Proverbs 23:24).

I have no greater joy than to hear of my children walking in the truth. (3 John 4)

Joy and Health: A joyful heart is good medicine. (Proverbs 17:22) [Building joy in the early months physically sets the foundation of the immune system. (Wilder)]

Joy is principally learned by *non-verbal* communication. As we saw earlier, the Joy Center is on the right side of the brain and communicates without words. Educators have long realized the importance of non-verbal exercises that can aid learning. When I was a high school Spanish teacher, I used marching, clapping, rapping, and throwing balls to help my students learn. In the same way, we build joy without words. Joy smiles are the best way. True joy smiles come from the Mother Core, the third center we looked at in the brain's control center. Cheesy camera smiles are not true joy smiles. Joy smiles light up the eyes and communicate to the other person that we are glad to be with them. Our eyes sparkle.

Kori's eyes sparkle with joy

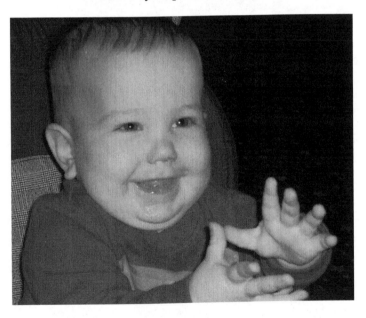

Ryan in medium joy

Singing is another great joy builder and aids learning as well. Poetry and rhymes build joy, as do proper touching and pleasant smells. Though words are not the best joy builders, voice tone plays a very significant part. High voice tones communicate joy and approval. Low tones indicate disapproval. Matching energy (synchronizing) also communicates that someone is the sparkle in our eyes. Playing with babies or pets and enjoying elderly people can fill us with joy. Any activity that encourages us to be glad to be together helps fill the Joy Buckets of all involved.

Joy is what develops the brain as God designed it. Dr. Wilder uses an analogy of camping to describe the building of joy. Joy Camp is our natural state, our destination each night (Ephesians 4:26) and where we want others to be with us. We set up Joy Camp at birth by the bonding methods mentioned earlier—smell, food, temperature, tone, and later eyes and faces. Joy Camp is where we feel safe, loved and have our needs met. We want the newborn baby to know Joy Camp as the *normal state* of being, the "destination" which he will seek and return to the rest of his life.

Joy Camp is on top of a tall mountain. Babies have to practice climbing that mountain all the time. The more they practice, the higher they can climb. The higher they can climb, the more capacity for joy they will have in their Joy Buckets (the Joy Center of the brain) to help them cope with distress. We want the Joy Bucket to be both large (capacity) and also full. I will say more about this later.

For this writing we are going to assume that the mother is the principle caretaker, the person who takes baby up Joy Mountain. Others of course can build joy with baby any time the baby desires. When the brain reaches its peak of joy building during the ninth month, baby will want to build joy up to *eight hours a day*. This makes it very important that mother is with the baby and that she is filled with joy herself. If mother is gone most of that time, baby will be cheated out of some of his capacity growth.

SYNCHRONIZING QUIET TOGETHER

Another aspect of building joy capacity in the brain is synchronizing quiet along with the joy. For this book we are defining synchronization as "matching energy levels and being on the same wave-length or same page as another." We have used Dr. Wilder's analogy of good music—timing, intensity and tone. We saw earlier that a good mother is to teach her baby how to synchronize his brain and how to synchronize with other people. The mother accomplishes this, as we said, by communicating with her infant right brain to right brain, left eye to left eye, at a rate of six times per second back and forth. This rate of interchange is below the conscious level and is totally *non-verbal* communication. Joy is built as the mother and infant interact, break away for rest, and re-connect. When the mother stays in tune with the baby's needs to either climb Joy Mountain or rest, they are synchronizing joy and quiet.

As the baby's joy intensity rises, the mother watches for the baby to reach his or her highest peak of joy. The baby will then look away to rest. The difference in a good and bad mother happens here. If the bond is about the baby, the good mother will allow her baby to rest, lower her heart rate, and wait on the baby to coast down in intensity before building the joy again. A bad mother will not allow the baby to rest, but will continue to stimulate the baby past what he is able to handle—until he cries. She may continue pressing the child to smile in order to look good to others. She may subconsciously try to get the

124   © 2007 Barbara Moon

baby to meet her needs for closeness. When a mother takes her baby beyond his or her capacity level of joy, the baby goes into overwhelm. Over time this contributes to problems associated with the three negative attachment styles, paving a path for problems down the road.

Synchronizing quiet together is just as vital as synchronizing joy. Dr. Allen Schore's studies indicate that too much stimulation is even more harmful than too little. (p. 19 LWM) Alternating joy and quiet allows the baby to learn to synchronize his own mind as well as his relationships. The baby learns to be energetic, to be able to calm himself, to build emotional capacity. As he rests after reaching the top of Joy Mountain, he learns that he can return to joy and eventually, with practice, he will be able to regulate his own emotions. (p. 20 LWM)

Quiet together is not the same as being left alone. Quiet together means the baby knows someone is there with him even though the arousal state is a resting one. Not allowing a baby to rest after his or her peak of joy is reached is the main predictor of future mental illness. (Schore) Again, this kind of interaction is about the adult's needs, not the baby's.

My daughter Jodi, (her family is in white on the back cover) shortly after having her first baby, passed along this important point about quiet and rest to her friends. As Connor began to smile and build joy, to interact with other people, Jodi would tell her friends to let him rest before going too high in intensity. She spread the word that going past the baby's capacity was very harmful. I don't know how many times growing up I saw an adult tickle a child until he or she cried or begged for mercy, forcing the child beyond his or her capacity into an overwhelmed state. This kind of harmful play is an example of de-synchronization. It should not be allowed. Healthy development is about both joy and quiet together. Joyful squeals of pleasure are part of building joy, climbing high up Joy Mountain, but it is up to the adult as the older brain to synchronize with the younger brain, and watch for that needed break to rest.

Greg and Kayli enjoy quiet together

SUMMARY

Joy is the only emotion that infants seek on their own. What this means is that your baby arrives already hardwired by God to look for eyes that sparkle and light up upon seeing him or her. Your infant will use body language, sounds and eyes to seek for that light in someone's eyes. If your baby arrives from Heaven looking for joy, what could be more important than having parents who are filled with joy that will spill over into the baby's heart? Because God has made us to be creatures of joy, being glad to be with him or her (joy) is what we want to use for training our child to handle the ups and downs of life. Climbing Joy Mountain develops emotional strength and capacity and a strong self. That capacity sustains the child through life's sufferings, mistakes, disappointments and losses. How she sees herself will be determined by what she sees on the faces that rear her; what she sees reflected in the eyes that behold her. Will she see someone who is glad to be with her, or will she see fear and anger? Will he be able to pack lots of joy up that mountain or will he be easily overwhelmed? Will he be strong under distress or weak and easily defeated? Their training on Joy Mountain the first year of life will greatly determine the answers to these questions about how children will live life and handle its disappointments and losses. When Mommy and Daddy synchronize joy and quiet, connection and aloneness, intensity and calm, while consistently meeting baby's needs for comfort and cuddling, the baby will thrive. A secure bond with both parents will set the stage for internalized security for life.

CHAPTER FIVE: RETURNING TO JOY

Goal: to understand the Big Six Emotions and how to return to joy.

INRODUCTION

As we have seen, the first year is all about building joy and learning to have quiet together. As the baby becomes able to synchronize at high joy levels, he or she is now ready to learn to return to joy from distress. Mother and baby have practiced climbing Joy Mountain during this first year, building greater and greater capacity for joy. Dr. Wilder calls this capacity our Joy Bucket. As mother and baby move into the next six months, which involves learning to return to joy from the negative emotions, the size and fullness of the Joy Bucket will determine how well the baby can regulate his emotions and handle distress. Joy strength determines the capacity to persevere during intense moments. Emotional training in the first two years is all about joy, quiet, returning to joy, and building and strengthening the Joy Center. All of these skills require joy-filled relationships.

Kori (age 1) is ready to work on return to joy

During this crucial two years, the mother and other close caretakers must have Joy Buckets of their own that are running over. It is vital that mother and daddy have support from each other and others in their community; that they have life giving experiences, so that their Joy Buckets will be full enough to fill the baby's Joy Bucket and help him or her build return to joy circuits in the brain. We can only learn return to joy in relationships that function in joy.

Mommy as the principle caretaker must guard against burning out, as she interacts constantly with the little one. Mommy has to find ways to have some time for herself to keep her own Joy Bucket full. She needs lots of encouragement, time with other Mommies, and dates with Daddy. If there is any hint of depression past the normal "baby blues," someone must intervene and get more help.

TWELVE TO EIGHTEEN MONTHS

As parents continue building joy and keeping the Joy Buckets full, return-to-joy building will begin around the first birthday. Around this first birthday, a good mother who has a well-trained Mother Core will intuitively know it is time to start upsetting her baby. Up until now we have done very little to upset baby, being careful to meet all needs as they arose. We were delighted to synchronize joy and quiet and practice climbing Joy Mountain together. Now mother and baby will work on returning to joy from negative emotions. Parents lovingly guide baby into and back out of these negative feelings so the brain can form "back to joy" circuits. (Wilder)

There are six basic negative emotions common to all cultures. (Joy is the seventh basic emotion) (Siegel). The six negatives are disgust, sad, fear, shame, anger and hopeless despair. Between the ages of twelve to eighteen months, baby's brain must learn a path back to joy from these basic six emotions. Dr Wilder defines "return to joy" as "reconnecting with someone who made me feel distressed." I have added to this definition "being glad to be with someone during distress and helping them stabilize and calm." For this to be successful, two things have to happen: the parent must share the bad feeling with the child (synchronize) and then return to joy (be glad to be together in the feeling and reconnect if needed.) The child's brain copies the parent's brain as the parent shows the child how to feel the feeling, quiet the feeling and stay relational and flexible at the same time. (p. 23 LWM) This experience makes a return to joy path that is stored in the Right Hemisphere. Returning to joy is another aspect of what I did in the van with the bee and with the bear mask.

The capacity strength for climbing back to joy will be directly related to the earlier strength developed climbing Joy Mountain with Mommy in the first year. When the path is there and joy strength is adequate, return to joy takes under ninety seconds.

Chris-and Kayli who's angry. ***Returned to joy in ten***
seconds.

Before talking more about this path back to joy in the brain, let's look at some definitions that will help us better understand these basic six emotions. These are taken from notes I've made at Dr. Wilder's conference on thriving:

We can note as we look at the following definitions and pictures of the Big Six emotions that the babies' emotions may seem mild compared to how we as adults view the emotions. Remember that the age for the baby to feel the emotions and build the path back to joy from them is twelve to eighteen months. These are foundational, right-brain circuits and under normal conditions, the baby will grow capacity and practice them over a long period before having to feel them more intensely as we do when older.

THE BIG SIX EMOTIONS

Disgust: *"Something is not giving me life here."* When Kayli and Kori, my twin granddaughters were around eighteen months, among many other crazy things they did were some disgusting ones. One day I caught the two of them in the bathroom. They had taken toilet paper and dipped and sloshed it up and down in the toilet, splashing water all over the floor, the seat and themselves. At the moment I arrived and opened the door (with my trusty camera in hand,) I snapped a picture of Kori with the wet toilet paper in her mouth. That is definitely an example of something that does not give life to either the participant or the observer.

Kayli and Kori -- Disgusting Fun

Also around the time the twins were this age, I cannot tell you the exact number of times that Greg, Chris or I had to wash babies, cribs and walls after their naps. You guessed it—poopy on everything. I estimate it to be over 30 times. In spite of us pinning and taping them into "straightjacket pj's" they did it so often that they learned to say, "No poopy da wall." We had lots of practice making that path back to joy from disgust.

Sad: *"Something important to me is lost. I lost some of my life."* Babies, adults and children of all ages feel sad when they lose something. It can be something small or large, tangible or intangible, seeming important or unimportant to others. It is good to grieve that loss while parents help children learn how to feel sad by sharing the sad and returning to joy.

Connor Got a "No" -- Sad

Fear: *"I want to 'get away.' Something bad is about to happen."* Below are pictures of one-year old Tyler, scared of a new experience. We placed her in a pile of leaves in order to take a pretty autumn picture. She was frightened. Mommy sat down beside her to synchronize and bring her back to joy from fear. In a later section, you will see the next picture I took. It is on page 141. Tyler is returning to joy, but because the right and left hemisphere of a baby's brain do not connect until the age of three, you can see joy on one side of her face and fear on the other.

Chris and Tyler -- Fear   ***Mommy reassures Tyler --***

Fear

Shame: *"I'm not bringing you joy and you are not glad to be with me here."* We can "not be glad to be with baby" when she brings us something disgusting, but shame can also arise any time someone is not glad to see us or we are not glad to be with them. Growing a path back to joy from shame is one of the most neglected and misunderstood paths, and not having that path back to joy can cause relationship problems later in life. When someone is "not glad to be with me" it can be very painful if one has no path back to joy from that feeling. Ideally over time, countless moments of not being glad to be together, but staying together and helping return to joy will build that path in your child's brain.

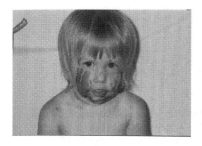 

Brenna -- A Self Portrait -- Shame   *Kori -- Busted – Shame*

Here is a catchy way to think about shame: "I'm not glad to be with you right now (shame), but I will be glad to be with you (joy) while I'm not glad to be with you, so we can share the distress and return to joy."

The goal of working on shame is to be able to be glad to be together again. There are times where behavior is not acceptable and the child/person should feel shame. Without a path back to joy from shame, getting a message that someone is not glad to be with me will cause the person to become defensive. Defensiveness and redirecting the "shame message" back on the sender is a good sign there is no strong path back from shame. If the other person also gets defensive, it could be a sign that neither has a good path back to joy from shame. Fatigue or low joy may be a factor, but consider the need to work on handling shame when you encounter defensiveness in another or yourself. Learn not to fear telling your child or others that you are not glad to be with them here because something is hindering your joy of being close. There is some behavior that needs correcting.

Anger: *"I need to protect myself & make it stop. I'm about to lose something important to me."* Anger rises when we are about to lose something that we don't want to lose. It may not even be ours to have, but we don't want to lose it. Again this something we are about to lose could be tangible or intangible.

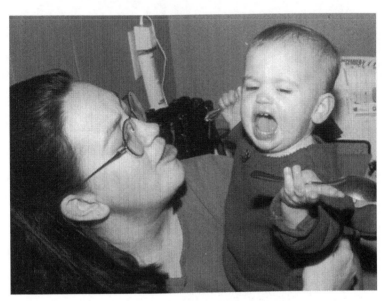

Kayli wants to keep the spoons – Anger

We want our children to be able to express anger in healthy ways. We do not want them to stuff or repress it: therefore, it's very important to help the little ones work on this path back to joy. I will talk about handling anger again in a later chapter.

Hopeless: *"I lack the time, capacity and resources to solve this. I'll never get back to joy."* Dr. Wilder points out that hopeless despair, like shame, can be one of the most difficult emotions to feel and from which to develop a path back to joy. Few people are willing to share

© 2007 Barbara Moon

this emotion and help the other person return to joy. It is important to remember, if you don't have the path back yourself, you cannot download it to your baby. It can be learned with a good mentor, but of course will take time. Also keep in mind that

Kori is devastated -- Hopeless Despair

the level of hopelessness that a baby is feeling is not deep depression but the feeling of not being able to get help. In adults it is sometimes dealt with by realizing it would be wise to "give up" and wait for guidance or help because one sees that the resources to handle the situation are not here right now.

From these working definitions of the Big Six, we can quickly see that returning to joy does not necessarily mean being happy, with everything fine and dandy. Joy means I am glad to be with you no matter the situation and I want to be with you so we can reconnect even if I am the one who distressed you, or I don't *feel* like being with you.

We want to stay relational and get back to calm. God upsets us quite often, but He is always glad to be with us and share in the upset.

In order to learn to return to joy, someone **HAS** to be glad to be with us **DURING** each the six emotions. The following are the basic components of returning to joy:

Share the distress

Be glad to be together

Stay relational

Use kind and comforting voice tone and touch

Help regulate emotions

Model how we act like ourselves

Have quiet together.

As you consider this list, let me share a true story that happened to one of my best friends and her family. Debbie is the same friend that gave you her testimony about "more is caught than taught". The Sellmann's story will illustrate what returning to joy is all about.

Scott, Debbie, Rebecca, and Andy

A RETURN TO JOY STORY

One night long ago, a wonderful family of four heard a huge storm over their neighborhood. Scott, Debbie, Andy and Becca listened as lightning flashed and thunder, mixed with blowing rain, crashed around their house. The thunder boomed, but the loudest roars were from the wind. A tornado was coming to their very street.

Quickly Scott and Debbie gathered their young children and rushed to the basement for safety. But they soon realized that the basement was not safe enough. They were going to have to take their children through a low door into a crawl space up under the house where Scott stored the lawn mower. It was full of cobwebs and the floor was nothing but dirt.

By now the children were whimpering with fear, but Daddy and Mommy assured them they would be together no matter what. After entering the crawl space, the parents huddled with a child in each of their laps. They were so glad to be together while this scary storm blew all around them.

Mommy began to sing softly to the children. While the storm raged above they comforted one another. The noise grew to crescendo as a tree crashed through their roof into the kitchen above. While all around their house the tornado tore up other trees, broke windows, stripped the neighborhood of roofs and scattered debris for miles, the precious family sat quietly together under the house.

Daddy prayed, Mommy sang and the children snuggled in their laps as they waited for the terrible, noisy storm to pass. Hours later the stillness outside echoed the quietness of the little family's creepy refuge and they crawled back to the opening to stare in amazement at the damage around them.

# # # #

After reading the story, as you refer to the list of components for returning to joy, ask yourself these questions: Did the Sellmann parents do each of these components? Were they glad to be together in the middle of a distressing situation? Was this returning to joy about happiness and being fine and dandy? It took some time for happiness to return, but joy (glad to be together) was there right in the middle of the situation.

When in a distressing situation, the synchronization that takes place between the person with the "older" brain who can remain calm and the younger brain that is distressed allows the younger brain to mimic the older brain. This happens through the non-verbal communication we have already discussed. The younger one learns what it is like to "act like myself." He gets internal answers to the question, "How is it like me and 'my people' to act in this kind of distress?"

Let's review what it means to "act like myself." Dr. Wilder says, "I am acting like myself when what I am doing matches who I am, when my actions reflect my heart, even during intense emotions." Children learn to go to joy/peace or fear in a situation by watching and downloading what the parents do during intense emotions. This is done rather subconsciously as they read the parents face, body language and other non-verbal cues. During the distress, joy (or lack of it) will determine if a person has the strength to "suffer well," thus passing on peace (or more fear) to others around them.

Jesus is our best example of acting like oneself during intense emotions. In Mark 3: 1-5 we read a story about Jesus being angry. This is not the story about turning the tables over in the Temple. That story does not give us an emotion word in the Greek, it simply states that Jesus did it. In the Mark story we have the Greek word for "rage"—*ogre*. As Jesus enters the synagogue He sees a man with a withered hand. The people were watching Him to see if He would heal on the Sabbath, which was against their laws. Jesus called the man to come to Him.

In verse 5 we find the Greek word for rage: "And after looking around at them with *anger*, grieved at their hardness of heart, He said to the man, 'Stretch out your hand.' And he stretched it out, and his hand was restored." Although Jesus was in a powerful rage, what did He do? He healed the man. If he had been at a picnic, what would He have done? He would have healed the man. If he had been teaching the multitudes, what would have happened? He would have healed the man. Jesus acted like Himself because it is like Him to heal, no matter which intense emotions He might be feeling. (Wilder, THRIVE Conference)

Our components of returning to joy contain another phrase that might need reviewing. What does it mean to "stay relational" under intense emotions? Again, Jesus is our best example. He both acted like Himself and stayed relational while He was on the Cross. No person has suffered more than He did on that day. But while feeling intense suffering, He talked to John and Mary. He sang Psalms and talked to His Heavenly Father. He forgave the people who were killing Him and shared hope with one of the thieves hanging beside Him. Staying relational means that when emotions are intense, I do not withdraw, shut down, panic, lose it, or attack someone. I might *feel like* or *wish* I could do one of these actions, but I do not follow through with the feeling. I stay relational, act like myself and suffer well.

Our look at returning to joy brings us to some important questions: why is it so important to have the return to joy circuits in the brain? What happens when a person does not have the path back to joy in his brain from one of the Big Six emotions? The answer the these questions is vital to our growth and maturity and how we relate to others, to God and ourselves. If we do not have a path back to joy from these negative emotions, we will avoid the pain that comes with those feelings instead of returning to joy in ninety seconds or less.

Pain is supposed to mean that "comfort is on the way," but I find that many people don't know this because they did not receive comfort as a child when they needed it. It is important to understand the problems that come with avoiding pain because avoiding pain is the opposite of suffering well. We do not want our children to avoid pain for several reasons. Avoiding pain causes relationship problems that are difficult to overcome and prevents us from maturing and reaching our full potential. Avoiding pain causes addictions to form later, when avoidance is a person's normal response to pain.

Addictions are anything that brings pleasure (a high) in order to avoid pain or anything that helps us dull or medicate pain (a low). The addiction controls us to the point that we cannot stop it even when there are negative consequences. When a child has not received what is necessary for thriving (love, comfort, re-connection) or has been abused, the child will have obvious or underlying pain throughout his emotional existence. Because he does not know how to face and feel the pain, he will turn to things that bring pleasure, such as alcohol, drugs, sex, food, spending or gambling. It does not take long for these pleasure-seeking activities to become an addiction that medicates the pain that the person does not even know he is hiding.

If a child does not learn to return to joy from one or more of the six emotions, avoidance of that emotion causes sidetracking to another easier emotion. For example a common emotion that is difficult to deal with is shame. If one does not have a return to joy path from shame, he will often sidetrack to anger. This is common in men. Women tend to avoid anger by sidetracking to sad and crying. Building return to joy paths in the brain prevents children from becoming "people pleasers" or "people haters," because they know how to repair conflicts and thus do not fear them.

When we know that return to joy is possible and likely after a problem, it takes the sting out of having a problem. Repair (return to joy), not prevention of ruptures (disconnections), is the key in a relationship. (Wilder) When we understand this principle, we won't dread ruptures and try to keep peace at all costs. We don't have to go into a rage or withdraw when we hit a bump with someone because we know that we can and will return to joy if we take the time and effort to work through the conflict. Again we can look at the life of Jesus for the best example of how life works. Hebrews 12:2 tells us that "for the joy set before Him, He endured the cross." Though Jesus endured more than anyone else ever has, ultimately being separated from His Father, He knew that He would return to joy.

Building return to joy circuits between twelve and eighteen months has an added bonus. These return-to-joy circuits also minimize the intensity of tantrums. Around sixteen months an "amplifier" turns on in the brain that intensifies the Big Six emotions—instead of anger we get rage and instead of fear we get terror and night terrors. If the baby's brain has return-to-joy circuits, the amplification of these emotions is just a harder work out to get back to joy from. If not, it causes suffering in the more intense moments. (p 26 LWM) Daddy plays a huge role during these months that help baby learn to regulate emotions. Daddy's "I'm gonna get you" games train the brain to regulate fear and aggression as long as Daddy knows when to stop and allow rest. Any stimulation that leads to crying would be harmful.

Deep satisfaction comes from sharing and building joy. God designed us for joy to be the basis of making it through hard times. As we give and receive life, everyone's emotional life grows to maturity and we will be more likely to reach our God given potential.

EIGHTEEN TO TWENTY-FOUR MONTHS

As we continue our journey through the Infant Stage, we can see that during the second half of the second year, the baby puts together her basic identity with the material we have given her as we synchronized and interacted together. We want that identity to be a joyful one. I call babies like this "joy babies." It thrills me to spot one while out shopping. Before putting together his or her joyful identity, babies handle each emotion separately, with each emotion having its own brain center. Around eighteen months, the "joyful identity" region (the Joy Center) attempts to grow a circuit that connects these six emotion centers into a "ring." After this takes place, the baby can be the same person no matter what he is feeling. This joy ring will later allow him to act like himself regardless of intense emotions. (p. 26 LWM)

Without the training in joy in the preceding years, these centers will remain separated and there will be no joy ring. This will cause de-synchronization when negative emotions get triggered. When older, people will say that the person is moody and acts differently when angry or scared. An incomplete joy ring is an invitation to behavior problems, mood swings, inability to self-regulate emotions, and addictions. We have already looked at another result of an unconnected joy ring—sidetracking to a different emotion. (p. 27 LWM)

As the end of the first two years draws near, we can see the importance of the work parents and babies have been doing building joy capacity and return to joy circuits that will increase joy strength and form the foundation for emotional health for a lifetime. Because there is so much at stake from these important tasks, let's review the two ways we build joy strength:

Climbing Joy Mountain	Returning to Joy Camp
Voice tone	Paths back from Big Six
Facial Expressions	Sing our way back
Smells, food	Psalms
Touch	Touch, I'm with you, you're safe
Temperature	Share distress
Singing	Stay relational
Pets	Pets
Babies, elders	Be glad to be together
Giving life	Synchronizing

Before we look at the other two years of the Infant Stage and how the brain continues to develop, let's remind ourselves again that there is good news for those of you who have children beyond the Infant Stage, or who may have yourselves grown up without great joy training. That good news is-- *the Joy Bucket never stops growing*! So spread joy smiles everywhere and build joy whenever you see a loved one's face. Startle people in the grocery store or Wal-Mart by smiling at them. Tell all the pregnant or new parents you know to build as much joy and quiet as possible the first two years, the years that the Designer designed as the best time.

AGE TWO TO THREE

In order to finish our journey through the Infant Stage and look at how the brain develops during those crucial years, I will speak briefly about two year olds and three year olds. In a later chapter, I will elaborate on that age group concerning discipline and give you lots of tips. For now I want to share how returning to joy can be helpful with what is commonly called the "terrible two's."

Before twelve months, a baby does not understand willfulness and/or disobedience. We don't do a lot of discipline during this time or label the baby as stubborn, willful or disobedient. During the second year, especially the second half, we will have encounters with the child that are more willful or disobedient. This upsurge in problems nearing that second birthday has caused many parents to mistakenly view the next few years as "terrible." (Wilder)

I would like to approach this view from a different angle by looking at a good point that Dr. Wilder makes about what is going on in the two year old child's brain. He tells us that a large portion of the problems causing conflict with the two year old is "parent error." Up until the second birthday, most of the brain development has been going on in the Right Hemisphere—the emotional side. "Now the Left Hemisphere has its growth spurt and will become one sixth of the adult brain. This verbal area lets us think in words about who we are... But when they are first learning language, children's brains cannot grasp a negative command. This can continue up to the age of five. This is particularly true when the child is under pressure or emotional." (pp. 26, 27 LWM)

In other words, twos (and sometimes older) do not hear "don't." This makes it necessary for us as parents to watch how we speak and how we give commands. It will help diminish conflict if we use positive commands such as, "Be kind. Be gentle. Let's pick up. That's Daddy's. Leave_____ alone," instead of "Don't _____." Using "no" as the first word of a command instead of "don't," does seem to work better and if you will listen, you'll notice that the toddlers themselves use "no" as a command. Connor (2) sometimes says, "No come, Mommy." Or, "No do that." And you will quickly notice that "no" is the toddler's favorite word as the answer to most questions you ask.

As we consider changing the way we give commands, let's look at where returning to joy fits with two year olds? What will help when and if we *do* get into one of those "terrible" moments? As we all know, children of this age need a safe place to explore, discover and grow. When all is going well and the area is safe, children will explore, discover and play with great enthusiasm. But when a child gets distressed and has no path back to joy from that emotion, the child stays in the distress--he cannot self-regulate. At that time, a parent might consider the distressed behavior to be disobedient or negative behavior. The child might be frustrated or cannot have his way for various reasons. We want to look at this problem as a "brain malfunction" before jumping to conclusions that the child is "bad" somehow. We don't call the two year old a baby or try to control her *before* returning her to joy. As Dr. Wilder says, "Many people give up on two year olds too quickly, leaving them outside of Joy Camp." (p. 30 LWM) It might be worth a try to get the child calm by synchronizing and being glad to be together instead of trying to control, lecture or punish.

It is very important to know that in distress with no path back to joy, or when the Joy Bucket is not full, the Logic Center (the Left Hemisphere) has shut down and the child is operating from the Joy Center where there are no words, only non-verbal communication. A child (or person) with his or her Logic Center off-line cannot "hear" instructions, threats or lectures. (They might hear a bribe, but we do not want to use bribery to train them.)

So what is a parent to do? When the child goes into overwhelming distress—exploring and thinking stop. The way to help the situation is to return him to joy first. Remember the list for return to joy tactics? Use them. Synchronize, share the distress, be glad to be together, stay calm and return to joy. Use your instructions and words when the emotions are not out of control, during a non-stressful time, *before* the melt down occurs or *wait* until after you have restored joy. They may or may not remember the instructions at first, but after many trials and errors, your calm training will pay off.

Keep in mind that words and instructions do not work when the Left Brain is off. Words and instructions just frustrate. (This applies to any age, even adults, by the way.) The number one priority is to return the child to joy. Obeying is the number two priority. (p. 30 LWM)

FROM THREE TO FOUR

Around the age of three, the Left and Right Hemispheres develop a connection, making it possible for the verbal and feeling halves of the infant's identity to discover each other. Before they connect it is actually possible to see two emotions on the same little face. Here is the picture of my granddaughter, Tyler where her face shows fear on one side and joy on the other while she was sitting in the pile of leaves that were scaring her. After Mommy got down beside her and assured her (non-verbally) that it was safe, she liked the leaves. But the camera caught her face in the middle of the change.

Chris with Tyler, halfway back to joy

After passing the third birthday and growing this connection between the two hemispheres, the child can begin to think about obeying when upset. (Around this time proper discipline will become vital). If the Left Hemisphere shuts down from distress it will operate as if the connection is not there. When the left side is connected and running, the child can now verbalize his or her feelings and we can reason with him a little better. She can talk about what is going on, even when upset. The child learns better how to act like herself while feeling intense emotions. The ability to talk about what he wants when distressed helps prevent the child from turning into a one-year old (because of overwhelm) when upset. A one year-old (regardless how old the body is) thinks only of what he is feeling, and words do not help. When the Left and Right hemispheres have not connected, whether developmentally or from neglect or mistreatment, the child does not develop properly. (p. 30 LWM)

According to Dr. Wilder, operating without the Left Hemisphere is similar to driving on a road where the bridge is out. If parents try to discipline or control the child with words, without the connection of the two hemispheres, disaster lies ahead. He says, speaking of the child before the age of three: "When it comes to maturity, sooner is not better. If you were exploring a road that was just being built and came to a river with a sign, 'Bridge to be built next year,' would you try to drive your family across the chasm?" (p. 30 LWM) In the same way, if a child (person) is past three and for some reason the Left hemisphere is undeveloped or shut down, he will act like a one-year old. Words do not help anyone who is acting like a one-year old. The bridge is out. (p. 31 LWM)

There is another capacity that develops around the age of three. The brain can now store long-term memory. Because he has the bridge between words and feelings and long- term memory, the child can now change what she thinks. What she thinks can help her to change her feelings and she can talk about what is going on. (p. 31 LWM) This is regulating emotions.

SUMMARY

This four-year journey of bonding, synchronizing, building joy and quiet, returning to joy and learning to regulate emotions is foundational for healthy relationships and good health. The baby comes with the equipment to learn and build, but someone has to teach him how to do all this, and practice it continually. We see the importance of Mommy building joy and quiet and return to joy. We see the importance of a secure bond with Daddy so that during the time from 12-18 months

© 2007 Barbara Moon

baby loves Daddy's emotional availability and learns to regulate fear, aggression and sexual impulses through "predator games." This secure bond of loving, protective care by Daddy internalizes security for life. During the year between three and four, we practice all the new development along with all the previous training and tasks for the Infant Stage of maturity, making sure that the needs are met and the tasks are learned. By age four the child is able to care for him or herself and he is ready to leave Mommy's world and venture out more into Daddy's. We continue to grow the Joy Bucket and keep it full, as life becomes increasingly more complex and distressing in the child's expanding world.

Fun in Daddy's world

NOTE: If you are reading for information only about infants at this time, please note that **Chapter Eight, Nana's Tips**, is another section that is divided by age ranges. There are practical tips beginning with newborns and ending with middle school. Teens are a separate chapter.

SECTION III -- THE PRACTICAL HOWS

CHAPTER SIX: DISCIPLINE

Goal: to move our children towards self control

INTRODUCTION

Disciplining children is a much-debated topic. I hope to narrow the debate for you as we build on what we already know about discipline while looking at some additional points to consider. From here on in the book, you will hear what I have gleaned from both my own years of parenting and what I have seen work as I helped many other parents. I want the "brain and joy" information to meld with what you and I already know, while we look at practical ways to apply it all. We will not synchronize with "naughtiness" but will instead discipline it. My hope and desire is that this book will be one that will help you know the difference as you keep it close at hand and refer to it often as your child grows and changes.

As a very young mother, I committed myself to God, desiring that He teach and guide me in my journey as a parent. He has been totally faithful to fulfill that desire, using many circumstances, many trials, and many different authors and teachers in the process. I will do my best to credit the ones from which I have learned.

So let's begin by defining two words—discipline and punishment. **Discipline** is "training that develops self control." **Punishment** means, "to cause pain for a crime." We often mix up the two ideas. This book will be about discipline, training that develops self- control, because that is our goal according to the Scriptures.

I like to fine tune this goal for discipline to say that we want to train our children in such a way that they will learn to obey the first time we speak in a normal tone of voice--and they will have a decent attitude. I use the words "decent attitude" because I am strong on being patient, loving, positive and graceful with children, giving them time to learn. We must consider that our training will take years and some of our goals are long-range goals. The key will be consistency over this long range. Military style discipline, controlling and rigid, does not produce a well-rounded, joy-filled child. An ignoring and excusing style of discipline can produce a bratty, destructive kind of child. So I want to keep our goals in mind that we looked at in Chapter One as we answered the question, "What do I want my child to be like when he or she leaves home?"

WHAT DOES SCRIPTURE SAY?

One of the most frequently used verses from Scripture concerning child rearing is found in Proverbs 22:6, "Train up a child in the way he should go and when he is old he will not depart from it." Here the word train can also be "discipline or dedicate" (train or dedicate for

© 2007 Barbara Moon

self-control.) If we read the verse with emphasis on the word "he," we quickly see that this training should be individual in many aspects, as I've already mentioned when talking about children being free to be themselves. No two children are alike, not even identical twins. The training and methods we use sometimes have to be adjusted to fit a certain child's needs or personality. Parents must stay flexible and observant (in tune with), listening to God's guidance about each child and his or her needs at a given time.

The last part of the verse brings hope for the future, as sometimes children will divert from their training and go astray. That is a topic that I will cover in the section about the teen years. Having a "straying" child is very painful for everyone. For parents, it can be a time of strengthening their faith as they cling to God, or it can become a place for bitterness and further rejection. For now, I want to concentrate on what we can do, with God's grace, to *prevent* straying children.

A MOTHER'S STORY

Recently I had lunch with my friend, Kathy Pittman. She has three grown boys who are fine young men, well educated, successful, talented and kind. I asked Kathy, "What do you think took place in your home that has contributed to how well your boys have turned out?" After thinking a moment, Kathy told me a few of her thoughts.

"I know that part of how my boys are now is that we had Jesus Christ as the center of our home. Jeff and I tried to walk what we talked. Church was important to us as a family and the boys had good training both at home and church. My time home schooling

them was a factor. That gave me extra time with them through the years. I believe that time was invaluable because they were able to see us living out our faith and to assimilate our values naturally, because we were together on a daily basis.

Another big factor, I think, was that we tried to consider each of the boys individually as to their talents, personalities and needs. We didn't lump them together, but accepted each one the way God has made him. We were diligent to encourage each one to reach his own potential in his own ways.

I added to Kathy's list the fact that the boys had a Dad who was very involved with them through the years. He spent time with them and poured himself into them. As far as I could see, he was a mature man. It was also important to me to know that, of the qualities Kathy and Jeff wanted their boys to have, they made certain those characteristics were part of their own lives. They not only worked in the church, they were in small groups that brought them accountability, community and a place to grow themselves.

What a blessing to see God's truth at work, to see the results in a family that follows Him and His ways. Thank you, Kathy, for sharing your reflections.

THE BRAIN AND DISCIPLINE

TAMING THE NUCLEUS ACCUMBENS

As you consider Kathy's story, notice that her family exhibits qualities of good discipline-- self-control and great modeling. They live at maturity levels consistent with their chronological ages. Dad

© 2007 Barbara Moon

apparently understands discipline for himself and each parent contributed his and her strengths to the whole. Without knowing the words, Jeff communicated and taught his boys a very important part of discipline.

This aspect of discipline and self-control is physically associated with the brain. That part of the brain is called the **"nucleus accumbens."** I'll refer to it as the **NA** for short. The nucleus accumbens is part of the survival center in the brain, sometimes called the pleasure center.

Taming the NA is an important step in child rearing. It needs to be tamed before puberty, because its cry, "I have to have _____ or I will surely die," will become amplified after puberty. If untamed at puberty, that amplified cry will increase the intensity of existing problems and contribute to forming addictions. Let's look at a Bible story that illustrates the problem of an untamed NA.

In Genesis 25:27-32, we find two brothers, Jacob and Esau. Esau, the older, famished from working in the fields, comes into the tent where his brother, Jacob, is stirring some fresh stew. "And Esau said to Jacob, 'Please let me have a swallow of that red stuff there, for I am famished.' But Jacob said, 'First sell me your birthright.' And Esau said, 'Behold, I am about to die; so of what use then is the birthright to me?' So Esau agreed to sell his birthright to Jacob, the younger brother."

In the Hebrew culture, the birthright belonged to the firstborn who was due a double portion of the father's inheritance, as well as being the one who would become the leader over the family. What was Esau thinking? Was he about to die? Of course not. His untamed NA was screaming for food and he traded his valuable birthright as the elder son for a quickly consumed bowl of stew.

The nucleus accumbens is located in the Attachment Center (Level 1) and is often used *unconsciously* to avoid attachment pain, the common factor in addictions. We feel attachment pain when we want to bond with or get close to someone who is not available or is unwilling. Attachment pain is the worst kind of emotional pain we can experience.

Attachment pain can be current pain from wanting to bond with an unavailable person or it can be old pain from childhood where our needs were not met through a secure and loving bond. Losing someone we love or feeling disappointment from a person's response to our needs can cause attachment pain. Wishing our parent(s) had responded or would now respond to our need with understanding and love can cause attachment pain. We either feel it or avoid it all through life. It is important to know what to do with attachment pain. We must face it, feel it and allow Jesus to heal it.

People with attachment pain and an untamed NA who have learned to avoid pain will use the NA, or pleasure center, to cover the pain. The most frequently used (chemical) pleasures to cover pain are drugs, alcohol, sex, and/or food, to which we can add spending and gambling. We all know how addictive these pleasures can be. An untamed NA loudly tells the person, "I must have this or I will surely die," while subconsciously using that desired pleasure to dull the pain of unmet closeness. It is relationship and closeness they are really looking for.

If accustomed to avoiding pain, the person might not even be aware that pain is there. He just goes after the addictive pleasure.

Discipline helps tame the NA, best tamed, as we said, before puberty. All religions have disciplines such as fasting, self-denial, solitude and abstinence. Training for self-control by taming the NA is principally a job for Dad. (Wilder) Daddy begins this process very early when baby wants Mommy and only Mommy will do, a function of the Attachment Center. Dad helps the baby calm without Mommy when she is unavailable. When the "one and only one" we want is not available, we feel pain and need comfort. If we don't receive comfort, it makes us want to avoid that pain in the future.

It is vital during the early years to help our children feel emotional pain while being comforted, so that they will not develop habits of avoiding the pain. We must teach them, "You will not surely die." If a child has no place to turn for comfort during his or her emotional pain, his NA will scream for something to cover the pain, something that brings pleasure. That is the beginning of an addiction that will only grow worse as the child matures. (NA ideas from Wilder, LWM)

Another early method of helping calm the NA is when we teach our children to "wait." Waiting has to be very short at first, but even toddlers can understand, "Just a minute." Infants' needs must be met very quickly, but as the child grows and becomes mobile and verbal, he can see that we have to dry our hands before we can get him a snack, and that we are making his peanut butter and jelly sandwich. As the child matures, the wait for help will lengthen and they can learn that instant gratification is not the way the world works.

Saving for a costly item helps train and teaches a child that she can't have everything she wants the moment she wants it. Even learning how time and the calendar work will encourage children that they do not have to answer the call of the NA. They learn that birthday parties and Christmas take a while to come around again. Taming the NA is part of learning to do hard things in the Child Stage of maturity. Tame it before puberty by being there to synchronize, calm, comfort and return to joy when upset occurs so that the child will know that "pain means comfort is on the way," and they will not learn that pain is something to avoid. Children must be good at producing joy and calming themselves so that they know how to survive the scream of the nucleus accumbens and be able turn off their brain circuits that set it screaming. (pp. 81-83 LWM)

CALMING THE BRAIN

Around the age of three or four, you can begin to teach your child a physical way to calm his brain. You must have this skill as part of your own life. It is called "Shalom (peace) My Body."[1] It can be made into a game to play whenever anyone gets upset and does not want to be relational. When the brain shuts down because of distress or upset, the relational circuits in the emotional control center cut off (Levels 4 and 3). We talked about this in Chapter Three. There are three physical exercises that we can do to restore the relational circuits. If you do them yourself, you will calm and if the child (or spouse) will do them

---

[1] "Shalom My Body" from www.thrivingrecovery.org pastor Ed Khouri's Belonging Module of Thriving Recovery.

they will calm down. It will be especially productive if you allow your children to "correct" you when you are upset and remind you to reset your RC's. They love it when we share our power like that. Here are the three exercises:

1) With your fingers or fists, lightly tap on each side of your chest (like Tarzan, but not so hard). Do it rhythmically to match your heartbeat while taking a deep breath. As you exhale, rub the same place on your chest as you say aloud, "Whenever I am afraid I will trust in You, Oh, Lord." (Psalm 56:3) You can substitute other words for "afraid" into the verse, such as "angry," "sad," "I want to run out the door," or "I want to scream at my children." (The vagus nerve runs from the brain to the abdomen on both sides of the chest there and it is closest to the surface at that point.) This will reset the RC's.

2) Just as newborn babies do the startle reflex, you can throw your hands up and backwards, head backwards at the same time, and loudly gasp a deep breath. Slowly bring hands and head back down while repeating the verse.

3) Take a deep breath while "yawning" to the left, release and look ahead, take a deep breath while "yawning" to the right," release and repeat the verse. Any of these three will help calm the brain, reset RC's. Number one seems to be most people's favorite.

There is a fourth method for calming the brain and resetting relational circuits. When we think about something that we appreciate, it physically helps the brain. Appreciation is anything that makes us feel like saying, "Ahhhh." Thinking of the beach, children laughing, having a campfire or beautiful parts of nature bring a smile to our faces and calm our brains. Here is the way to incorporate this into your family's arsenal for calming:

Together with the children who are old enough, everyone closes their eyes and thinks of something that makes them feel good and want to say, "Ahhh." Then each person gives their memory a name of one or two words. We open our eyes and each tells their name. If desired, everyone can also describe their appreciation picture. Explain that when anyone gets upset, this will be one of the ways we can help each other calm. We will want to be kind and not pushy about it. When it is appropriate, we can use the "appreciation name" to help someone calm. Children can also know our appreciation memories' names and remind us when we are upset. Again, they will like this use of power. It is helpful to have two or three of these for each person. **(See Appendix A for use of calming exercises during healing.)**

DISCIPLINE TIPS

TRAINING IS LONG TERM

Training a child in the way he should go is a very long and slow process. We have to look at the fact that we have over twelve years to influence and train. Much of the foundation is laid in the first three to five years, but the process continues much longer. Try not to look at parenting your child as if the child has to know "everything" today. Think about any new job or sport that we want to learn. It takes time and practice and no one becomes an expert instantly. This helps us be more patient with ourselves and with the children, as we keep our eyes on the goal down the road, while consistently training for that goal.

Jobs and sports take consistent training, little by little increasing the difficulty and the understanding of the whole. Consistency and remaining calm are as important to discipline as a patient coach or trainer is to a new sport or job. Calm, consistent training will over time bring about the results that you have written for your goals in Chapter One. And keep in mind how long it takes to master a new sport, skill or job. Continually look for balance as good coaches do—just enough hard work to learn the skill without discouragement and enough praise to keep the heart loving the journey.

CONSISTENCY

One of the most important traits a parent can exhibit when parenting is consistency. If you struggle with consistency and self-control in your own life, it would be good to get help and work on that as you parent. Children see in us what is really there, not what we tell them we want them to see. They are so intelligent and very observant of every weakness we can have. They will take advantage of that at every possible moment. Because of this, it appears that they want their own way all the time. That is true to a point, but a bigger truth is that they want secure, consistent boundaries that communicate to them, "You are safe here and you can depend on me to take care of you—even if you're trying to tell me you want it your way." We can communicate this with clear procedures, clear consequences, and clear follow-through.

Consistency is tied to the bonding styles that we talked about in Chapter Four. If the parent's style is consistently dismissive the children feel insecure, fearful and ignored. If the parents are consistently distracted, the children feel insecure, fearful, and clingy. As I have said before, parents struggling with the disorganized style with consistent anger and/or fear may need to ask for help from others.

In order to discipline well, the consistency has to be loving and unchanged by circumstances, flighty whims, and moods of the parents. Discipline cannot be based on bribery for good behavior. This is what I mean by consistency—that the children know what is expected and most every time the consequences are timed and carried out the same way. Mommy and Daddy don't make idle threats that everyone in hearing distance knows will not be done. They don't command something over and over without carrying through to see it is done. Mommy and Daddy don't yell, scream and never ask forgiveness when they blow it. Mommy and Daddy don't say, "Do what I say," and then not practice it themselves. Consistent parents can be depended on to mean what they say and model it as best they can, admitting and asking for forgiveness when they don't. All of us *will* be consistent—but which kind of consistent do we want to be?

DAD AND MOM UNITED

Mommy and Daddy must also be consistently united in their attitudes, efforts and methods of discipline. This means that Mom and Dad have discussed and come to some agreements about how they will discipline. But most of all it means that neither will undermine the other <u>during</u> an encounter with the children. A parent who interferes with the other parent's moment of discipline to correct that parent will send a message to the child that splits his loyalty. The child can feel that one parent is for him and the other is against him. This will be worse as the child gets older. If a parent observes a problem with the other parent during an encounter with the child, this must be discussed out of the presence of the children. If the parent doing the disciplining realizes he or she was out of line, then they need to seek the child's forgiveness and humbly take the input from the spouse.

Supporting the other parent during discipline is definitely helpful, especially if one parent is the principle caretaker and the other parent backs her (or him) up. In our family we have an inside joke that comes from a children's song. In the song, the little ducks go out to play and do not come back when mother duck calls them. Then daddy duck "QUACKS!" and all the little ducks come running back. It can be very helpful for Daddy to "QUACK," to help get the little ducks' attention when they might not be paying attention to Mommy.

TIME OUT

It seems that these days, "Time Out" is the most common form of early discipline. It can take many forms and names. Jo Jo, the Supernanny, gives various names to the places she teaches for Time Out, such as the "naughty stool," the "naughty mat" or the "naughty steps." I have a friend, Scott, who calls Time Out the "think chair." These are places for removing the child from a negative or upset situation so he can get calm and think.

When I learned the way God designed the brain to synchronize, I changed my views about using Time Out. I realized that being alone did not precipitate synchronization, because it is impossible to synchronize with a person that we are not with. I asked Chris if we could change our form of Time Out to fit better with the new brain research. She agreed. Tyler was now about seven and did not often need Time Out. Kayli and Kori were around four and Brenna was about three.

The form of Time Out we had been using since the twins were around two and half and Tyler was about five went something like this. When needed, Time Out was in an alcove in our kitchen that goes to the garage door where the girls were unable to see the rest of us in the kitchen or playroom. They had to stay in that space and sit without screaming until the timer bell rang, which was set for the amount of minutes of their age. It had taken some training to get them to go to Time Out without balking, but when necessary they were placed there and told to stay. As they matured we added two things to talk about after the bell rang--"What did you do?" and "What can you do next time?" This was part of returning to joy.

The change we made after learning about synchronization was to stop sending the girls to Time Out alone. Now one of us would go there with her so that we could synchronize with her. Chris and I had to hide our smiles the first time or two when one of the girls found herself in the corner with an adult. They could not figure out why Mommy or Nana was in Time Out, sitting on the floor and being glad to be together in the distress before returning to joy. We saw a big change in the amount of time spent in that corner. I am not certain if it was because the children had matured enough to not need as many Time Outs, or if the increase in all around synchronizing with them kept the Joy Buckets fuller. Whatever it was, we realized one day that we were seldom using Time Out any more. We continued other kinds of consequences and still do, but Time Outs became very infrequent.

In order to help new parents that have never tried Time Out, I would like to describe the process here that should work well beginning around the age of twenty to twenty four months. Your little one should be able to understand most of what you say by this time, even if he or she can't talk well. The following instructions will be useful if your child is doing fairly well at listening to you and obeying. I will speak to full blown tantrums in the next section. Use Time Out if synchronizing and calming, or distracting to another activity, do not work. When older, use for disobedience when you are certain that is the issue.

Decide what behavior you want to address, such as whining, screaming, or hitting. Tell the child that she will have to sit in Time Out when she does these things. It might take a while for the new words to have meaning, so proceed calmly and patiently. Pick a place in the room that you are in the most, a place such as one end of the couch, a place where you can see each other when she is sitting there. Connor, my youngest grandson (2) thought it was fun at first and would even tell us, "I go sit down" when he thought he needed Time Out. After a while he began to understand and was not quite so eager to go to Time Out.

Let's say that the child is falling apart with some kind of temper like screaming. Calmly pick her up and carry her over to the "spot" on the couch and sit her down. She can have her blankie or stuffed animal or pacifier. Say something like, "Sit in Time Out." You want to sit across from her where she can see you. Stay there about sixty seconds if very young—at the most the amount of minutes she is old. If she tries to get down, calmly sit her back on the spot and start the time over (in your head). You will not talk to her during this time. If your child is fighting you, hitting you, screaming at you or any other form of defiance, please refer to the next section. You will not be able to follow the steps here until you fix the tantrum problem.

When she is calm or you feel she can handle words, very briefly say, "No scream," or "We have to be kind," whatever is appropriate. You can move beside her for this and even hold her. As she matures enough to understand, you can begin asking, "What did you do?" Use short positive phrases to communicate what it is not okay to do. When you think she is repentant and understands to her level, return her to joy, smile, giggle, and say it's okay to play now.

If she wanted something she can't have, do not give in. If she still needs to obey somehow, follow through with that. If you will be consistent in quickly and calmly taking her to that spot, stay there and synchronize face to face (it is okay to show you are not pleased) until she is calm, you should have good results. Jodi and Rick saw much improvement once Connor (2) understood the process.

By whatever name we call Time Out, it has a common goal and purpose—to separate the child from his activities, to calm the child and/or get him to focus on a need. If you have been leaving your child alone in Time Out, it might be worth a try to go there with him and synchronize the upset and bring him back to joy and calm and then use words to instruct or guide.

CALMING TANTRUMS

If your child is fighting you verbally or physically when you try to use Time Out, you will need to work on that before being able to discipline whatever caused him or her to go to Time Out. Try using one of the body exercises above as it may help. If you go to your spot and the child will not stay there after you put them back several times, that will be your first battle to win. Keep putting them back until they stay no matter how long it takes. When they believe you mean it, they will stay. If you consider it a tantrum, follow these steps.

For "breaking" tantrums, we are going to rename our Time Out spot as the "Calming Spot." You are going to stay there with the child until he or she is calm. At first it might take a very long time, depending on how defiant the child is. Keep putting him back on that spot over and over until he stays. Ignore the screaming until the next step. The most important thing you need to remember is that you, the parent, are not going to talk. You are not going to give any instructions during a tantrum.

Talking during a brain meltdown is an interaction that tries to teach the Left side of the brain to control the Right side. It does not work and can cause relational problems down the road later in life. The emotional brain works by synchronization, not intellectual control.

Even if you do not understand this, trust me that it is not good parenting practice. Parents must help with return to joy skills from the Big Six emotions and with synchronization. If you are not good at it yourself, it will be difficult to teach it to your child.

You may say a time or two, "Stay there" or something like that. You will need to sit where the child can see your face and synchronize with him by watching his face. Your face should appear to be mildly upset to neutral with him, but not scowling. Do not talk until he remains on the calming spot and calms. Watch for his face to change from rage to sad. If it does, change your face to synchronize sad with him. Wait for him to be completely calm. Do not let him up or into your lap until then. (If the child is hitting and/or kicking you, you might have to hold him tightly in your lap to avoid this. Children should NEVER be allowed to hit and kick parents.)

When he is calm, you can hold him and talk briefly about the issue that sent him there before the tantrum, whatever caused the tantrum if you want to. At this point the discipline is not the issue and you both may be drained and have forgotten about the issue. Usually children melt down because they received a "No" about something, they had to share, or they didn't get their way. It can be easy for parents to give in all the time to avoid conflicts.

After you see improvement in the length of time it takes to calm, begin working on "No screaming or hitting in your calming spot." You will need to explain this before the need happens during a regular part of the day. Then verbally reinforce it one or two times during the calming time, but still do not talk much at all until he is calm. If he or she wants you to hold them, say something like, "When you are calm, I will hold you."

Don't keep saying it, just sit and synchronize.

The goal for Time Out is to go there, sit there without a tantrum, think about why I'm there, and then talk about it afterwards. There is no place for a screaming, hitting, raging, verbally abusive fit. (They might not be using swear words, but the tone is the same.)

After you have worked through these issues, then do the regular Time Out steps above. The emphasis in both places is that you are going to stay calm with the child, be glad to be together in the sense that you are there calmly, synchronize, eye to eye if possible, without talking to him or her before they are calm. They will not hear you when they are in a raging tantrum and barely will hear you when upset and crying without it being a tantrum. So save your breath and teach them how to stay calm in intense emotions and/or how to get to calm that they can eventually do on their own.

If your child is throwing tantrums (more than just getting upset) it is usually a lack of return to joy skills and a lack of having that return path back from one of the Big Six emotions. If you are unable to break this habit of tantrums, there is something lacking in your attitude or skills. Ask a more mature parent for some help. Bad behavior takes place when it is *allowed*.

AFTER THE DISCIPLINE

There are some important follow-ups to Time Out, or other consequences, that are sometimes easy to overlook. I mentioned the two questions that are good to ask the child at the end of discipline time. After discussing the questions, the child may have unfinished business, such as still needing to obey something that he did not do, pick up toys or ask someone for forgiveness. The discipline is not finished until these have been done.

Remember we must be practicing and modeling asking for forgiveness in our own lives when we discipline wrongly or don't synchronize, saying, "Will you forgive me?" instead of "I'm sorry," giving the other person a place to answer. If the other is not ready to forgive (which seldom happens in loving families) they can take more time and then come back and say, "I am ready to forgive you now." Just such an event happened last year when Kori was about six.

Margie, our friend who was living with us at the time, and I had taken Kori for a special day. On the way home, for some reason I don't remember, Margie spoke harshly to Kori. It got very quiet in the back seat. In a few moments, Margie asked Kori for forgiveness. It was still quiet in the back seat. I asked Kori if she was not ready to forgive and she answered "no" in a very small voice. I told her that was okay, that she could forgive when she was ready. A few more miles and minutes down the road, we heard Kori say, "I am ready to forgive you now, Auntie Margie." And she did. Margie told her thank you and we continued our trek back from the store.

USING CONSEQUENCES

Proper consequences are a great teacher for all of us. The definition of consequences is "a logical result." The definition of punishment is "to cause pain for a crime." Good parents use consequences not punishment. Yes, consequences bring pain, but when used correctly, the child learns the logical result of what they did and the responsibility is upon his or her shoulders instead of the parents'.

Tyler, now 10, behaves very well and has only been in trouble at school two times; the first when she was in second grade. Chris went to school with her, sat down with the teacher and had Tyler to ask the teacher's forgiveness. It was very difficult, but Tyler did it, and got the message that her behavior was her responsibility. The teacher was so impressed that she had tears in her eyes. Recently Tyler again had some trouble and had to seek forgiveness from a teacher. This time, Tyler was mature enough to go to the teacher by herself and apologize.

Most of your consequences will be dealt with at home and it is vital at any age that you discover the "coin of the realm" for your children when consequences are needed. What is most valuable to them at their given age? Is it playing with a particular toy, watching a certain TV program, riding bikes, playing with friends, talking on the phone, playing computer games? These are the coins that he or she will have to pay with when needing a motivating consequence. Consequences that are not valuable to the child do not work. For elementary age children and up, we have found that going to bed early is a great consequence. Staying up is very valuable to them. It is easy to say, "Well, for that, you will have to go to bed early tonight." You can add half hours as needed if you get too much protesting. Going to bed thirty minutes early can be an all around, easy to administer consequence.

Make certain that the instructions about behavior and consequences are clear: "If you _____, this will happen." Then make certain that you follow through with consistency. I know adults that go to work late day after day, goof off instead of working, get threatened and then don't change—because the threatened consequence never happens. One can be sure that this is the story of their lives and not paying consequences creates a very dysfunctional adult.

A child who consistently hears, "If _____ happens, then _____," will not only be more likely to behave but will at the same time learn cause and effect—a very useful skill for life. Consequences are most effective when they fit the "misdeed." Save drastic consequences for huge problems like running out into the street, lying, defiance or stealing.

If consequences are too harsh, the child may be "provoked to wrath." In Ephesians 6:4, we read, "Fathers, do not provoke (exasperate) your children to wrath." The idea here is that something the parent is doing causes the child to be angry with the parent and not feel loved. The child is not truly obedient with a decent attitude, but rather stubborn inside (or outside). This can set up strongholds of anger and stubbornness in the heart that will bloom into huge problems later in life. Proper discipline is done in love and produces "the peaceful fruit of righteousness." (Hebrews 12:11)

Because I feel so strongly about the harm done by improper discipline and have seen the results in many lives, I have come up with what I call *Eight Commandments for Everyone*, though of course the

178   © 2007 Barbara Moon

list is not all inclusive. These seven admonitions, when taken to heart, will help eliminate much provoking to wrath as we deal with our children, thus eliminating many feelings of rejection.

EIGHT COMMANDMENTS FOR EVERYONE

Please don't bully

Please don't call names

Please don't use too much sarcasm

Please don't use put downs

Please don't yell or curse

Please don't threaten

Please don't ignore anyone's "no."

Please don't withdraw your love & shut others out

I cannot emphasize too strongly the importance of eliminating abusive anger, sarcasm and other forms of verbal abuse from your life and home. Abusive or uncontrolled anger *physically damages the brain* of the recipient. It is physical, not just mental or emotional. It makes a "spot" on the brain that can be triggered throughout life. It is associated with the *disorganized bond* that we talked about in Chapter Four, when a person wants to get close to (or bond with) someone they are afraid of. Wrong expressions of anger bring fear into any relationship and the relationship cannot function correctly. Dr. Wilder calls this dysfunctional condition a **Disorganized Attachment moment (DA)**.

I began to understand **DA moments** first hand from Dr. Wilder, when I experienced one last year. It was not a pleasant lesson. A DA moment is a given moment or situation when we are afraid of someone we want or need to get close to. The fear can be for many reasons—fear of rejection, fear of disapproval, fear of more anger, fear of disappointment, fear of humiliation.

Because few people recognize this brain malfunction, there is little training about it. No one wants to experience it or even talk about it. A DA moment is very painful. As we look around and observe or hear others talking about the fear they have with someone they want to get close to, we will see that DA moments are everywhere.

The desire or need to connect is taking place in the Attachment Center, but when fear is present in that desire or need, it causes attachment pain, which you will remember is the worst kind. Fear prevents the connection, causes attachment pain, harms the relationship and/or moves towards an addiction to medicate the pain.

The fear involved in DA moments can have levels of intensity varying from mild to extreme. Mild DA moments are common and easier to face. Here are a couple of examples of a mild DA moment: You have to tell your pastor that you can no longer serve on a committee. You feel afraid and maybe worried about what he will think of you, but it is most likely mild enough that you will plow through the fear and talk to him. Or, your mother is coming for a visit, and you are afraid that she might disagree with something you do with your child while she is there. You have a low level of dread about the coming visit. In both examples, you want to connect or draw close, but fear is involved.

Although many fear-based interactions can be mild, when the conditions are right, a disagreement or misunderstanding can quickly escalate to a Disorganized Attachment moment with extra-high levels of fear and anger, triggered because of the "spot" programmed into our brains by the abusive anger and sarcasm we have received in the past. When the body temperature changes during these emotions, (and the spot is there) the brain will heat up, and not only will the relational circuits go off, but chemical changes also will make the brain operate differently than it does when we are not highly angry or afraid. The relational circuits will shut off, but the melt down will be more intense and the ways in which we are used to relating and repairing will not work at this time. Techniques we are accustomed to using for repair don't work. It is like operating a computer where you are working on Microsoft Word and it suddenly changes to Star Office. It would do no good to continue trying to work with Word. You would just get garbage. In the midst of a DA moment we try to act like we would if still in our regular ways of relating (Word), but nothing we are used to doing works the same in the DA moment (Star). Not being able to repair the relationship brings more pain and frustration.

An intense DA moment is much more difficult and painful to experience with the person who originally caused the "spot" with their anger and fear towards you. It will take a lot of work with outside help to avoid these "spots" getting triggered if you are still in a relationship with that person. Not wanting to cause such a brain "spot" should be a big motivation for us as parents to avoid uncontrolled and abusive anger, so that these kinds of triggers will not get programmed into the child's brain. We do not even want to think about what happens to a child that lives constantly in this kind of anger-filled environment.

As humans we were not designed to be in this DA state of mind. We hate it and are supposed to hate it. It is unnatural and is a result of the Fall of Man--a brain malfunction. We cannot work things out by usual methods nor make it work by trying harder. It's not designed to work because it is not natural--we are freaked out and the brain is fried.

Understanding that nothing we are used to doing will work at that moment will help us to stop analyzing the problem and get some help from someone who is objective. The more we understand how DA moments work and how they don't work, and the more we realize the potential for conflict they carry, the better we will be able to avoid them. *Not fearing ruptures or conflict* will help us avoid a DA moment. Believing we can face the fear involved with wanting to connect and draw close, along with *return to joy,* is the key to working out of a DA moment.

When the DA gets triggered in the Attachment Center, we cannot un-foul the circuit nor expect *usual methods* of calming to work. This moment of intense anger and fear is very powerful. We do not *have* to follow through the emotions and do the action that is connected to the trigger, but the pull to do so will be very strong. This powerful emotional pull needs the greater power of the Holy Spirit to bring us through the fear and anger to joy and peace. Reliance on the Holy Spirit and getting objective help are the paths out of a DA moment cycle if one gets triggered. Hopefully as one or both seek help to return to calm, the relationship will become a better one.

As parents we must find healthy ways to deal with our anger and acknowledge it as a problem. Then we will be less likely to pressure our children with fear and anger. One of the best places I found for helping children learn better ways to deal with anger was in Dr. Ross Campbell's book, *How to Really Love Your Teenage,* Chapter Seven. Although in this chapter Dr. Campbell is speaking about teens, I feel that it can be helpful to consider for training throughout childhood. Dr. Campbell uses the analogy of a ladder, an "anger ladder," to illustrate fifteen ways that anger can be expressed.

Dr. Campbell's anger ladder starts at the bottom with the worst ways to handle anger. I will not speak about them in detail here, but only list them, beginning with the worst way and going in order up the ladder to the best ways.

"Passive aggressive behavior, physical abuse, emotionally destructive behavior, verbal abuse, destroying property, throwing objects, expressing unrelated complaints, displacing anger to other sources, cursing, unpleasant and loud behavior, thinking logically and constructively, holding to the primary complaint, focusing anger on source only, seeking resolution, pleasant behavior." (p. 67)

I highly recommend this book along with Dr. Campbell's other book that I will mention later, *How to Really Love Your Child.*

SPEAKING POSITIVELY

In place of fear and anger, and to avoid causing a DA spot, we as parents want to see and speak positively as much as possible with our children. Remember the importance of voice tone in building joy?

Remember that it is so often not *what* we say, but *how* we say it that impacts another. It might take some self-discipline on parents' part to begin using voice tones and phrases that are positive, such as, "I like the way you are (playing together)" [an action], or "You are so (helpful) today" [a character quality].

Whenever possible, share with another family member or friend *in front of* the child what he did special or positive that day. Brag about the good character your children show, rather than only pointing out when they do something special in a sport or other performance. When you notice a positive change in some behavior or character quality you have been working on with the child, be sure to tell him or her. Your praise will reinforce the positive.

FILLING THE EMOTIONAL TANK

We have talked at length about the importance of joy and filling the Joy Bucket. In the 1980's, I read and referred often to a book that I found to be very helpful as I was rearing my children. I want to share a few words from that book here to emphasize and underline the importance of building joy and emotional health. In his other book, *How To Really Love Your Child*, Dr. Ross Campbell lists four aspects of parenting that he advocates for "filling the child's emotional tank," what we have been calling "filling the Joy Bucket."

Dr. Campbell encourages parents to use "eye contact, physical affection, proper discipline and focused attention" as ways to fill the emotional tank, as ways to convey love. (p. 36) I was very motivated to show love to my children and I took this idea of an emotional tank very seriously. It seemed to me that I did fairly well with eye contact, physical affection, and discipline, but busyness could certainly get in the way of focused attention. As I began to "concentrate" on these four ways to convey love, I began to notice that a few minutes of focused attention would go a long way toward filling the emotional tank (the Joy Bucket). Whenever I spent about 10 minutes reading to or talking with one of my children, they would go play alone for a while.

To further incorporate filling the emotional tank into my parenting, I found it helpful to ask myself a question whenever a child was acting out in negative behavior. If another parent asked me about her child, I often asked the same question--"Is the emotional tank empty?" If doing one or more of the four fillers helped the situation, it was easy to see that an empty tank was the problem. I could refill the tank instead of assuming the child was just acting out.

I still ask this question today about the Joy Bucket—no matter who seems to be "acting out," child or adult or myself. Looking at negative behavior as a possible empty Joy Bucket helps me see the other person "through Heaven's eyes" instead of thinking about and reacting to them as if they are bad. Down through the years dealing with both children and in counseling adults, I have found this principle to be true--that most negative behavior comes from deep wounds and feelings of not being loved, not belonging, not being accepted. An empty Joy Bucket greatly affects behavior. As we said in Chapters 3 and 4, it is much easier to fill the child's bucket every day than to try later to fill many, many years of emptiness, neglect and abuse--and to fix the problems associated with that emptiness.

A GRACE-FILLED FAMILY

Along with building joy and feelings of love, a very important part of family life reflects the very family of God—that of giving grace, favor that is not deserved. Giving grace to those around us draws them to God and His ways. Children who grow up in a family filled with grace are more likely to want to know God.

A grace-filled family separates *who* the family members *are* from *what* the members (and others) *do*. One very easy way to do this is by the words we use, especially when disciplining the children. Since lying is one of the first sins committed by us humans (Psalm 58:3), we can begin early to teach and model grace by saying things like, "We don't like lying in our home. We don't want any lying around here and we won't have any lying around here." The opposite of grace-filled phrases will sound more like, "We don't like liars in our home, we don't want any liars and we won't have any liars around here." Just this simple change in one word makes a huge difference in how a child will view himself. It is vital to communicate that the actions are unacceptable, not the person.

There is another phrase commonly used by parents and teachers that helps communicate the difference in actions and personhood. This phrase has taken the place of one used in days past that did not help to distinguish this difference. That phrase is "good job" used in place of "good boy" or "good girl." Children are realists enough to know that they are not always good, so they may not believe us when they hear, "You are such a good boy (girl) for helping pick up your toys." But they can be proud of themselves when they know that what they did was done well.

We can also encourage and affirm personhood by affirming good character, saying things such as, "I like the way you were kind to your sister." Or "That was such a helpful thing you did." It is more helpful to affirm specific qualities that we want the child to have and exhibit than to just throw out, "good boy or girl."

Helping each other do hard things is another sign of a grace-filled family. Remember that learning to do hard things is part of maturing during the Child Stage of life. As we train the child to pick up after himself, help with chores around the house, do homework, and learn to relate well with others, we don't simply order the child to do them, but we share the tasks until skills are learned. During the learning, a grace-filled family always leaves lots of room for trial and error and practice, without yelling or condemnation for mistakes. There is discipline with love and instruction done in a spirit of togetherness. When failures come they are met with love and concern, not rejection.

Children need room to fail while still in the safe confines of a loving home. Perfectionism has no place in a grace-filled family. Living with perfectionism breeds many problems down the road and is a killer of joy all along the way. We will never achieve perfection or find it in any other person except God. If perfection is the standard, children only feel unworthy, unimportant and inadequate.

Sometimes disciplining with grace can be very powerful. It works very well to introduce children to the idea of grace after they have partially "paid" a consequence for an offense. Depending on the event and the attitude of the child, a consequence can be shortened in order to teach about grace. For example, if the consequence is three days without computer games, and the child has been having a good attitude about the whole incident, you can talk to the child about God's grace to us when we fail/sin and that today you want to show her grace by taking one day off the consequence. We won't do this every time, but we can do it now and then as an expression of grace. The child will internalize a deep message about God's grace, acceptance and love.

PARENTAL DECISIONS BEFORE THE NEED

As your baby becomes mobile and verbal, you will find that there are certain problems that children have in common and are prone to do. It is very helpful to have a united, consistent front from you as parents before these activities begin. You will either deal with them or not, but they will arise.

Bickering

Where two or more are gathered, there shall be bickering also. We don't even have to have two gathered, as we can even bicker quite well within ourselves alone. So children will bicker and quarrel. Decide how much of this you will allow and how much you will referee. When it gets physical, that is a different story, but for verbal bickering, there are various ways to handle it. Some parents refuse to referee.

Dr. Wilder shares in *Living With Men* how he used to sit his two boys at the kitchen table when they had a disagreement. It was up to the boys to work out their conflicts. Upon bringing a dispute to their parents, they were told to sit at the table until it was resolved. Neither one could get up until the other one gave them permission. The sessions varied in loudness and length. It was preparation for fairness. They quickly realized the value of mutually satisfying solutions. Sometimes their solution was to ask for adult help. (p. 63 LWM)

Some parents give consequences to both or all siblings when they fuss and cannot work it out alone, while other parents separate the quibblers for a period of time. It is good to have your own family limit and guideline to this common problem.

Whining

Whining is a tone of voice that can be very attention getting and annoying. It will happen. It usually grows when a child has the feeling he is being ignored. It escalates because it works. The annoyance brings attention from parents and reinforces the whining. Some kids whine more than others. It needs to be nipped in the bud by consistent reminders to "Use your words," or " I can't understand whining," or using Time Out. As we focus on a child's questions and sometimes seemingly endless demands, they don't have to whine to be noticed. As they grow we can teach them about not interrupting and waiting, but in the early years of language development, whining gets reinforced very easily when the whine gets the attention, the cookie, the water, or even the negative response. This applies to screaming or tantrums as well.

Physical Violence

I cannot believe my eyes these days when I see (or hear about) parents that allow their children to hit, bite, slap or kick them. This has to be broken immediately, as soon as it happens. Hitting adults is not funny, and if allowed, it will turn into a form of defiance that will only get worse and worse. Hitting at parents can begin sometimes right after, or even before, the first birthday. A strong, "No!" and grabbing firmly on the little hand that is slapping will deter the behavior and begin to teach that it is not allowed. Speaking firmly goes a long way with a child who already wants to please you. The tone of a firm voice that means business is <u>lower</u> than a voice that is playing. The lower tone does not have to be harsh or a yell, but it does indicate, "I mean what I say." Although an infant batting at our eyeglasses is not hitting, the firm voice tone will work for that problem as well.

I have watched a couple of generations of parents and children, and I find that I can often predict how a child will be as a teenager when I see him or her with the parents before the age of two and half or three. What a child does at two or three will not be funny at thirteen, fifteen or seventeen. Make a commitment to deal with inappropriate behavior when it begins. (I will speak about spanking in the next section.)

What if your child hits or bites *himself*? This does happen and must be addressed. We want to teach our child to love and respect him or herself just as we want them to love and respect others. We quite often "love our neighbor the same way we love ourselves," and sometimes that is not a positive. Consistently speak to any self-hurting that you see. Remind the child to "Love (his name). Be kind to (her name)." If parents can take a moment to analyze when the behavior occurs, here are a few questions they might ask themselves and each other. "Are we being too strict so that the child is not 'free' to express his feelings and is taking something out on himself? Is the child sensing that we are not in agreement on some issue of discipline or allowed behavior? Is the Joy Bucket full and functioning?" Sometimes children who are truly "joy babies" will do this type behavior. It is worth checking into with these questions if it happens too often, but does not necessarily mean that the parents have failed somehow as long as it is temporary and/or infrequent.

It is helpful as parents to also decide early on what we will do with physical fighting among the children. I did not want my children to do any kind of physical contact when angry. I loved seeing them wrestle with each other, with Dad, with uncles or friends, but I did not want them to hit, kick, bite and slap. It was not part of our family values and as far as I was concerned not allowed. If physical fights happened when I was not around and was not told, that I don't know about, but when I was around, I highly discouraged physical fighting.

I will leave it to you fathers to decide what to tell your boys (and maybe even your daughters) about defensive fighting when bullied. If your child is attacked by a bully, you should immediately look into the situation and bring it to an end. This is part of protecting your family. It is especially affective if Dad takes care of it. But the point I am making here is for you to take time to think about these things before they arise so that you will know how you feel and what you think about them.

SUMMARY

The easiest way to discipline is to make the simple rules, post them, refer to them, and consistently use them, nipping problems in the bud before they blossom. Make it fun to use the body exercises to keep everyone's RC's on and most importantly, be consistent, kind, joyful and as grace-filled as possible. Children thrive when they feel secure, loved and safe. Consistent, joy-filled, proper discipline builds a foundation for that security.

And he who begets a wise son (daughter) will be glad in him (her). Proverbs 23:24b

CHAPTER SEVEN: TO SPANK OR NOT TO SPANK—THAT IS THE QUESTION

Goal: to consider a loving method of spanking

INTRODUCTION

Spanking is probably one of the most debated questions in child rearing. Television talk show hosts often speak of the dangers and negatives of spanking. Parents have become paranoid about discipline of any sort in public for fear of being accused of child abuse. This politically correct debate has resulted in a generation (or two) of unruly, insecure children that hit, bite, scream at and disobey their parents. Super nannies have had to be imported from Great Britain to help bring some of these children to normal control. It is my opinion that proper spanking can be helpfully used to train young children. My emphasis is on the word PROPER.

A proper spanking cannot be done in a hurry or in anger! It may take up to twenty minutes. But when done properly it can shorten the length of time to get a point across about unacceptable behavior. This chapter and its ideas will apply to children between the ages of two and a half to three to around seven or eight. It is usually not necessary to spank much before or after these ages, **if** you have followed other aspects of loving discipline and joy building. (Around the age of nine to twelve months, some babies start to fight having a diaper change. You might have to "pop" the little leg with your hand and say, "No!" This will usually solve the problem.) Younger than two, children can usually be distracted from a negative situation. As we looked at in the section on "terrible twos," returning them to joy is imperative before discipline. If discipline has been done well, children older than six to eight seldom need a spanking. It is my desire to put forth a method that is neither abusive nor harmful. It is not anything akin to the old days of taking a child to the wood shed or sending them out for a switch. Please prayerfully consider this method before deciding against it.

In order to help you consider spanking as a method of discipline, I want you to hear a personal testimony from Chris. She can say it best in her own words.

A PERSONAL TESTIMONY

Like most people my age or older, spanking was a very negative experience. A spanking required that a part of my body be "sacrificed" in order to appease the parental god, for a sin that I either did do, or at least got blamed for doing. Spanking was done with almost any object and for almost any issue. I often felt shamed and then had to swallow that feeling, along with feelings of anger or rejection. As a result, I swore I would never spank my children. I could surely find a way that would avoid such an extreme form of discipline.

Then my first child was born and turned two. All of a sudden my pleasant child turned on me. I tried talking to her, Time Outs, and more talking to her. Nothing worked. So I called my mother-in-law (Barbara) to seek advice and cringed when she told me I was going to

194

have to spank. 'Not that!' I thought. But down inside I knew she was right because I had heard her talk about a different way to do it. I asked her to walk me through the steps of how to spank the proper way. A knot welled up in my stomach but I determined I would give it a try the next time it seemed necessary.

The first time I spanked Tyler, I thought I was going to throw up, but I continued believing that this was very different from the experiences that I'd had. The next time I had to spank, I felt a little more confident, but the response from Tyler was not the same as it had been the first time. She did not want me to hold her; she fought me and pushed me away. This was not part of the plan and I thought, 'Uh-oh. Now what do I do?' So I called 'Mom' again and explained the situation.

If I thought what she told me the first time was hard, this time it felt a thousand times worse. What did she tell me? She said if Tyler would not sit in my lap, I had to turn Tyler back over my lap and spank her a few more times until she submitted to my love. I prayed inside that this would never happen again so that I would never have to follow through with this new information. But we all know what happened, right? The next time Tyler needed a spanking, we had to go through two rounds.

I was so relieved and surprised that then Tyler melted into me afterwards and we were able to return to joy. Pretty soon I became more comfortable with this type of discipline and I found as Tyler grew up more, I did not have to spank as often. She knew I meant business.

But I got a rude reawakening after I had Kayli and Kori and they turned two. Suddenly I felt as if I were spanking someone all day long—and I felt that way for quite a while. (We have a whole book on the shenanigans they pulled.) When my twins were sixteen months, I had my fourth daughter, Brenna. She waited until she was about 3 ½ to test me and I had to use this method with her as well. Of course, I used other methods along the way with all of them, but I am now a firm believer in spanking, as long as it is done correctly and lovingly.

So how are things now that the girls are 10, 7, 7, and 5 1/2? I hardly ever have to spank them and haven't for a while. I only use spanking for severe offenses like lying or physically harming someone (usually one of the sisters.) We have always given ten whacks for lying and as I reflect on it, lying was really not a problem very often.

Growing up, I never would have thought that I would be a firm believer in spanking, but having four loving, well-adjusted, fun-to-be-with, joy-filled daughters is proof to me that what God's word says about spanking is true.

Now that you have heard a testimony to the method and a testimony to the outcome, I hope that you will consider further instructions. Below are the thoughts, cautions and steps that I gave to Chris that day when she called me at the end of her rope.

WHEN TO SPANK

We must never spank when we are angry. If you do not have enough self-control to wait until you are calm, do not spank. Spanking is not the same as hitting. Hitting is done spontaneously and angrily. It can be very harmful. Spanking has a method and a plan.

Always spank, age appropriately, when the child is defiant, has lied, or stolen something. Save spanking for the "big things." The definition of defiant is "daring or bold opposition to authority, open disregard or contempt." This can be manifested as a simple "No!" or hitting at you from a toddler, the stomp of a foot, sticking out the tongue or a contemptuous look on the face of an elementary age child. When taken seriously as a "big offense" and treated consistently as such, this behavior will not continue into the older years. Teens will try defiance again at times, but it is usually milder in a teen when it was addressed properly in the younger years. I will address teen issues in a later chapter.

As we consider all forms of discipline, we want to keep in mind that we are training over a long period of time. Sometimes defiance is just "saving face" and can be ignored now and then. If you stay in tune with the Lord, you will know when to spank.

WHY SPANK AT ALL?

I see a couple of reasons for spanking. The first and foremost is when Time Out or trying to calm tantrums is not working. Proper spankings clear the air and allow life to go on with joy. The offense is over and done with and must not be brought up again as a point of shame. Spankings are swift and to the point. When reserved for major offenses and done correctly and lovingly, they send a loud and clear message: **this behavior will not be tolerated**. The possibility of a spanking is usually a motivating factor and will help a child to gain self-control.

Another reason for spanking is contrary to what we are told by many television celebrities and famous authors. Spanking is Biblical. The following are several verses that you can study and pray over. Keep in mind the definition we are using for discipline: *training that develops self- control.*

Note: The word "rod" in these verses indicates a stick (wood). In Proverbs 26:3, we are told, "A whip (leather) is for the horse . . . ."

Proverbs 13:24 He who spares his rod hates his son. But he who loves him disciplines him diligently.

Proverbs 22:15 Foolishness is bound in the heart of a child; the rod of discipline will remove it from him.

Proverbs 23:13 Do not hold back discipline from the child. Although you beat him with the rod, he will not die.

Note: There are two words in the proverbs for "beat." One means "to strike," the other means, "to crush." This word above is "strike," not "crush."

Proverbs 29:15 The rod and reproof give wisdom, but a child who gets his own way brings shame to his mother.

Proverbs 29:17 Correct your son and he will give you comfort.

Proverbs 15:10 Stern discipline is for him who forsakes the way.

Proverbs 3:11, 12 My son, do not reject the discipline of the Lord or loathe his reproof. For whom the Lord loves He reproves. Even as a father the son in whom he delights.

The Proverbs are a great place to discover God's views of child rearing. Mine the gems there for yourself until they are part of your life.

Hebrews 12:5-13 is a good passage to look at in order to understand how God disciplines us.

HOW TO SPANK PROPERLY

I cannot emphasize enough how important the following steps are for a proper spanking. It is not the only method we will use for discipline, but when used, some form of these steps is helpful in order not to bring harm. These steps contain the differences between the writers and teachers who agree with spanking and those who don't. We who believe in spanking advocate the procedure differently than what most people consider as a spanking.

The first thing we need to do is make clear to the children what behaviors are spanking offenses and what the procedure for spanking will be. We do this before it is needed, not during the emotion. This is a "teaching time" as to what is expected and what will happen. We will give reminders along the way until the pattern is set and then they will know, as the procedure is followed each time. If begun early the procedure will evolve with time, but if you are beginning this with a child that has not been trained with it, the following is a guideline to discuss with the children. If you are beginning around two and a half to three, you can talk about it on that level.

THE INSTRUCTIONS TO THE CHILD

When you do certain behaviors (whatever our family considers) you will get a spanking.

I will not warn you with a spanking more than once.

I will take you to the (dining room, bedroom). You will go without fighting me.

You can take your blanket or other security item.

I will use a (wooden spoon, a paddle). [*We do not use our hands to spank. Hands are for loving touches.*]

I will tell you clearly why we are going for the spanking.

You will lie across my lap (or on the bed) *Note for parent—the child keeps his or her clothes on!*

You will not be allowed to put your hands or feet over your bottom. You cannot scream and fight me.

You will get the number of whacks according to how old you are. (Except for lying if your family decides. Chris and Greg gave 10 whacks for lying).

You will cry softly, not scream.

After the spanking I will hold you on my lap, or beside me, while you cry (for a reasonable time).

After you have cried I will ask you two questions. "What did you do?" "What can you do differently next time?"

We will return to joy and then you will have to (ask forgiveness from sibling, etc., still pick up toys, etc., whatever is needed to finish the incident.)

In the beginning you will most likely have some "fighting, some hands and feet on buttocks, etc." It is important to continue the training as you go. We proscribe the whacks just hard enough to precipitate crying, real crying, not pretending. If the child does not cry, you have not done the spanking well. Please keep in mind the verse that we've already looked at: "Fathers, do not provoke (exasperate) your children to wrath." (Ephesians 6: 4) When a child refuses to cry and stubbornly thinks inside, or says aloud, "I won't cry; you can't make me cry," he has been provoked to wrath. This is a terrible pattern to set up in a child and forms a very negative pattern of stubbornness for the adult he or she will become.

The most important part of this spanking method, the one that we never hear about on television or from most books, is the time of holding the child on your lap after the spanking. During this time, we do not talk. We do not lecture. We just sit and hold them and comfort them. We are glad to be together in the distress. This is part of the training-- that we want our children to come to us for help, even if we are the one who "hurt" them—that they can be with the one who hurts them and not run away or put up a wall-- because we will return to joy.

After a reasonable amount of crying, we want to ask the two questions and get to an understanding of what happened, on the child's level. Sometimes they will say they do not know what they did. Talk it through. Remember you are glad to be together and you will return to joy together by loving on the child, laughing together, giving more comfort and assurance of your love. Then finish the steps needed to remedy the situation that brought on the spanking. They will still need to obey.

Most spanking should take place in a designated area that is private, even in the home. This depends somewhat on the age of the child. It could just be in the next room for a younger child. Older children need to be taken to a more private room. We are not out to humiliate the child. Finding the paddle or wooden spoon and going to another room can also give the parent time to cool down if needed.

What if a child needs a spanking when we are out in public, at a store or a restaurant? There are various ways to handle this. If you can avoid a spanking by using talk, do so. If a serious offense occurs, you might have to go to your car or to the restroom to handle it. This seldom has to be done more than once or twice as the child sees you mean what you say. If the child is old enough to understand, you can tell them you will deal with them later at home. If you are consistently doing proper discipline at home, public issues should be very rare. We want the child to learn to obey our voice, the first time. That is the goal.

Again, we never spank in anger. The parent must take time to calm him or herself before spanking. If we lose it and strike out in a way that doesn't follow the procedure, we must ask forgiveness for doing it wrongly. Sometimes we don't spank correctly, but the spanking was needed. We can tell the child something like, "I was wrong to spank you that way, but you did need the spanking. Will you forgive me for doing it the wrong way?" Then continue the procedure that would come after the spanking.

SUMMARY

Spanking is just one of many ways to discipline, but when needed and done properly, it sends a strong message. The message is grace-filled and loving, the way God disciplines us—I love you, but this kind of behavior is not acceptable. (Hebrews 12:5-11) We separate who the person is from what they do. We do not strike out in anger at just any appendage that is reachable. We administer a spanking in a calm way that ends with comfort and taking responsibility for actions. We practice self-control while modeling and training self-control into the child.

CHAPTER EIGHT: NANA'S TIPS—BY AGE GROUP

Goal: to have a collection of suggestions that will help cut down on stress, disorganization and conflict while helping you reach the goals from Chapter One.

INTRODUCTION

Parenting is one of the few major endeavors that requires such little training before taking on huge responsibilities. I wonder how the public would react if our men and women in blue were issued a gun, a radio and a car without any instructions prior to going out on the streets. What about a surgeon who could operate without a license? Becoming a parent is as important as any other job we might have in life, but because it happens without needing credentials or having to apply for a license of any kind, good parenting depends on us to educate ourselves. We can study the Scriptures, read books and go to seminars.

Another great way to take self-teaching courses is through benefiting from the experience of others who have parented before us. A student in this school, like any other school, must be teachable and open and ask questions. Answering questions from moms and dads is one of my favorite things to do. And I love it that they are asking questions.

For this chapter I want to speak to a variety of questions that new parents have as well as speak to issues that arise as the children grow up. I am drawing from years of proven experiences and observations. Every age range that a child grows through can make us feel like we are a "new" parent all over again. As I did previously, I have divided these comprehensive tips into age groups, beginning with infancy and going through the middle school age. I will speak about teens in a later chapter.

INFANTS: BIRTH-TWELVE MONTHS

I love newborns and it gives me great joy to help new moms and dads. I wish I could be with every one of you in person and help you get a good start. It is a blessing to help as you explore this new and often frightening experience of bringing a new baby into the world. I hope you will use this section, these other tips, and the section on joy as a handbook that you refer to over and over. I trust that you will find some ways here to help your transition from womb to cradle.

BEFORE THE BIRTH OF YOUR FIRST CHILD

Because I am passionate about mothers staying home with their children, I want to talk first about a very important transition that takes place even before the transition from the womb. Understanding this transition will make being a new mom somewhat easier. The credit for understanding this section goes to my daughter, Jodi. Jodi spent ten years in her career before having her first son. She found the transition from a career in an office to being a career mom much more difficult than she had anticipated. She told me one day that going to work was much easier than staying home with a baby. Some months later she realized that having a career had inadvertently trained her to think and operate in ways that were <u>opposite</u> to how she would have to think and operate in order to be a good mom. I want to share her list with you and encourage you to pass it on to other young women who want to take some time out to rear their children. The list will include other changes that occur with having a new baby. Try to see the humor in it as you read.

IN THE WORK PLACE, VERSUS BEING A FIRST-TIME MOMMY

In the work place you are rewarded for your work quickly with a paycheck and sometimes praise. The rewards for rearing a child are far into the future.

In the work place you get regular breaks. With a new baby, you get very few at all, day or night.

When having problems with co-workers, you are taught to negotiate. One day you will find yourself trying to negotiate with a two-year old.

If you have a problem with a co-worker, you can walk away. The new baby is ever-present and demanding.

At your job, you know what is expected of you. Most of the time you will have no clue what to do with a new baby.

At the office there are plenty of people to talk to and interact with. At home with a new baby, your life will, at first, revolve around burps and poops.

On the job, you will have short-term, measurable goals that someone will recognize are achieved. A new baby will not give you any feedback and you will see no quick results for your sacrifices.

At the end of the workday, you can do whatever you want. Baby will demand you do everything he wants.

Before baby you can go out any time you please. After baby, you may feel trapped and alone.

After work, home is a place to have a good meal and to prop your feet up with your spouse. With a new baby you will have a good meal when a friend brings it by--and forget about propping up your feet.

I thank Jodi for this list (and my friend Jakki Leatherberry added a couple of ideas.) In this day and time, I hope it will help prepare some for this drastic transition. Becoming a parent is the road towards becoming more unselfish. If you desire to be a good parent, you will have to travel that road over and over. Good parents "give without expecting anything in return." They lay down their lives for their children. The rewards are often intangible; rewards such as joy, love, pride, progress and hugs, but these far outweigh the rewards in the material world. I encourage you mothers to stay home if at all possible and diligently work towards the future goal of seeing your children be as close as possible to those goals that you wrote down in Chapter One. Now let's look at some tips for those days after the new baby arrives.

HEALING PRAYERS FOR THE NICU AND C-SECTIONS

If your little bundle of joy was delivered by C-Section and/or had to be in the NICU, he or she had an unusual beginning. Any unusual event at birth can interfere with bonding. I have found it very important to pray over babies who have been in these situations, or any situation that kept them from being with the parents immediately. It is not a difficult or frightening prayer, just one of faith and healing. The parents (or a person you know who is a person of prayer) can pray aloud, in the presence of the baby, for Jesus to heal any hurts or wounds that might have happened because of any difficulty during birth or immediately after that made it unusual or prevented immediate bonding in any way.

If the baby was in NICU, he or she was not held as often and as soon as if she had been in the room with the parents. Ask and thank Jesus for healing any hurts or any sense of not being wanted that might have wounded the little heart. These prayers are for and about the baby. They are not about what the parents were feeling or how distraught they may have been that unusual events happened. These prayers are about what the baby might have felt. The parents can say, "I'm sorry that you weren't with us," or anything else that might apply. If there is disappointment in the gender of the child, make sure that there is prayer for healing any negative thoughts or words that were said about that, before or after the birth. If you were blessed to have your baby through in-vitro fertilization or adoption, it might be good to cover that unusual beginning as well. Ask and thank Jesus to heal anything that might hinder your baby's emotional growth.

I have seen babies just a few days or weeks old who would not cuddle well until someone prayed these kinds of prayers over them. What do we have to lose by praying for any emotional healing that might be needed? Our God loves to answer these kinds of prayers.

Speaking of cuddling, I must say that you cannot hold and rock your infant too much. It is an old wives tale that holding too much will spoil a baby. This is not true those first months. Hold and rock and hold some more. This is how that early bonding takes place and can never be repeated. (Remember how important smell and temperature are?) Very soon the eyes will focus and this is where and how we build and develop the Joy Center. You cannot spend too much time building joy and quiet together during that first year.

NURSING

I cannot encourage you enough to try breastfeeding. If you decide to try, determine to give it all you can. Talk with a friend who has made it through. Know that it might not be easy, but worth the effort. When you and baby figure it out, it will be easier than bottle-feeding. Doctors recommend it as a way to help avoid allergies to all kinds of things. The first weeks will be very time consuming.

If you follow some of my suggestions in this section on infants and you take the "joy stuff" to heart, you will find nursing to be a vital part of making a secure bond. If you don't worry about scheduling and how much the baby is getting, but simply feed on demand for a while, you will be glad. I know mothers with nine to ten pound babies who were able to nurse successfully.

The first time that you might need help is around the third day when true milk comes in. In the hospital stay, which now is only a day or so, you will not have milk in the breasts, only colostrums. You may leave the hospital having had help from the nurse only to find when the milk comes in that it is a different matter. The baby might have a more difficult time attaching, even though he or she did at the hospital. Let go of your modesty and allow another mother or grandmother to help you figure it out. I have done that several times through the years and seen the joy that nursing can bring to all involved. Persevere and don't give up if you really want to do it.

LACTOSE INTOLERANCE

If you have any suspicion that your baby is crying too much and you have a sense that it might be from pain, please talk to your doctor about lactose intolerance. All four of Chris' girls were lactose intolerant, even to breast milk. She did not know it with the first one and nursed her for ten months. Tyler often cried after feedings, though she was a happy, joyful baby otherwise. When the twins, Kayli and Kori, were born, Chris tried to nurse them and as soon as the colostrum was gone and milk was there, they began to cry. She changed them to soymilk and they stopped crying the next day. Then Brenna came along and the same thing happened. During that time I was the nanny for another set of twins, Avery and Arden. Avery cried daily for weeks until her mother switched her to soymilk and Avery became a different child overnight. Lactose intolerance might not be the reason for the baby's crying, but if it is, it's a very easy problem to solve. You can also buy formula that is milk based but is lactose free.

IN THE HOSPITAL & FIRST WEEK HOME

When all goes as expected your stay in the hospital won't be a long one. It might help you to have a few ideas in mind for those days and the following week or two. Company is a big issue. Only you and your spouse will know how much and with whom you can be comfortable, as far as company, at the hospital and home. The important thing is for you to get rest whenever possible and not have added stress. If you have doubts about lots of company, especially if from out of town, you will have to verbalize this and accept that some people might feel offended at first. But you and the new baby will do best with lots of time to bond and adjust. You will probably want and need some help, but you can decide who and when.

If you are tired and not sleeping much, don't be ashamed to ask for help. As time passes, please call other parents and ask them questions. This is a very big and new adventure you are experiencing. If you have determined to breastfeed, don't give up. It will get easier.

PACIFIERS AND SECURITY ITEMS

I cannot encourage you enough to try a pacifier. Newborns sleep quite a bit a first, but that does not last, and it can become more and more difficult to soothe them. Many new parents say, "My baby won't take a pacifier." Some babies take them in the hospital and never let go. But if your newborn does not love the passy, keep in mind that it is a skill that can be taught, and you will not be sorry. If you already have a thumb-sucker when you get home from the hospital, you might not be able to change the baby to a pacifier. But it is much easier to take a pacifier away than it is a thumb.

The best reason for using a pacifier is that it is much easier to quiet the baby when needed. It is easier to put them to bed and it usually helps them be quieter in the car. It is easier to leave them with a sitter or in the nursery at church when they take a pacifier.

If the baby spits out the pacifier, keep trying. Hold it in the baby's mouth with your finger or try what we call the "passy hold." Hold the baby cuddled on one of your arms (the opposite arm than the one that you use all the time) with the baby's arm that is close to you behind your arm, down to your side. It will dangle or the baby will hold on to your shirt. The baby's face will be very close to your chest. Turn the baby slightly toward you and put the pacifier in her mouth with her mouth (holding the pacifier) and her face up against your chest. (Leave breathing room of course.) As you hold the baby in this manner, the pacifier is up against your chest and will be held in the baby's mouth. You might have to keep pushing it back in at first. Early on, they lose it easily, but after a few weeks, they can hold it themselves. Babies love this kind of snuggly holding and it works well when you are sitting down or standing. It can be a good way to get them to sleep.

If you decide to put a sleeping infant down while you have been holding him, hold onto the pacifier with your hand as you lay him down. Keep it from falling out until the baby returns to soundly sleeping.

When the baby is on her back or in the swing or car seat, you can roll a cloth diaper into a long roll and place it around the front of the face, on the chest, to help hold the pacifier. (Be sure the cloth does not go up on the face.) Just keep trying it; giving the pacifier often throughout the day, and most of the time, he will learn to keep it in his mouth.

Another important item to teach the baby to love is some kind of security blanket. Some babies end up loving a cloth diaper (and they know the special ones from all others) while other babies love a blanket or even a stuffed animal. Since parents are told to put nothing in the cribs, a blanket is probably the easiest because they usually have to have some cover. If you want the baby to get attached to a blanket, hold the blanket over your shoulder, touching the baby, while you are nursing or giving a bottle or rocking and holding her. Keep that blanket around all the time and she will get attached. Then she will have something that always smells like home and mommy whenever she is out--in the car, traveling and sleeping in a strange crib or just going to a friend's house or to church.

In my family, my mother has bought a "night-night blankie" for each of her 19 grandchildren and now her (I think) 29 great-grandchildren. She always buys the blankets that have a silky-ribbon on the edge and every single child (grown or still young) loves (or used to love) that silky edge. They use it for self- comfort and most of them want to take the blanket wherever they go. These security items are not to be taken lightly and made fun of. They feel comforting and smell like home and sometimes they are even needed at college.

Pink girl blankies   ***Blue boy blankies***

In my family's opinion, the best blanket is a cotton thermal blanket with a silky edge. If you cannot find one with a silky edge, get a blanket from Penney's and buy the ribbon from Wal-Mart and have a seamstress sew it around the blanket. Your baby will rub the silk and self-comfort.

OTHER SOOTHING TECHNIQUES

Here are a few tips for soothing babies, especially newborns. They all begin with the letter "S." In the hospital, the nurses will show you how to **swaddle**. Do this for the first few days or weeks that the baby is not moving about. Most like to be wrapped tightly at first.

The pacifier brings us to the next "S"—**sucking.** Sucking is very soothing to babies, so keep trying the pacifier. Another thing babies usually love is to **swing** and this can be done with a baby swing you buy or by swinging them in your arms. Being on their **stomachs** is soothing, as well, and you can lay them over one of your arms on their stomach or over your knees while sitting. You can put them on their stomach close by you after you see that they can pick their head up and turn it over. Doctors recommend sleeping on the back, but lots of tummy time from the beginning is helpful to develop muscles that will get ignored if baby is never put on the stomach. Learning to crawl is vital to development and tummy time encourages the use of those muscles. If babies are never put on their stomachs, they will protest later when you try to encourage it. Lots of tummy time will also help prevent a flat head. I highly recommend tummy sleeping after the baby can pick up his or her head and turn it over. Doctors now vary on their recommendations.

The last "S" is **shushing.** I read about this one in a book entitled, *The Happiest Baby on the Block* by Dr. Harvey Karp. This soothing method works well in the early weeks. Hold the baby with his or her ear close to your mouth and make a rather loud "shushing" noise, rhythmically—shuh, shuh, shuh, shuh. It mimics the sounds inside the womb and helps the baby quiet.

Another technique for quieting a newborn is to hold the baby's hands. While on his back, put your forefingers inside his fist, take your hands that are holding his, and place the baby's hands beside his ears, against the surface he is lying on. This works especially well during the first weeks when the baby still has the startle reflex and gets easily upset at diaper changes. Most every newborn cries when having his diaper or clothes changed.

From the beginning, use a small fan or other type of machine that makes "white noise" in the baby's room when he is sleeping. This will block out the regular household noise and will be even more helpful when the child is older and napping or going to bed earlier than the rest of the household. It will not interfere with the monitor. It will become a habit and can (or must) be taken with you on trips where surroundings are strange and have different noises than those at home.

BOREDOM

Babies get bored just like the rest of us. Their attention span is very short. Forget the décor in your living area and have lots of different places to move the baby around. Use a baby swing, a bouncy chair, tummy time on a colorful floor mat, room to roll around on the floor, gyms that hang over the baby while on his back, and exersaucers. Some babies will begin to push up on their legs as early as three to four months. They will like the saucer before they can sit alone. Use the floor often. You can put a big quilt out if it bothers you to have the baby on the carpet. The more he can explore the better.

WATCH THE LIGHT

As you place your infant in the crib or in a bouncy chair or car seat and he or she is going to be in that position for a while, or over and over, notice that she may be turning her head towards a mobile, a window, or other light. If, for instance, she stays in the car seat or other device to sleep and you leave it sitting in the same place, she will turn her head towards light (like a plant does) and one side of the head will flatten. Just take the device and turn it around daily so she looks the other way. The same will work in the crib. Parents tend to lay the infant with his or her head at the same end of the crib every time. Just change that direction now and then so that the baby is looking each way at the mobile or the window or other light. After a while he will turn his own head and move around more. If you use tummy time, that will help as well to avoid a flat head.

READ READ READ

Read, read, and read. Begin reading to your baby as soon as he can see and look around. Buy the board books that babies can handle without tearing them. If we take a moment to think about it, reading to children encompasses several of the building-joy directives. We are sitting quietly together, we are touching, we are using pleasant and varied voice tones, and we most always feel close and calm.

If you read often, you won't be sorry when you see that babies can learn letters of the alphabet before their second birthday. Reading will increase vocabulary and set the foundation for a good beginning for school that will come before you blink. You can begin going to the library before the second birthday and books make great gift requests.

TIPS FOR TWINS--OR MORE

If you find out you are going to have twins—or more—you will be shocked and excited at the same time. You will not have a clue what is before you and neither will anyone else who has never had or helped with newborn twins. You <u>will</u> need help and you will want help for a long time. Here are a few tips for this double pleasure:

If your twins are identical, and really close to the same size, put some kind of mark on their feet (or an ankle name bracelet) so that you won't get them mixed up at first. It won't take long for you to know them apart, but you will be surprised that it can be easy to mix them up.

For nursing and/or bottle-feeding, buy two Boppies™, which are pillows that hold a newborn. The pillows will help you balance the babies without holding on to both of them at the same time. You will have to figure it out if you are nursing. If you are bottle-feeding by yourself, which will happen, you can use a Boppy™ on each side of you while sitting on the couch. You can then hold a bottle in each baby's mouth at the same time.

If you don't want to buy anything, you can sit on the couch and lay each baby by your legs, or on a regular bed pillow, before they get too big to move around. When that day comes, you can prop the bottles while sitting on the floor, but stay by the babies, watching and touching them.

As you can see by these tips, it is easier to have them on the same schedule. Sometimes you might be able to feed one then the other, but then you are feeding all day long. The first few weeks may be a nightmare.

Some twins sleep well in the same crib when first home and some do not. If one awakens or disturbs the other, go ahead and separate them for sleeping. They can be together when awake. You will need two of just about everything—cribs, car seats, swings, saucers, high chairs. Get a double *umbrella* stroller because you will use it for years and they are easier to put in and out of the car.

When the babies begin to eat solids or cereal, just use one spoon to feed them both. They will be swapping germs all day long anyway. It is useless to try to separate toys and other things, like bottles and pacifiers that they will put in their mouths.

For personality development, be careful about treating your twins as if they are one person. Dressing alike is cute when small, but each must be his or her own person. Allow them the freedom to develop as who God made them to be. Even identical twins are usually different in many ways, and this is healthy.

Kayli and Kori   **Avery and Arden**

DISCIPLINE

Babies younger than twelve months and up to about twenty months do not need much of what we commonly call discipline. The best way to deal with problems is to distract them to another area, another toy, or another activity. There will be lots of distracting and some "no's." One of the earliest problems is spitting food after they begin to eat solids. Your voice tone and face can show disapproval with a firm, "No spit." You can stop giving them ammunition (food) for a minute and then try again. Determine if they are full. As they begin to use a sippy cup and feed themselves, they will drop cups and food on the floor, or even throw them. Use the same strategy—cup out of reach, no more cheerios on the tray, a firm, "No throw."

It is best at this age to have as few "no's" as possible. Again forgo the décor and baby-proof the area that the baby will be in. Keep firm "no's" for knocking off your eyeglasses, hitting you on the nose, and spitting food.

WHAT ABOUT SICKNESS?

The first time your baby has a fever, you will be frightened. It will be fine to take her to the doctor. You will learn over time when to call the doctor, go to the doctor or just wait. Since I am not a medical person, I will only give a guideline or two here. If you are ever in doubt, at least call the pediatrician's office or nurse line. They are accustomed to calls.

It is not good to give over the counter meds to any child under two without your doctor telling you to do so. He will tell you what kind for what symptoms. When children are older, you will know what you can give for a fresh fever or cold symptoms. When they are very young, I would call the first day with a fever or at least the second. When older, if they are not better after about three days, call or go in. You will not be able to diagnose strep or an ear infection.

The struggle comes when the children are older and get a fever. Doctors do not give meds for viruses, but strep throat and ear infections will not go away if untreated. This creates a debate in your mind about taking a child in to the office. When in doubt, go in. It is better to spend money and time and be told it is just a virus than to wait and discover it is something serious.

SCHEDULES

I have already mentioned that there are some parenting books that advise parents to do the opposite of what brain research shows is needed for the developing brain. The principle area that this advice crosses with the brain research is in the area of scheduling and bedtime. Some of these authors advocate putting even a newborn baby in the crib to go to sleep when the parents decide it's time, and leaving them there to cry if they don't go to sleep. They advise this same type of schedule for feeding. The parent decides when the baby/child will eat and sleep.

I highly disagree with this kind of parenting and believe it is exactly the opposite of what is good for the baby and how God designed the brain. This method is like two of the attachment styles we looked at in Chapter Four--the Dismissive and the Distracted bonding styles. If you remember, these bonds are about the parent not about the baby. They are *not* based on synchronizing. Not synchronizing causes great emotional pain.

In the Dismissive bond, the baby feels that no one will ever dependably synchronize with him, so he gives up and pretends to be fine. He looks good on the outside because he doesn't cause "trouble." In the Distracted, the baby does not know when the parent will synchronize, so he stays alert and clingy so as not to miss out when it does come. He has to please the parent. These books that push for the parent to schedule the child so rigidly, generally produce a child who looks fine and doesn't cause trouble. Either way, it might not build joy, resilience and strong immunity systems that come from a secure bond where the baby's needs are met with timely joy.

The new brain research on joy bonding calls for a baby to be fed when he is hungry. I believe that newborns should be fed on demand and worked *slowly* into a schedule. Keep this especially in mind if you are nursing. The infant will eventually come to a schedule that falls into about an every- three to four-hour feeding. (If you have a preemie, you might have to wake the baby to feed her. Your doctor will tell you.) But those first few weeks and months, a baby's cry should be comforted as soon as possible. Sometimes a baby will cry even when you are trying to comfort. This is different than putting him in the crib to cry alone. It has to do with your attitude of "Trying to help" versus "Don't bother me." We don't let them "cry it out" before close to the end of the first year. There may be a time for that by processing it slowly, but not in the beginning.

As the baby is working *slowly* into a feeding and sleeping schedule there are a few tips that will help this process. After the first few weeks of feeding on demand, you should notice that the time between feeding lengthens. Sometimes you can stretch the time for a few minutes if the baby is awakening early, by giving the pacifier a few times. This is especially helpful at night to help the baby learn that night is for sleeping longer. It can be helpful to try to keep the baby awake for a while after a feeding so that the sleeping time will end later in the cycle. Just don't let him cry unnecessarily. Babies eat when they are hungry and stop when they are full. Only he is going to know when that is until you get in touch with his rhythms. Most infants (after they stop sleeping almost all the time) will eat and stay awake about two hours after a feeding, play, and then take a nap. The naps will vary in length, so just go by the baby's needs. One way to know that baby is getting hungry, sleepy or bored is that he will begin to "hum" or "sing." This is a signal to change the place he's playing, feed him or put him to sleep, according to where he is in the flow of the process. Heed this signal quickly to avoid escalating to crying.

IN THE NIGHT

When you get up at night with the little one, don't turn a bright light on and talk and goo at her while you change the diaper and feed her. Let nighttime be different than daytime. Keep trying to lengthen the times between feedings at night, but please don't let a young baby cry unnecessarily. Some babies do not sleep all night for many months and it can be very difficult, but I do not feel it is good to let them cry in order to bring that about.

BEDTIME

As the baby matures, you can begin to form a pattern for bedtime that will carry over even into school years. The pattern should include Daddy as much as possible, especially when the children are older. It is good for Daddy to be certain that everyone is in Joy Camp before bedtime. When Daddy's presence brings quiet together time at the end of the day, the family thrives with security.

This routine will be good to begin around three to four months of age, but especially helpful towards the middle of the first year. Decide for your family, according to when the household gets up, what is a good bedtime. Let's say that the family gets moving about 7 AM. 7 to 8 PM is a good bedtime. This will give you parents some time to unwind and to be together. Beginning this pattern early will not guarantee that you have no bedtime problems (I will speak to that in a later section), but it will go a long way towards making bedtime easier. If during these months you have spent lots of time building joy and spending quiet together, the baby should be on his way to being able to self-comfort.

A PATTERN FOR BEDTIME

About thirty minutes before bedtime, give the baby/child a bath. The bath will help relax him. Have playtime before the bath so that all time after the bath is low key. After bathing and dressing, prepare the room by turning on the monitor and fan if you are using them. Take time to rock the baby and read some books. You cannot start reading to your child too early. After the stories, say prayers and sing "Jesus Loves Me" or another quiet song. (As your child grows, you will be surprised how young they learn to pray, modeling after your prayers, of course.) You might want to turn off the light and rock some more. Then give hugs and kisses and put the child in the crib. Say, "Good night" and walk out. Young babies and children do not need a nightlight or the door open. Most begin to ask for one, or to have the door open, closer to three years of age. That request should be honored.

BEDTIME PROBLEMS (WHILE STILL IN A CRIB)

Everyone has an opinion about how much and how often to go back into the baby's room if they fuss when put to bed. That depends on the child and the age of the child. Infants don't usually cry when left. Even when older, with some babies, you can go back to give the pacifier or comfort and leave again with no problem. With others it is not so easy. I do not feel that it is good to let a baby "cry it out" much before the first birthday, but other than that, it is very difficult to give a set rule. After a few weeks or months you should be able to distinguish types of crying—anger, pain, short-term fussing. This will help you determine whether or not to return to the room. When you leave the room the first time, be very firm and matter of fact that it is bedtime. You can even say something like, "Goodnight, Mommy (Daddy) is going out now. See you in the morning."

There may come a time during the second year that you have to let the baby cry after put to bed. Since most children can understand and even speak many words by this time, these tips will apply to that age: Determine a time limit, five to ten minutes that you will wait. It will feel like hours the first time. Do not go back in for that set time in order to see if the baby will settle down. We want her to learn to self-comfort. Have several pacifiers in the crib or hook one on to the pj's if you feel comfortable doing that. (Be certain it cannot get around the neck.) If you have been using the blanket or other security item, this will be helpful also. If you go back into the room, don't talk except to speak firmly, "You're okay. It's time for bed." Lay the child back down after being sure they have their security items (and that he does not have a dirty diaper), and walk out. You might get an even louder scream of anger. Somewhere you have to decide when and if you will let them cry it out. Into that second year it will not be a trauma and usually only takes one or two days. Bedtime problems only get worse and worse, so it is good to build this pattern and stick to your guns. (I will speak later about bedtime problems that occur after leaving the crib.)

TWELVE TO EIGHTEEN MONTHS

DON'T FORGET "RETURN TO JOY"

Twelve to eighteen months is a very key time in the development of your child and his or her brain. As we have briefly looked at before, this is the time when Daddy trains for fear and aggression. A securely attached baby will be more interested in Daddy than Mommy sometimes. This is a positive. This is the also the time when Mommy begins to teach returning to joy, which she and baby will practice for life with all those around them. Learning how to repair disconnections is vital to future mental and emotional health and a basis for good relationships. It's imperative to keep in mind that this God-designed window of opportunity is a short six months. Return to joy can be taught at later ages, but this is the ideal time from the Creator and is much easier done during this window. Remember there are six basic emotions that I have defined in Chapter Five from which t learn return to joy.

DON'T FORGET "SYNCHRONIZING"

Synchronizing is the other important brain function that we never stop working on and doing with others. It can become more difficult as the child grows and begins to talk and begins to need discipline.

(Remember, we do not synchronize with "naughty," we discipline "naughty." The process of discipline will involve synchronization, but we do not want to communicate that "naughty" is okay or funny. Hitting and sassing adults is not funny.)

It is easy to forget to synchronize, be glad to be together and return to joy when needed, when the child is not that sweet, little precious that he was in the first few months. So we want to consider the best solution and be diligent to notice the child's emotional state and look at his world through his eyes. What is he or she feeling? How can you best deal with chaotic and negative situations that are increasingly more intense? What can you do to minimize upset and avoid battles that can lead to more upset?

MINIMIZING UPSET

The following are a few tips that will help minimize upset at this age, but will also work as well a bit younger and much older.

For as long as you can, use distractions to avoid escalating to "naughty." Young children can be creatively distracted.

Play children's music CD's or tapes in the car. Not only will the children learn good music, but they will also learn about Jesus and popular songs about Him. Listening to music gives them something to focus on.

Use your voice tone with firm "No's." There is no need to yell; simply lower your voice tone. Low tones are for discipline. I call the low tone my "teacher voice," as schoolteachers use that firm voice tone to keep control in the classroom. Begin to notice the tones you are using. As you practice lowering your tone, it will become easier, but you don't want to overuse the low tones. Use high tones for building joy, having fun, and loving the children,

Do not ask questions to which the child has no choice. For example, "Are you ready to pick up your toys?" "Are you ready to go to bed?" Children are seldom ever ready to pick up or go to bed. Instead use phrases such as, "It's time to _____," "Let's _____," when your child does not have a choice.

Begin to give choices when they are age appropriate and guided by you, but don't give a choice if they *can't* choose. Examples of age appropriate choices guided by you would be the type of snack available, a choice between two shirts or two outfits, the type of sandwich for lunch or which book to read. Keep the issues simple so they don't escalate into major battles. I will say more about that in a later section.

Continue a schedule. Don't let the child get hungry, but be careful not to teach her that she can eat all day long. Most children need protein at three meals a day plus a morning and afternoon snack. Keep sugar to a minimum. It is false energy.

Never leave the house without a snack and water. You never know how long you might be gone or what may happen. Children (and adults) get cranky when hungry and tired.

If your little Houdini begins to tear off his diaper, especially at nap or when it is a nice dirty one, simply duct tape the diaper and hope for the best. When Chris and Greg's twins were this age, we had to put their zippered pj's on backwards and/or safety pin the top of the zipper to the pj's. Even that did not always work.

Besides reading stories at night, read during the day. Use time for reading as a short Joy-Bucket filler, as a quick break when someone is cranky or upset. It is a great way to have quiet together. We never stop building joy, quiet together and return to joy.

LANGUAGE DEVELOPMENT

You have been talking to your baby since before birth and especially as you interact with him or her in joy. I have a simple tip for helping children learn to talk that, as I have observed over the years, many new parents don't seem to know. Some children talk very young—many words by twelve months with sentences and paragraphs by two. Others say very little until well after two. You don't need to worry if your child is not talking much by eighteen months to two, (as long as other development is normal) but this tip seems to help the process. As your baby begins to play and then become mobile, use one-word sentences with him or her.

Children (and people learning new languages) understand way more than they can say. For example, when your little one picks up a ball, say, "Ball," instead of saying, "Look at the red ball." The idea is to begin with one word at a time most of the day. For English, you will usually add a color or a "possessive" next, such as, "red ball," "daddy's shoe," "mommy's eye." This does not mean you never talk in regular sentences; it's simply a tip to shorten your sentences, especially when having direct interaction. If you live in a bi-lingual home (or culture) and your child is hearing more than one language all the time, this may slow him down a bit, but don't stop using any language you want him to know. He or she will get both languages by about the age of three. Their young brains can handle it, as it is easier to learn languages before puberty.

SAFETY

Keeping your child safe is a given. During this age span she will begin walking. Baby-proof the house again because now she can pull up on furniture and soon she will walk. Use cabinet hooks in the kitchen. Cover the outlets. There is a safety product for just about anything you can think of. Gate any stairwells. Watch out for the stove and dishwasher (knives sticking up). Never go out in the car without the proper car seat, and <u>never</u> leave the child alone in the car. Keep household doors locked that can lead to danger outside. Teach them to go backwards down any stairs if they don't have help.

We could go on and on about all the possible ways for a toddler to get hurt and we all know that accidents will happen, no matter how hard we try to avoid them. But I caution you, please don't grow overprotective and keep your little one from exploring and getting dirty and going lots of places with you. This is how they learn. New environments bring new challenges and possibilities for growth that the four walls of your house will never provide, even if the playroom has every kind of toy imaginable.

Kayli & Kori love to get dirty   ***Brenna slides with joy***

EIGHTEEN MONTHS TO TWO

PARENTS ARE BOSS

These six months are such an adorable age. The child begins to play more, he learns many words, he begins to walk well without help and he can begin to have tantrums. The emotional amplifier has come on line in the brain and molehills can become mountains. It is imperative for parents to be the boss and for that to be established early. It is easy to pick up two to five year olds and move them to obey you, but it is a little difficult to do that with a twelve to fifteen year old. Become a benevolent boss.

GET UP TO CORRECT

As you are teaching your child to obey, it is helpful to get up to correct her now that she is mobile. You can continue to distract him, move him to another place, to try a different activity, or go outside for a while. It does not work as well to sit on the couch and give orders.

© 2007 Barbara Moon

Just giving orders will not help a young child learn to obey the first time.

LIMIT TV AND DVD'S

Limit television and DVD's. Notice how your child behaves while watching these. He turns into a zombie. He quits moving around and playing. She no longer relates with you. Use television for very short periods such as when you are making dinner. Please don't let it be a babysitter.

THE PASSY FAIRY IS COMING

Close to the end of this period or maybe in another few months, you will want to think about taking the pacifier away. You can begin weaning from it by leaving it in the bed and just using it for bedtime an/or in the car. When you are ready, you can cut a tiny hole in all of them and when the baby sucks on it, it won't work. You can tell her it's broken. I know some moms who have told the child that the "passy fairy" took it after she threw them all away. Avery and Arden's mom told her girls that they had to give it to the trash man on their third birthday. None of these methods seem to cause any huge trauma, although sometimes there might be a short period of mourning the loss.

NIP WHINING IN THE BUD

During this age, children may begin to whine. Whining is a learned behavior and must be nipped in the bud. It can only get worse. If you give in when they whine, it reinforces the whining. Say something like, "Use your words." Or, "I don't understand whining." Do your best not to let the habit form. The best way is to answer or attend to the child the first or second time they want something. This does not mean to cater to them. You will slowly teach them to wait. It does mean don't ignore them until the asking escalates. Remember to synchronize and calm.

A FOOD TIP

You may notice around this age that your child begins to take his peanut butter and jelly sandwich apart while eating it. Many times when they do this, the children only eat the jelly side. Here is a tip for helping get that protein down the hatch: Instead of putting peanut butter on one side and jelly on the other, put a little peanut butter on both sides before spreading the jelly. That way when he takes it apart to eat the jelly, he will get more of the peanut butter. He'll probably lick as much of the jelly as he can, but perhaps he will bite the bread and get it all.

TANTRUMS IN PUBLIC

If your child begins to have tantrums out at the store or a restaurant, you might have to go out to the car or to the restroom to calm her. When possible, make errand trips and other outings when the child *is not hungry or tired.* Always have an easy snack and a drink in your child's bag. If you go out when the child is hungry or tired, you will be asking for trouble and you might lose it easier yourself.

It is not good to bribe children to behave. We are beginning the training for them to obey when we speak in a normal voice. As you consistently and calmly train your little one, self-control and obedience will grow. Remember to synchronize and return to joy when upsets come. Return to joy before giving instructions and take the time for everyone to calm again.

TWO TO THREE

DO TWO'S HAVE TO BE TERRIBLE?

Now you are fast approaching the most challenging time of childrearing, the time often called the "terrible two's." You might find tht it does not begin until the child is nearing three, but a change will come. In Chapter Five, from Dr. Wilder's wisdom, I have already spoken about how important it is to remember that returning to joy is the key to discipline at this age. Two's do not hear words and instructions when their brains are desynchronized nor do they hear commands that begin with "don't." Use *positive* commands or short "No_____" commands. Continue to give appropriate choices, because he will definitely know what he prefers. Pick your battles. If you have given a "no," you will often get a protest. Don't find yourself trying to negotiate with a two year old or telling him something over and over. Teach that your no means no. If you find yourself in a confrontation, you might have to remove the child from the situation for a moment (a short Time Out with you there) and then began again. Closer to three you might find that your Time Out methods are not working as well.

Check Chapter Seven again. Closer to three is a very critical time in discipline and if you are not diligent you may set the stage for heavy defiance and "bratty" behavior. What you do around three and up to about five will greatly determine how your child is going to behave all the way through elementary age. It is the time to be firm and consistent and when you will do most of your work to train him to obey your voice the first time with a good attitude.

BEGINNING MANNERS

Even at this young age, you can begin to teach manners such as "please" and "thank-you." If it is part of your family values, you can teach, "Yes, Ma'am and No, Sir, etc." You might at least want to work on saying "Yes" instead of "Yep" and "Yeah." You will not even know all the things you say until you hear them coming out of that little mouth.

ART TIME

Introduce art items such as play dough, crayons, paints and glue as a great way to limit TV. At first you will have to sit with the child to do these things. The attention span will be short, but towards the age of three these activities will be greatly enjoyed. Have a box with dress-up clothes and lots of items with which to pretend. Play music and let them dance. Pretending is the child's "work/job" for now. These indoor activities will take the place of TV and benefit the child's development as well.

BEDTIME PROBLEMS IN BIG-KID BEDS

Around the age of two, you might find your toddler out of his crib. You might hear a loud thump and then a cry. He has figured out how to climb out of the crib. Now is the time to make a change. If you are not ready to move your child to a "big girl or big boy bed," you can try a couple of different things first. If your crib has a movable side, let the side down and leave it down. She can climb in and out without falling. If it is a convertible bed, take the side off. If the child is still closer to two, you might have to rig up a rail of sorts to prevent him falling out of the side-less crib. Most youth beds have a rail.

Now that the child can get in and out of bed at will, whether that's because the side is down or a she's in a big kid bed, you will have a new problem. She will first need to learn to stay in the room. There are different ways to approach this training. **(Explain any procedure before doing it the first time.)** Begin by making the room safer. Look around and think about what the child might try to do while alone. Most will just play with toys or books. Then go through your regular routine of bath, books, and prayers, putting the child in her bed, going out, and closing the door. If you already have knob covers on the inside, then the child won't be able to get out. If you don't, lock the door from the outside. The child can get up and play in the room, but not come out. There may be a protest at first, but most of the time the child will play a while and then get back into the bed himself. Be sure to check on him before you go to bed and unlock the door. If you have been building joy and disciplining consistently all along, this transition should not be a big problem. I have also seen this transition fix existing problems.

If the child is older and you feel that locking the door is harsh, you can try sitting in a chair or on the floor close to the door inside the child's room. You will not talk, but sit quietly (hide your eyes) until they go to sleep. If they get up, you first tell them to get back in bed, and then put them back there if necessary. You can move outside the room in a few nights. This may work and it may backfire. Eventually the child needs to go to bed alone and they can be great manipulators at bedtime. They will want drinks, potty breaks, toys, and will cry to get you to give in about bedtime. They will suddenly have aches and pains the likes of which you have never heard. Stay firm and consistent.

Consistency and firmness will help the transition if a problem arises; it will escalate if ignored. If you do not train the child to stay in his own bed, you will definitely find him in yours. Your voice tone and consistency will make it clear that you mean business and she has to stay in her bed.

FACING FEARS

Around the age of three, many children ask for a nightlight or for the door to be left open. It is good to allow the light and /or the door open (unless you have to do the locked door procedure). Fears are likely becoming a more common part of life as the child notices more and more of the world around him. Typical fears need to be nipped in the bud by calm reassurance, by synchronizing and by using the three-way focus we looked at in Chapter Three. A three-way focus is when a more mature person synchronizes with the child's fear while observing or talking about the fearful object or event, calming the fear and working through it while glad to be together. This same procedure should be used for nightmares as well.

When the child faces and comes through a fearful event, and returns to joy, there is no trauma. We synchronize with him, calm him and help him face what happened, or go through it again with us if that is appropriate. Let's look at an example. Your child is frightened of a dog, not bitten, just not sure about this new thing he sees. Because of the three-way focus possible in the Joy Center you help him look at the dog and even touch it. He synchronizes with you and your lack of fear and, from a safe place, he learns about dogs. Or your child might become frightened upon seeing someone in a costume, or from getting splashed in the pool or ocean. Your reactions to these typical childhood fears teach the child what to think about them.

What about if the fear is somehow hurtful? How can we avoid that becoming a trauma? We can find help for that answer back in Chapter Three where we talked about stories and telling the truth about events (the *Eight Below* movie and the Sellmann family tornado). If an event is very scary and/or hurtful, talking about it over time will diminish the possibility of a trauma. The key here about fearful events is synchronization with a greater mind, joint focus with that greater mind in order to process the event, and returning to joy. We are glad to be together here in this event or as we process it later.

I WANT THAT, MOMMY, AND THAT, AND THAT...

As you run errands and your child watches more television, he or she will quickly learn about all the great stuff out there in the stores.

Don't give in to demands and requests for something every time you go out. Train him early that your "no" means "no" and that not having everything we want, when we want it, is part of life. Remember that self-control is a principle aspect of discipline.

POTTY TRAINING

Well, I dreaded getting to this subject as much as you do, if you haven't already. There are some great books out that will speak at length and only about potty training. Some of the methods work and some don't. My philosophy can be summed up in one sentence: "Don't do it until the child is ready." It is time consuming to push and prod the issue and in the end it is usually Mommy who is trained.

Children mature and are ready to co-operate with potty training at all different ages and with very different attitudes. Some are easy and some are not. Some figure it out in one day and others take a year. The less fuss you can make the better for everyone. And never spank or punish for accidents during potty training. If all is normal, he won't go to Kindergarten without being trained.

Here is an example of what I mean by the child "being ready." At some point around the age of two you may have already purchased a potty chair if you want to try that. It is familiar. You have hopefully allowed the child to be in the bathroom with you along the way. You have talked about the topic and he has some words about the subject. He might even be telling you after he goes in the diaper. Be cool. No big deal here. We'll slowly work into it.

So you pick a morning (warm weather works best) that you will be home for a while and you put the big girl or big boy underwear on your little one. You talk all about it. You don't put other pants, shorts or jeans on him or her. You can try the "training in one day" method (see book list) or you can just see what she does. Whenever you get the desired response, give a couple of M and M's or Skittles. If you have to clean up more than three or four messes, she isn't ready. Put the diaper back on and try again in a week or more. The object is for her to tell you or go before the accident.

It is quite common for a child in training to hide to have a bowel movement. Usually they will get that action in the right spot after learning first to urinate in the potty. If the child goes at a certain time, you may be able to "catch" it by sitting him on the potty and reading a book.

For boys it seemed to me to be easier to teach them to stand up from the beginning. Daddy can demonstrate if he will. Be sure that the stool you use is not too high. Some stools that you can purchase are too tall. If you are out at the mall, a store or a restaurant with your little boy, stand him on the top of your feet and he will be able to reach quite well.

I personally think that pull-ups do not help some children potty train. They feel just like a diaper to the child and she is used to "going" in the diaper. There are pull-ups for sale now that give a signal to the child, but I don't know if they work or not. But using pull-ups is easier if they don't hinder the process and for certain you will want to put one on the child if you are going out and they are not yet consistent about telling you! Needing to go potty while in the car will be a very annoying occurrence for a good while. With little ones, we never leave the house without making sure everyone has gone to the bathroom.

It is not a good idea to put a child to bed without a diaper for a nap or at nighttime for several weeks or even months after you have begun the training. Some children stay dry in bed first, but most take longer to get to that point. Don't ever use shame or punishment for accidents.

You can probably see why this was not an easy topic to address. There are no rules or guarantees for easy success. For me, the most important thing is to stay calm and helpful, realizing it may take some time, believing it will happen.

ANOTHER BABY ARRIVES

Somewhere around this age range of two to three another baby may arrive in your home. It may be sooner or it may be later. The first bundle of joy is about to feel some new feelings. He or she has had all the attention from two doting parents. Now he will have to share Mommy and Daddy. It is good to talk about getting a new brother or sister before the event arrives. Little ones like to pretend with a doll or stuffed animal. Close to the time, talk about the fact that Mommy will be gone and who will keep the child left at home. Talk about how they might wake up and someone else will be there. Of course it should be someone they are bonded with. Be sure to tell the child that the baby won't be able to play with him or her for a while.

Depending on your child and your circumstances, it is good to bring the older sibling to the hospital to see you and the baby unless you feel that will be more upsetting for her to have to leave you there. Have the person who is bringing her talk about it first.

When you return home, allow the older one to do as much as possible with you as you care for the new baby. Let him stand on a chair by you as you bathe the new baby. The more you include her, the easier it will be for her to adjust. You want to set a good stage for preventing sibling rivalry. Avoid ignoring or reprimanding the older sibling too much when caring for the new baby. Read to him while you nurse the new one. Let him help if you are using a bottle. If the older child wants to hold the baby, let him do so while you sit right there. Usually at the toddler stage they don't want to hold the baby for more than a few seconds. Watch out that they don't squeeze too hard or say, "I'm finished," and push the baby away.

If after all these major changes in your little one's life, he or she seems to revert to a younger age, don't worry. She might want to wear a diaper again or drink from a bottle. He might talk baby talk and want you to hold him like a baby. These behaviors are normal and will pass as you synchronize with the new feelings she is having and continue to assure her that she is loved and appreciated. Don't make a big deal about it or call your older child names. Having a new baby, regardless of the age of the older sibs, is a time for transitioning slowly. Give lots of grace for a few days.

THREE TO FIVE

SHARING

Sharing is one of the first life-giving things a little one does. They share joy smiles with us as we smile at each other, they share their cookies and they want us to play and pretend with them. Most likely you have been working on sharing since your baby could interact at all with others either at home, church, or at play dates. As he matures and recognizes that possessions belong to different people, sharing does not come as naturally as it did when he was tiny. I love the seagulls in the movie "Nemo." They hilariously sum up a young child's philosophy: "Mine; mine, mine; mine."

Slowly but surely, if you train your child, sharing will become more a part of his life. As children grow and mature, the objects for sharing increase in complexity. By three to five, sharing computer time and TV shows can be an issue when there is more than one child in your family. A great method to promote sharing without having arguments and fights is to use a timer. You can use a small kitchen timer or the timer on the microwave. Set the timer for the number of minutes appropriate to the activity to be shared. Tell the children, "When the bell rings, it is _____'s turn." This takes the refereeing from your shoulders and makes it impersonal. Generally children do not complain with this method.

Now and then there is a time for not sharing. When one child receives something new and the siblings did not receive anything (birthday presents, get-well gifts, and treasures from school) I feel it is good to allow the child a short time of not sharing, if they do not want to share. Usually after the newness wears off, they are not as possessive when siblings want a turn. It is good for the other child to learn that each one of us can have a time for our own things. It is also important to teach siblings to take care of others' possessions. This is a good time to instill those qualities.

PREVENTING RIVALRY

Right along with sharing issues we find the problem of sibling rivalry. The best way to prevent or eliminate rivalry is by not negatively comparing your child to anyone else, especially a sibling. You will not have rivalry if each child is loved, accepted and impressed with how much you value him or her for being who they are. Do your best to make no room for comparing your child to anyone in a way that would communicate being of lesser value. Being certain that each child contributes to the family and being certain that no one feels left out also prevent rivalry.

Avery (top) and Arden

Children benefit as well from having "extra" moms and dads who delight in them and make them feel special. This helps prevent rivalry. Discouraging grandparents or other relatives from showing partiality or preferences also helps. If you find someone showing partiality to one of your children, you will need to speak to that person. It can be very damaging to both that child and to the child that gets ignored.

If you have more than one child, do your best to make time for Mommy or Daddy to spend special time alone with each child, no less than once a week whenever possible. Our culture is so busy that we often find it difficult to spend daily time alone or give focused attention to each child, even when we know that it works wonders for all children. So we catch a moment here and there as best we can. But special time alone works best outside the home. If you have more than two children, you might have to make a schedule to put on the

246

refrigerator in order to keep track of taking turns to go on errands. Make a chart with each name and a place after the names to note or check off when that child had a "special day" and where they went. Even if the child only gets one time every few weeks outside the home, this will benefit everyone. When you have a child alone in the car with you they have your undivided attention and will usually talk your ear off. At this age, they don't really care where they go with you as long as they have you to themselves. In the section on older children we will look at some options other than errands.

TELLING STORIES

As we spend time with our children, we want them to learn about their heritage, what it is like us and our people to do in life's various situations. We teach this through stories of us, stories of our family and stories of God's family. Children love to hear stories about their parents when the parents were children. They love to hear stories about themselves when they were younger. We can use photo albums to tell stories about the past. We can tell stories while traveling in the car or before bedtime. We can watch old family videos together. Telling stories has always been a way to pass down heritage.

Become a story telling family in order for your child to know you and your people better. By five to six, children can begin to understand how the family tree works. They like to hear about this. As we read Bible stories, they learn about God's family, of which we as believers are a part. The Bible stories teach what it is like us to do when trials come, when joy blooms, when sadness pervades. We want to model and instill in the child that we turn to God for everything, that He is always good, that He is always faithful. These internal and sometimes subtle lessons will be part of the adult your child will be in the future. Internalizing values through stories will help our children be able to stay relational and act like themselves when hard times come in life.

WHAT'S REALITY?

Around the age of five, children begin to distinguish what is real and what is pretend. They are better able to understand their emotions. Until this age, children believe that whatever they are feeling is what is true. Words will not always change that belief. The child needs someone he trusts to truthfully explain things that are going on, to help him know what is real or imagined. As the child grows, he goes through a process of imagining and then testing that against reality, with many failures and comparisons. A good trustworthy parent tells the child the meaning of the successes, failures and comparisons. This helps the child distinguish what is real and what is pretend. (p. 62 LWM)

HARD THINGS

Towards the end of the range from three to five, we want to ascertain that our child is moving out of the Infant Stage and ready for the Child Stage of maturity. A huge factor for this move up the maturity ladder is learning to do hard things. At the age of five, children develop the capacity to do things they don't feel like doing. Up to this point, children think everyone only does what he feels like doing. Now they are able to choose to do something hard that they do not feel like doing. For the next seven years, we will practice doing hard things. (p. 59 LWM) Although we have been helping the child do some age appropriate "hard things" all along, now we can stretch them a little more.

We can help children practice doing what they do not feel like doing by helping them feel good about the task—to anticipate the hard thing because we associate it with something pleasant—such as, "I will read you a story when you get in bed."(p. 60) Other times we will help them by making the hard thing more appealing than another situation—such as dessert after eating (p. 60 LWM)

As we encourage this move for the child to stop going by how she feels, we must be careful that we gear the hard things to the appropriate age and not make things too hard too soon. If we push too hard too soon, the child will become discouraged and maybe even quit trying. Dr. Wilder says that much of the practice for doing hard things comes towards the end of the Child Stage around the Middle School years. (p. 60 LWM) Keep your child's age and individual development in mind, while at the same time encouraging her to stretch her abilities and tasks all along the way.

WHAT SATISFIES?

Learning I can do hard things brings great satisfaction. It feels good to accomplish a difficult task. Teaching what satisfies and what is life giving is vital during this time. (Remember that you as the parent must know these things for yourself.) At this age level, children can learn how life giving it is to help around the house as they do chores.

He can hear praise for the good jobs he does. He will learn to receive and give kindness. She will give thanks to others around her and learn to share. As she waits on you for a moment when you are busy and receives some "no's" at the store, she will learn that she will not surely die if she does not receive instant gratification. If you model that it is not necessary to have every whim of fashion and be the center of attention, she will learn that fads and popularity are not the means of satisfaction. Receiving and giving life to others is what satisfies.

SWIMMING LESSONS

Giving your child swimming lessons during the preschool years is not a waste of time or money, especially if you live in an area where there are bodies of water such as canals, lakes, ponds, and pools. Children can learn to swim earlier than three, but they can learn easily and well by the age of three. I say this because I teach children this age to swim and what to do if they fall into a body of water. It is safer to know what to do in the water and to either face the fear of getting their faces wet, or never develop that fear in the first place, than it is to have a fatal accident. Knowing how to swim is a life and death skill.

Kayli and Kori can swim at two and half

LET'S TALK ABOUT MONEY

Your child's first lessons about money begin with how you model this part of life in front of him or her. Remember, "More is caught than taught." Around the age of five, you can begin to teach a little about money and how it works. We want to teach the children 10-10-80--to give ten percent, save ten percent and spend eighty percent. You can get three jars and label them with the words "give," "save," and "spend." When the children get money for a birthday or if you begin an allowance, they can learn to divide the money among the three jars.

As you are training about the value of money and how to spend it, you can take the child to a dollar store and tell them they can pick out (three) things. It will be a challenge for them to narrow their choices down to your number. If you are at a regular store, you can give them an amount and help them narrow it down as you say, "Well, that's too much, but this is within the amount."

When it is age appropriate, you can have them take their "giving" to church or put some into the Salvation Army kettles around town at Christmas. They can use it to buy something to go in one of the Christmas charity shoebox events. At first the child may not understand that the gifts you are buying for the needy child are for someone else, but you can work that out by letting them buy a little something for themselves at the same time. It takes a little explaining at this young age about charitable giving, but that is part of the training. We let them help fill the shoeboxes as we talk about children that do not have anything to play with and sometimes not even enough food. When the war in Iraq began, I took my four granddaughters with me to buy supplies for the soldiers. They were quite young, but that experience became one of the stories that we tell now and then.

PRAYER AND MONSTERS

As part of the bedtime routine, we are already praying with the children and helping them learn how to pray aloud. Occasionally, parents will need to pray *over* a child that is distressed or exhibiting behavioral problems. I mentioned this type of prayer in the section on infants if the newborn was delivered by C-section and/or was in the NICU. If a child is behaving in an unusual manner, we need to ask ourselves a few questions? The first question to ask would be, "Is the Joy Bucket full?" Many times if we recognize that it is not full, filling the Joy Bucket with some joy-making focused attention will solve the

© 2007 Barbara Moon

problem. We also might ask ourselves, "Has anything happened that could be considered a traumatic event?" In that case, we would need to spend some time with the child and find out his or her feelings and give comfort and get healing. Be sure to emphasize that Jesus is always with us even though we cannot see Him.

If there is yet a problem that these two questions did not solve, then we might ask ourselves, "Could there be something spiritually negative going on here?" If we as parents check our own life and we are not allowing the enemy any place to come into our home, then we can pray over the child and command anything that is bothering the child, or our family, to leave in the name of Jesus Christ. We do this in the child's room while the child is asleep. As the parent of a young child, you have the Spiritual authority over the child. (When the child is older, he or she will have to be engaged in the prayer by his or her choice. In that case, we pray *for* the child if they are in some type of rebellion and do not want to co-operate.) If you are uneasy with this type of prayer, then ask a friend or minister you know to help you.

As you can see, I believe that the enemy of our souls is real and can harass us. I feel that it never hurts to take this into account and ask the Lord Jesus to intervene. Greg and Chris have taught their four girls that the enemy is real. So when the girls began to talk about "monsters in my room," Greg and Chris taught them to command the monsters to leave. Our culture accepts that it's part of childhood to have monsters in the room, even to the point of making a movie about it. What if it were true that the enemy wants to influence, scare and attack children at this young age? It would be just like him. What if it were true that children could learn early that Jesus is bigger than the monsters and they don't have to be afraid of them? That is the truth I want children to know. Though it may seem scary to you, it is something to think about and consider.

Prayer Warrior Dads, Jim and Greg

PATIENCE, PATIENCE, PATIENCE

These preschool years, all of them, will try your patience. As my daughter, Jodi and her friend, Melanie, both mothers of two year olds, agreed with each other last week, "Raising a child is hard. It's a lot harder than going to an office every day." This is a true statement in many ways. Any moment with little ones can bring about upset and difficulty. Parents play many roles simultaneously and often have to make instant executive decisions. A day flows from joyful delight to creative discipline moment by moment. These years are vital to the child's personality, almost formed by the age of three, as to what he thinks about himself, about God, about values and about the world. And it will be very difficult in the following years to undo these imbedded beliefs if they are not the beliefs we hoped for. What a responsibility, but wonderful privilege it is to have a part in molding a person. Don't try to do it alone, without God and the Scriptures. Remind yourself often that *you* are this child's window to the world and that you are the model he is watching. Tap into Jesus who is your patience and cling to Him when you want to run out the door. And be sure to get some time for yourself and keep your own Joy Bucket full.

A TIME SAVER

Until at least kindergarten and maybe even first grade, buy shoes with Velcro. You will not believe how many times a child takes his shoes off and on in a given day. It will save you lots of time and frustration. Be sure they can really tie their own shoes before getting laces.

THE ELEMENTARY YEARS

Your little bundle of joy is skipping to the huge yellow school bus and you are holding back the tears. These days, that journey begins younger and younger. Maybe you opted to take your child to a private Pre-K and Kindergarten and now she is going to "big school" on the big bus. Don't they look so tiny climbing up those steps? Maybe you are opting for private school altogether or you are going to drive that precious one to public school and she won't have to ride the bus. Whatever your decision, unless you opt to home school, the time you have with your child is going to change drastically. No longer will you have hours and hours to pour into him. Someone else will be influencing him up to seven hours a day.

The elementary years are quite different from the preschool/toddler years. Independence and individuation increase with the passing years and discipline becomes more complex. The "control" you have over aspects of your child's life may decrease as her world broadens. You may no longer be the "authority" on all subjects that you once were, as your child branches outward to teachers, coaches and instructors. This is a very busy time as everyone pursues more and more activities outside the home. You may very well feel like, and fit the profile of, a soccer mom or a ball dad. You may have to fight for family time together, rushing home to get supper, rushing out to various sports practices, lessons or events, and rushing to get everyone bathed and in bed. Multiply that exponentially if you have more than two kids.

During all this rushing around to do life, one of the most important events of the day may quickly fall by the wayside—dinner as a family. It seems that this practice is almost extinct. Many parents both work outside the home, and mothers seldom cook anymore. I would highly encourage you to fit this old-time practice into your schedule whenever possible. It is invaluable to building and keeping relationships with your children and each other. The dinner hour should not be a time for conflict and reprimanding, but rather a time for finding out what each family member enjoyed most about his or her day. My son, Jim and his wife Elizabeth, (their family is in blue on the back cover) ask their kids at the dinner table, "What was your favorite part of the day?" This question prompts conversation and keeps the dinner discussion positive and joy building.

The elementary years will be vital to the training time that you have left before the teen years. Since the children are more able to take care of themselves, you may think you can finally have more time for yourself. You may be tempted to slack off on relationship building, joy and quiet, and synchronization. That is the worst path you can take. It is almost impossible to fill in the relationship building time lost between third or fourth grade and high school, because the teen is supposed to individuate even more as she increases independence from you. Your long-range goal is to see the child develop healthy independence from earthly parents at the same time he or she is developing strong dependence on the Heavenly Father. This will not happen if you skip these elementary years just because you all are extra busy and the children can do more for themselves.

Being extra busy makes it a certainty that we can all use some helpful tips, so let's look at some ideas that will help the busyness and chaos that often accompany the elementary years. Then we will take a look at the middle school and teen-age years.

TIPS FOR AGES 5 TO 10

USING THE IMMANUEL PROCESS FOR HEALING[2]

---

[2] For more information on this prayer process, see www.kclehman.com and www.lifemodel.org Books: *Outsmarting Yourself,* by Dr. Karl Lehman,

Your child is going to encounter painful events. By this age, she may already have. I encourage you to order the booklet footnoted below and take some time to study it. Children can learn to take their pain to Jesus and have Him help and heal those wounds. In Chapter Three we talked about how to avoid traumas, especially in the early years by using the three-way focus to process through a fearful event. That works, but as the child grows older, he or she can learn to go to Jesus personally. It will be important for you as the parent to know how to do this or to know someone who can help you or the child. I will give the basic components here and if it interests you, you can order the booklet and other material that will give more details.

When you know that someone has encountered a painful moment or has an unresolved trauma, first ask if they are willing to ask Jesus about it. If so, make sure the relational circuits are on by doing one of the "Shalom My Body" exercises from Chapter Six under Calming the Brain. Then ask them to look for a memory when they knew Jesus was with them (or an appreciation memory). Upon connecting with Jesus in a spirit of prayer, age appropriately, talk to Jesus about the painful event. You can ask Him to show the child where He was when it happened. He will show them. You can ask Him, "What do you want (name) to know about this?" Sit quietly and help the child, but do not give them suggestions. If it is appropriate, you can ask Jesus to show the child, "What did (name) believe about himself/herself when this happened?" After Jesus shows them this, you can ask Him, "Please show (name) what You think about that, Jesus."[3] This will uncover any

---

Share Immanuel booklet, by Dr. James Wilder and Chris Coursey.

lies believed and replace them with God's truth. When you feel the person has found peace about the painful memory, thank Jesus and close the prayer. Process a little with them after they open their eyes. We want to develop an Immanuel Lifestyle that will keep both us and our children healed and free.

(See Appendix A for both the calming exercises and healing prayer together.)

PAY THEN PLAY

As your child begins the school years, homework can become an issue. Much of the training you will be instilling at this time will under gird your child into adulthood and doing hard things is a vital part of that training. Kevin Meyers, Senior Pastor of Crossroads Community Church in Lawrenceville, Georgia, coined a great phrase to help us remember the importance of this training: "Pay then Play." This idea applies to homework, music practice, sports, cleaning up, and life in general. As your child begins to come home with homework (or you are teacher and they are doing it all at home), make a family "rule" that the children arrive home, have a snack and maybe a short few minutes of down time and then they do homework. No TV, computer or other playing until homework is done. You are forming a habit that will carry over into high school, college and then life. Another good way to

---

[3] This question and the next come from the material of Dr. Ed Smith who trains counselors in Theophostic Prayer Ministry, Campbellsville, KY: New Creation Publishing.

help the children with "pay then play" is to say something like, "*After* you _____, *then* we/you can _____."

ENCOURAGE ACTIVITY

Limit TV and computer games in general. Encourage reading, reading, and reading. Encourage art, music, and outdoors play. Give lots of opportunities for creative activities that don't necessarily cost money. If you can afford to, encourage active sports and summertime swimming. Do family activities that are physically motivating.

Four girls in a tree

Erica flies on the Big Wheel

TIMING TASKS

Watch your child's development as she grows and take care to find a balance between expecting too little and expecting too much too soon. Finding this balance is part of synchronizing--knowing each individual child and his needs and abilities. Giving tasks too early can be discouraging.

Children are not to parent the parents nor are they to parent their siblings. If you expect your older child to do too much with the youngest, you might put too much pressure on the older one. If a child does not have time to play and do some things on his own, this will cause pressure he is not built to handle. Children should not have to work to support the family. Children should do chores, but not be treated as Cinderella was. Of course older children do many things to help with and entertain the younger ones, but they should not be responsible for the younger siblings or take the caretaker's place. Children are to help, but they are not equipped to run the show and carry the responsibility.

Cheers for Elysia – Time to be a kid

MONEY

Continue lessons about money, increasing the complexity of what the child understands about each of the three categories, using the three jars labeled give, save, spend. Elementary age children can understand tithing, giving ten percent to God, if that is part of your beliefs. I remember in my own life setting aside a dime for every dollar I received. When I grew up, got a real job and got married, it was part of life to continue tithing. I also learned how to save for that special item that I wanted to buy.

As your children begin to understand the value of money and what can be done with it, watch out for "stealing" around the house. At first it may only be part of learning whose stuff is whose and how not to bother others' possessions, but it can grow into a problem if not dealt with. One day, Chris discovered that one of the twins (five years old at the time) had taken several items from one of her sisters and put them in her own toy box. While Kori was at school, Chris stripped her room of everything that belonged to her and hid it—even the bed covers. After school when everyone was in the living area, Chris declared aloud--to the air--that someone had taken things that did not belong to them and they might have to go to jail. The little culprit quickly and loudly confessed with much repentance and was just as quickly assured by Mommy that she would not have to go to jail. Everyone got the point and in a day or two the possessions were returned to the penitent twin. After that, there was no more trouble in the family with taking others' possessions.

While you are broadening the lessons about money, create extra ways for the children to earn money that are not associated with allowance. Kayli wanted to buy a certain book at her school's book fair and she earned the ten dollars by helping out around the house. Of course, I was delighted to pay well for a few small tasks in order to encourage Kayli to earn money for extras.

Extra chores earn extra cash. I feel that allowances shouldn't be associated with basic chores, but there are differing opinions on this. It seems to me that allowances should be given freely and chores should be done with a good attitude and not for pay. I also feel that children should not be paid for good grades but that good grades should come from an intrinsic desire to do their best, although these are not issues I feel strongly enough to argue about

As your children grow up, you can be certain that they will ask for and want many things that you cannot (or do not want to) afford. This will increase even more in the teen years. We will need to teach them various ways to handle this wanting. They can learn to save and wait. They can learn that they don't have to have everything they see. And we can teach them early on that they can pray for things that the family cannot afford. Part of that training will be to learn that God is not "Santa Claus" and does not just give us everything we think about. At the same time, they can learn that He loves us and pours out blessings upon us, even more than we can imagine.

When Greg was in the eighth grade, Izod shirts were the desired commodities in his circle. We told him that we could not buy such expensive items, but he could ask God for one. That Christmas, he received four Izod shirts that we did not furnish. As he grew older and began to spend his own money on items, he quickly learned that designer clothes were not any better than ordinary brands. He could buy more for his money if he did not have to keep up with the other students.

LONG TRIPS

Many of today's parents probably don't have the problems with car or airplane trips that those of us did in days gone by. New cars come equipped with DVD or Video players. I call these devices "baby crack." In reality any TV or movie equipment could be named so, but for sure on a trip when that portable or attached DVD player comes out, even the babies turn into little zombies. We have to remind them to blink. So use sparingly.

If you would like to relate during a trip, here are a few suggestions: Before the trip, go to a dollar store and pick up several inexpensive items that you can give out during the trip. Crayons, books, sticker books, small toys, white paper, and even play dough work well. You can buy small lap trays that fit right over the child's lap in a car seat. Keep the items in a surprise bag and get them out over the trip as attention span decreases. Use the movies only for a short time. Play children's songs on the CD player and tell family and made-up stories. You will find that you will have to take more breaks than if you were only traveling with adults. Dads, you can practice patience with this.

Years ago I found a great suggestion for trips in a book by John Rosemond, author of *Six Points for Raising Happy and Healthy Children.* He suggests giving each child three to five tickets (depending on the length of the trip) at the beginning of the trip. (I have also done this with dimes or quarters, depending on the ages of the children.) Clearly state the rules for which the child will lose a ticket. If a child misbehaves, he immediately loses a ticket. Bickering brings a loss to all involved, no matter who started it. At the end of the trip is an activity that the children love to do and will be highly motivated to keep the privilege of doing. If they have no ticket left, they cannot do that activity that day, or some form of it, depending on when the arrival takes place. This puts the responsibility upon the children to behave. The consequence is quick and obvious and they can quickly calculate how many tickets they have left. Rosemond says that when they instigated this design, they had the quietest trip they had ever taken. (pp. 92, 93)

PICK YOUR BATTLES

Along with helping the children take responsibility for their behavior, we parents want to be careful to pick our battles according to their importance. What is important will vary with each family, but some issues are common. How the child wears his or her hair can be a battle to avoid. Some clothing issues can be avoided as to wearer's style. How the child dresses for church may be negotiable, among choices, according to your family's ideas. What they have to eat, or the amount, might be negotiable. Keep in mind that you want to save the big battles for the big issues. There will be fewer battles if you try to avoid giving too many nit picking little orders and rules. Allow your children as much leeway as possible to express their own sense of style and preference. This is part of accepting them as who they are and not giving in to perfectionism. You might have to say no, but don't reject the child for his desire.

Bob and Amy (family in black on the back cover) had an occasion to practice this principle when my grandson, Josh, was about nine years old. Josh asked his parents if he could get his ear pierced. Bob and Amy did not laugh at Josh or deride him for his legitimate desire and request. But neither did they allow him to do it. They explained that he needed to be older. Josh accepted the "no" and did not dig in and argue because Dad and Mom did not reject Josh or laugh at his idea. Later when Josh wanted to grow his hair long, Bob and Amy agreed to that.

Free to be Josh

If modesty is a value in your family, then begin to model and teach it early in order to lessen battles later. If you don't want your young teenage girl to wear a bikini, don't put a bikini on her when she is two. When she leaves home, she may decide to wear one, but you can be part of that decision up until that time. Most children naturally become modest around four or five and we can just work with that as well as

266

modeling modesty. In the teen years, modes of dress may become a bigger issue, but it can be easier to deal with if modesty has been taught in the early years.

PARENTS STAY UNITED

Just as it was in the earlier years, it is vital that parents do not undermine each other in front of the children. As they grow older, more and more children see and understand subtleties and innuendos around them. Work out your differences privately if you want your children to feel secure. Support each other, back up what the other is saying and come to compromises where you differ—out of ear range of the children. Children want to know that their environment is safe and secure. Even if your family has had a marital split, the children will benefit from seeing their parents "united" about their welfare and circumstances.

ALLOW LOGICAL CONSEQUENCES

Don't pad the pavement all along the way and prevent your child from learning from mistakes and paying the consequences. When my son, Bob, was in the second grade, he forgot his lunch off and on over a few weeks. At the beginning, I took the lunch bag down to the school and delivered it to his room. On occasion the teacher loaned him lunch money. One day I sent a note to the teacher and told her not to give him any more lunch money the next time he forgot his lunch. I also asked her not to give him anything to eat. You guessed it. He forgot his lunch again and came home that day having had nothing to eat all

267

day. It was hard to watch and I know it was hard for the teacher as well, but Bob never forgot his lunch again.

SEX EDUCATION, DATING AND DRUGS

Around the age of eight or nine, parents need to have that difficult talk with their girls. It is good if both parents are there. You may find that your child already knows more than you wanted her to know when you have the talk. Other children have told her all about the subject. Because we live in a sex-saturated society, children see, hear and know too much too soon.

Puberty is beginning much younger these days and girls need to know what to expect before it happens. They do not need to know everything at this time, but if you want to be the one to tell them, do it earlier rather than later. Boys generally can wait until closer to 11 or 12. They too will have plenty of "locker room talk" so you may also have to tell them sooner.

Begin early talking about dating, drugs, smoking and other topics that you hope you won't have to deal with for a long time. In other words, give the game plan before the hormones kick in. Your family can decide what age is appropriate for various types of dating and give that information out casually before it is needed. Some families want boys to ask the father if he can date the daughter.

At this age, before they will actually play the game, it is a great time for Daddy-Daughter dates and Mother-Son dates. You will model for your child how a girl should be treated and how a guy should behave.

If you have not already done so, this is a good age to begin praying for your children's future spouses. Talk to God about what kind of person you want them to have, as you continue to help mold your child into the kind of person that one deserves. Pray for that future son or daughter-in-law as if you know them.

MISCELLANEOUS TIPS FOR LARGE FAMILIES

If you have a **large family** and your house has bedrooms upstairs, get a laundry basket and put it by the entrance door where children can put their shoes when they take them off. You will not believe how many shoes can be all over the place until you have four kids with two or three different pairs of shoes each. It is very frustrating and time consuming to make them take shoes up and down the stairs many times a day.

Put a small basket on the steps with each child's name on it. As they bring home school art, change from their pj's, or bring toys down, you can put their things into the basket and have the children put everything away upstairs every few days.

If your house has limited storage space and each child has bunches of stuff, purchase the long flat plastic boxes that are made to hold wrapping paper. Keep the box under the child's bed. That way they can keep their things that they don't want in a community toy box separated from the siblings' things.

When you buy new (or used or hand me downs from a friend) clothes, use a permanent marker to put each child's initial on a tag inside his or her clothes. Or you can put a dot on the tag according to the child's place in the family. (One dot for the oldest, two for the next, three, etc. When you pass them down, add a dot). This really speeds up doing laundry, folding and sorting, especially if an "outsider" might be helping you. Have a central place to put dirty laundry. Some children change clothes more than once a day. It is helpful to teach them very young to pick up after themselves and put the laundry in a certain place.

When sorting seasonal clothing, store part of the off-season clothes in a white garbage bag that you label as to size and season, keeping only what you decide to pass down or may wear the next year. Put what you are not keeping in a separate bag to give away. You will see what to do with the other part of the off-season clothing in the following suggestion.

If you follow this suggestion or some form of it, in most areas you only have to change the seasons twice. Let's assume that each child has a dresser with five drawers. In the top drawer you keep underwear and socks. In the second drawer you keep pajamas (all of the current season's with two or three from the off-season). In the third drawer you keep shirts of the current season. In the fourth drawer you keep pants/shorts of the current season. In the fifth drawer, you keep *some of both* the shirts and pants/shorts of the off-season. This way you will have access to the season that is changing either way—hot or cold-- because you have access to both extremes. As summer ends, in some regions we have warm and cold days. As spring comes, we have cold and warm. With this set up you do not have to go hunting through the attic or storage for the new season's clothes as the weather begins to change but has not yet turned completely. You have a few for the coming season in the bottom drawer and will only have to do the big exchanges twice a year once the season has truly changed. Usually closets will hold both seasons of hang-up clothes and you can sort and give away or pass down these at the two times you exchange.

LOOK AT THEIR WORLD THROUGH THEIR EYES

Looking at the world through your child's eyes is a vital practice with all ages and like timing tasks, it is part of synchronizing. When we consider the other person's point of view, it is very comforting and it precipitates understanding. Wanting to be understood (even if disagreed with) is extremely important to almost everyone. Listening, seeing through another's eyes and trying to understand how they are feeling can vastly diminish conflict. This does not mean that we have to agree with the other or even take away consequences. But it does pave the way to easier resolutions when we synchronize before lecturing. Remember: words don't help when a person is melted down. Synchronize and return to joy, be glad to be together to work out whatever is going on. Watch your child's face and body language. What does he or she see and hear in a situation? How is it affecting him? Is it bigger to her than it would be to you as an adult? How is your child reacting to what you are saying in a discussion? Carefully observe what is going on in their world, from their perspective, and how is it affecting them, so that you can work together to solve the problem, get comfort, or accept something that can't change.

FAMILY RULES

Remember during these elementary years to continue to work on the family rules we talked about in Chapter One—obey, be kind, respect others. Keep the rules simple with consistent consequences. Continue to work on manners, whining, and facing fears. Most likely your child will go off to school for most of the day. What you have done up to this time will be tried and proven as he or she spends much of the day away from you.

During the elementary years, your child will begin to bump into situations that tempt them away from your rules. They may not even desire to go against them, but sometimes to "stand alone" can be difficult. Tell your kids that they can "blame Mommy and Daddy" for the things they cannot do or are not part of your family values. Then you parents can be the "bad guys" and the kids can save face. This can carry over into the teens.

SUMMARY

We have covered a lot of years so far in this chapter, with tips for most. The infant grows so quickly into a toddler and then time flies to the pre school years. The child changes every day. The elementary years are busy and chaotic. They are full of activities, more changes and tons of variety. Children of all ages love fun, fun, and more fun. Loosen up and be silly with them. They will be out of the nest before you know it. Tell lots of stories about your family, both before and since they were born. Give them a sense of their heritage, of what it is like you and your people to do in different situations. Fill in the history of your families, being honest and open as best you can. Keep a balance with sports and music so that the family won't suffer from lack of together time. Give lots of grace when failures happen, peppered with love and empathy—even tell another story of how <u>you</u> failed in a much similar way. Use focused attention to build constant joy so that everyone will have the capacity to endure trials, suffering well in difficult times that come along. Include the children in as much as they can understand and tell the truth about the hard things that happen through life. Teach them early to love God and talk to Him so that when they are old they will not depart from Him. Stay on your knees because middle school is on the horizon and you will need that lifeline to God even more than before.

THE MIDDLE YEARS TO TEENS

The dreaded age is upon you. You remember your own middle school years and you've heard all the horror stories from older parents. Who could possibly choose willingly to teach a roomful of seventh or eighth graders? Who in their right mind would want to be a middle school pastor? Can't we just send them off to Grandma when they get to this age?

Jake in Middle School

We do joke about these middle years and it does seem to me to be true that people who work in any way with this age group are some of the most called and blessed in the community. My own son, Jim, was a middle school pastor for eleven years. At that time, he knew of few others specializing in this age group at church. Even today, there are few middle school groups. It is my opinion that one reason Jim was called and drawn to this age group is because he had a significant life-changing encounter with Jesus Christ when he was eleven. He had become a believer when he was seven, but one night, at the age of eleven he sat in our living room in Huntsville, Alabama, and listened to a newly appointed staff member of Campus Crusade for Christ teaching about following Jesus with all your heart. As Jim listened, the Lord Jesus became real to him in a way that set him on the path to be a true disciple. We saw changes that were unexplainable outside of an encounter with the Living God. Somewhere deep inside, Jim must have nurtured the belief that a child so young could truly follow Jesus, until after college, the One he was following designed circumstances that led him to become the catalyst for hundreds of other young middle schoolers to take that same path. The middle years can be difficult, but with God all things are possible and the horror stories and rumors you have heard do not have to be part of your home.

TIPS FOR TWEENS

NO HYPOCRISY

As your child grows older, they also are growing wiser—especially in recognizing when you are being hypocritical. Having tweens is more than ever a time for honesty and humility on parents' part. Remember our emphasis from the very beginning of our study here that, "More is caught than taught." There is no place for little white lies or shrugging off responsibility. They <u>will</u> notice and proceed to fault you for most any kind of dishonesty, even if they only fault you in their minds. Hypocrisy will affect your child on a deep level, even though you may never hear a word about it while they are young. Parents have to be on their knees to walk what they talk and continue modeling the outcomes they want to see in their children's lives.

Josh and Aaron -- Tweens at the beach

PICK YOUR BATTLES

Just as it was important in the elementary (and even the toddler) years, it is helpful to the pick battles you want to have with middle schoolers. Wait for the big issues before coming down strict and hard. We don't have to wage war over fads and hairdos. Remember Josh wanting an earring? Mom and Dad said no to those at the age of nine, but now Josh and Aaron both have long hair and are able to choose more of their personal styles and preferences.

Like fads and hairdos, neither do we have to make mountains out of children's messy rooms. Work out a plan that will keep the battles to a minimum. Let them keep the door shut if you can't stand to look at it. If they don't pick up dirty clothes, what would be the logical consequence?

Avoid battles over homework assignments. At this age begin putting more of the responsibility on the child. Leave room for the kids to learn from their own mistakes and pay the consequences of not turning in homework or practicing their instruments, or putting their clothes and towels in the laundry. As John Rosemond says, "When he leaves his shoelaces loose all the time, let his face meet the sidewalk instead of nagging him to tie them--" a catchy way of saying, "Let them learn the hard way." (p. 96 *Six Point Plan*)

Don't bail children out of every problem that comes along. That's why we have so many adults that do not take responsibility for their actions. Be careful not to blame others, or allow the child to, for problems that arise, because that teaches children that they are victims. Be on your child's side, but check out stories about "that teacher doesn't like me," or "she picks on me," or "the dog ate my homework."

SIBLING RIVALRY

Let's look again at preventing sibling rivalry now that your children are older. In the other section on sibling rivalry, I recommended not comparing children in any negative ways. I would give the same advice again. Intellectual, athletic, and musical abilities are some of the areas in which parents can easily slip into comparing, especially if siblings are the same gender. All of us must also be careful not to enjoy one child's personality over another's and thus not spread our attention evenly. Allow all the children to choose whenever possible what activities they want to attend or excel in. Encourage individuality when possible, and find interests and characteristics to brag and talk about with each one.

If by chance you have a child gifted in an area and that brings lots of attention his or her way, this can be a time to teach the others in the family to appreciate and be glad for others' accomplishments and abilities. This is an unselfish characteristic and might take a while to grow in a young person, but it is a great characteristic to have—the opposite of jealousy, which can damage any relationship in life. Again, when each person knows he is loved, valued and appreciated for who he is, sibling rivalry will not be a huge problem.

CHARACTER

Keep an eye out for character qualities you can still work on. Much of the child's character is formed very young, but if you can do it *without nagging,* continue working on whatever you can. These middle years, and the teen years, are the time for backing off a bit. What used to be guidance can become nagging. There is a fine line between helping your child and rejecting him or her by constantly picking at every mistake or thing you disagree with. This fine line is another place that keeps us on our knees as we try to distinguish what to accept unconditionally and what to speak to in love.

PARENT DATES

Getting time alone with each parent increases in importance in these middle and teen years. The young people will benefit even more from the parent "dates," because time spent together will discourage sibling rivalry and encourage feelings of love and acceptance. It will also benefit the young person greatly if the mentoring time for Bible study and life skills increases and becomes consistent. I will elaborate on mentoring in the last chapter.

Erica and Daddy (Jim)

RESPECT MATURITY CHANGES

Remember the admonition in Chapter Six about not being sarcastic and verbally hurtful? As your child grows into a tween and then a teen, please respect the changes in their maturity, both emotionally and physically. This is not a time for hurtful teasing or name-calling. This is a time to stop using baby names or baby talk if the child is bothered by it. This is a time for supporting your child's preferences and interests, even if they do not fit the dreams you had for your child. Remember that during this block of time, everything is changing both outside and inside the child. Support, love and encouragement go a lot further in promoting a good relationship than do teasing, putdowns and rejection. You will avoid many of the stereotypical negatives associated with mother/daughter and father/son problems when you respect your changing child and move more and more towards accepting them unconditionally.

SUMMARY

Your middle school child is on a threshold of huge changes, with ups and downs from roller coaster hormones, to trials and errors towards independence. An "identity change" is upon him. During the middle school years, he will reach the end of the Child Stage and begin moving into the Adult Stage. Check your maturity list of needs and tasks for holes that might need filling before he moves up again. Keep the joy and grace flowing with your eyes open to his or her needs for understanding as they struggle to cross that threshold into another stage of life. Maintaining your relationship is vital, though some modifications as to how you interact may be necessary. See her heart and accept her as her Heavenly Father does. Be there as a *quieter* guide than you were in the early years, ready to listen more and speak less as his world broadens and expands.

But everyone must be quick to hear, slow to speak and slow to anger. (James 1: 19)

CHAPTER NINE: THE TEEN YEARS

Goal: to understand the importance of individuation and letting

go

INTRODUCTION

Your child is turning into a teen. In the *Life Model*, thirteen begins the Adult Stage with its needs and tasks. This change brings a whole new approach for relating to your child. Now his focus will be less at home and more on his peers as he forms a group identity. In the coming years he will need to learn how to take care of more than one person at a time and achieve mutual satisfaction in a relationship. He will need to feel important in his community. Now he will learn to bring others back to joy at the same time he is returning to joy. During these next years through high school, college, the armed forces and/or a job, he must be able to protect others from himself and know how his behavior affects history. Somewhere along the line he will determine if he will bring life or death in a sexual relationship. Remember Dr. Wilder's example from Chapter Two about choices in the "back seat of a car" that can help determine adult or child level maturity?

As you just read through these aspects of the Adult Stage, being reminded of the tasks that they will need to accomplish in order to mature, you may have felt overwhelmed--and even more so when you realize that parents are part of the process as guides along the way.

What I desire to do here is at least lighten your load somewhat, as we look at a few points that can help us relate a bit differently while moving through the teen and young adult years. I want to share some points that I found helpful with my own concerns as the parent of teenagers. The concerns and questions have changed very little today. But most of all, I want to encourage you to trust God and walk with Him through every phase and trial that comes with having a teenager.

The first concern that comes to my mind as we look at the teen years is for those parents who are just now reading a parenting book and they feel they have done very little to bring their child up in the Lord and His ways. Your teen may be troubled and difficult to deal with. Maybe you just became a Christian. Maybe you just got your own life straightened out. Maybe you did your best *as* a Christian and still your child is rebellious and pushing you away. For whatever reason a child may be rebellious, your pain is huge. What, if anything, will help? I hope that gaining some understanding of the teen years will comfort your pain.

I know first hand that living with a rebellious teenager brings conflict, chaos and pain to everyone involved. It's useless to blame oneself or to blame each other. At best we just want to avoid hopeless despair and get past the problem. We have to turn to God. He is the best help we can find.

IS IT TRULY REBELLION?

In order to soften the edges of pain we feel with a rebellious teen, I would like to approach the problem from two directions by asking a two-part question: is the teen in "true rebellion" or is he or she trying to individuate? As I understood the role that individuation plays during the teen years it helped me tremendously as I hit bumps with my own teens. Individuation is an aspect of the teen years that I learned about from John and Paula Sandford, founders of Elijah House, a counseling ministry in Idaho, and authors of the book, *Transformation of the Inner Man.*

The Sandfords include individuation in their discussion of three lessons that children should learn during their teen years. These three lessons go right along with the Adult maturity tasks we looked at in Chapter One and have just mentioned at the beginning of this chapter. These lessons are necessary for the teen to form a group identity, to be able to "leave and cleave" in marriage and to have healthy relationships throughout life. The three lessons are individuation, internalization and incorporation. Let's first define each of these separately.

Individuation is the process that involves separating oneself from all formative influences and becoming one's own person. (p. 330 *Transformation of the IM*) This process can be a difficult task as the teen struggles to become his own person while remaining part of a family. But without individuation, a person cannot incorporate (form a group identity) healthily.

Incorporation means to become part of a group (community, family, marriage) and to have sensitivity to the desires and wishes of others. Individuation is necessary for healthy incorporation because only a truly free person can give himself to a group and accept the give and take of a healthy relationship. (p. 330 TIM) When we look at the

Adult tasks in the *Life Model*, we can see how many of those tasks involve incorporation with others.

Internalization is the other necessary ingredient for healthy incorporation. First the teen must individuate (cut free) and then he must internalize for himself all that he has seen, heard and learned about life. The values he's been taught must become his own, often by painful inner wrestling. There is no shortcut. (p. 331 TIM)

This entire process takes courage on the part of the teen and patience on the part of parents. Various forms of individuation have been in process since birth--separation from the womb followed by, "I can do it myself," around the age of two. Now in the teen years, individuation will come to fullness. It will take time and patience. The teen will go back and forth between his desire to stand against his parents and the need to remain in the safety of childhood. He has to stand against the very people he loves and admires. (p.332 TIM)

Just because the teen wrestles does not mean that all your training was useless. Very often the fact that the teen has the courage to individuate and internalize is proof that you did a good job. Let that be part of what you hold on to during difficult circumstances.

As they separate, examine and test all values for themselves, sometimes consciously and other times subconsciously, teens may be asking themselves, "Is God real? Do I want to follow Him? What do I believe about Him, about politics, about the world and life?" Each teen must wrestle with questions like these and have the freedom to search and make them his or her own. This is not an easy process and has to be "felt" down deep in the spirit. "Incidents have to happen which reveal to the teen, often by pain and loss, where his heart really stands." (p. 333)

Timing is as important to this threefold process as it was to the windows best suited for brain development. God has ordained that individuation, internalization and incorporation should take place in the teen years. The worst thing that parents can do as the process begins is to clamp down, tighten up rules, lecture, nag and attack. It is vital to stay supportive and let go as much as possible, allowing plenty of room for unconditional acceptance as he tries to discover what he truly wants and believes. If we clamp down and tighten up, the teen may have to "defend the very things he might have used to discover reality and come to sensibility." Then he may have to go to worse depths in order to break loose. He might get stuck in ways that he would not have taken if everyone had not come down so hard. (p. 335 TIM) "Let them go," say the Sandfords. "This does not mean permissiveness. Rules must remain. We speak of an *inner* letting go expressed outwardly as compassion and understanding." (p. 340 TIM)

Let me elaborate for a moment on what I feel that inner and outer letting go may look like and later I will share some stories to illustrate both. Inner letting go is an attitude that comes from your heart. It means that you allow your teen (or anyone) to follow his or her own journey. It means that you do not reject the person for choices, ideas, preferences or directions that they have. You might not agree, but you do not reject the person. You interact without strife and put-downs. There is no way that parents can do this without trusting God. And to trust God, we must know what He is like. During the teen years, especially, we must be leaning on the Heavenly Father who is full of grace and mercy and faithfulness.

How you speak to and interact with a person with whom you disagree characterizes outward letting go. Will you nag and belittle, or communicate compassion and understanding? You may need to allow more freedom of movement in and out of your home. You may have to lighten up on rules.

It's possible to let go outwardly and not let go inwardly, or vice versa. As your teen grows to adulthood, much of what he or she does will not be "any of your business." Some parents never let go inwardly and that causes many extended family problems. Some parents never let go outwardly and a teen may move towards rebelling. Parents' willingness to let go is a huge factor in the process of individuation.

Preventing individuation at the proper time in the teen years will brew deep underlying trouble that will likely erupt at a later time— when there is a spouse and children involved. Many family problems arise when a father or mother decides to act like a teenager--partying, carousing and as the Sandfords say, "opting for the wild life." (p. 339) If a person has to individuate later than the teen years, it will take tons of help, counseling and repair to get them and others involved through the mess. Wise parents will turn loose at the ordained time.

In the New Testament there is a great example of individuation and how it is best handled. That is the story in Luke 15 of the prodigal son. John Sandford gives a clear interpretation of this story. The younger son left home with his inheritance, which was the same as wishing his father were dead. He took hold of what was his in order to individuate and internalize. It cost him everything--a very hard lesson to learn. What happened when the son returned is the place in the story where we want to concentrate. Most of us have had teaching about the father's forgiveness and restoration and how he is like God waiting for our return. That is, of course, very key and important. But let's look at the story from a different angle. What can we learn from the fact that the father gave his son the ring, a new robe and a celebration? John Sandford says that the father recognized that the son had become his own man and was now qualified to rule. Not just in spite of his rebellion, but also because of it, the father rejoiced that his boy had come through it all and returned a man (p.333).

Sandford completes the story with strong words. "The remark of the elder brother is easily seen by any experienced counselor as that of an   un-individuated child: 'Look! For so many years I have been serving you, and I have never neglected a command of yours and you have never given me a kid, that I might be merry with my friends, but when this son of yours came, who has devoured your wealth with harlots, you killed the fatted calf for him.'" (Luke 15: 29-30) Internalization means that as much as a teen may admire his parents and desire to keep their moral ways, he must not simply do so [blindly and without examination] or he fails to become his own person. He must examine morality for himself, test and see." (p. 333)

This discussion brings Sandford to another heavy point. "Can Jesus' comparison of the prodigal and elder sons say among other things, that He views maturation in Christ as more valuable than being good? Suppose we have two children, one who stumbled many times and returned through it all to be wise and free, while the other is a

© 2007 Barbara Moon

model of good behavior, but with whom we can't be fully real because he is always performing to please us. Which son are we more relaxed with? Which one is truly a son? Which is like a servant trying to please us? The one who has become a son is the one with whom we have a depth of fellowship the performer knows nothing about." (Paraphrased, p 340 TIM)

As I began to learn these ideas from the Sandfords, I had to chew on them, pray about them and examine them. They resonated deep in my heart and brought hope to my pain whenever I encountered an issue that seemed wayward or rebellious in my teens. Both John and Paula, and I, can testify today that these truths work. During the time that their book came out and they were building a worldwide ministry, one of their sons was wayward and rebellious. I listened to his story on cassette and soaked in John's admonition to "keep the relationship no matter the behavior (by not rejecting or condemning the teen) so that when he or she is ready to return, *you* will be standing there as the one they come back to." Today, their son is the head of Elijah House.

And today my "teens" that individuated and internalized have incorporated well with their spouses and community while owning most all the values their father and I desired for them. I thank God for the lessons that John and Paula taught me about wayward teens. Those years were some of the most painful I've lived through, but God's grace and my understanding of individuation kept the pain bearable as I clung to Him. I had to let go. I had to know what God is like and trust Him, believing that He loves my children more than I do.

Letting go was like tearing out part of my heart. As I let go both inwardly and outwardly, letting go meant saying to two of my teens,

"This is your life. You have to live it yourself. You have to pay your consequences. You know what we believe and value. So as you go your way, (late high school on) all we ask is that you don't break any laws or go against any of our values *while on our property*. What you do other places will be your decision, but we expect you to honor us here." Letting go meant that I had to love unconditionally, respect strange decisions, watch silently and pray. It meant that no matter how much it hurt to watch, I had to leave them in God's hands. The only way to walk with a wayward, individuating teen is on your knees. (I will share three stories about this in a later section)

DO THEY HAVE TO REBEL?

As we continue to look at this topic, let's look at another question. "Can a young person individuate and internalize without rebellion and immorality? The answer to that question is a wonderful, "Yes." The Sandfords are in no way condoning or glorifying sin. But as John says, ". . . if a child cannot individuate any other way, I am sure the Lord would rather he rebel and so become his own rather than remain a performing Pharisee. I believe our Lord paid the price on the cross for sons to become sons, not servants only." (p. 340) John and Paula tell their stories in order to give a word of hope and faith to those whose teens are still rebelling.

At the beginning of this section, I proposed that we look at "rebellion" from two directions: Is a teen in "true rebellion" or is he or she trying to individuate? I would like to narrow our definitions and propose that there are degrees of rebellion and individuation, and call those degrees "true rebellion" and "waywardness." True rebellion would be the intense end of individuation while waywardness is a milder form. Let's look more closely now at "true rebellion." What are some factors that affect the degree of individuation that makes the child wayward versus turning him to rebellion?

It seems to me that one factor that distinguishes degrees of intensity in individuation would have to do with the level of involvement we have had as parents--how we have disciplined and how we have brought God into the preteen years. According to the Sandfords and other experts, all children need to individuate, internalize and incorporate. On the lesser end of the intensity scale, some teens who have been reared in the Lord, with parents that walked the talk and filled the home with joy and grace, will only need low levels of "waywardness." This might simply take place in the teen's mental wrestlings. It might take the form of disagreeing with parental admonitions, leaning towards a different political party or bucking against going to church for a season. Moving along on the scale of intensity might bring lying, sneaking, arguing and disrespect, but all in all, the young person seems to be able to remain in the family setting.

Another factor that may keep the intensity mild would be the teen's own walk with God, which could already be strong by this age. Some teens never really rebel against God even though they may question things taught by earthly authorities. Abusing drugs, behaving violently or running away from home would be examples of true rebellion.

TRUE REBELLION

True rebellion can come from many factors, most of which in my opinion involve childhood pain. Type A and Type B traumas affect the growing child and if unhealed can explode into extreme behavior when the child reaches the teens. Children that have suffered neglect, abuse or apathy from caregivers can be primed for rebellion. The availability of free time, mobility in vehicles and influential friends are all contributors to true rebellion, sometimes brought about even when parents did their best. All people have a free will that they can exercise whenever they wish.

But I do lean towards the underlying problem in most rebellion being deep wounds and pain, most likely unrecognized and/or unresolved attachment pain. Since my focus for this book is on prevention, I will not take the necessary time here to speak further about the deep needs and wounds that may be contributing to true rebellion. If you are experiencing true rebellion with your teen, you need continual help from a counselor and your community. At the end of this section I will list some good books to help you where prevention failed or you might have been ignorant of how to tap into God's power as your child grew up, but you need more than a book. Let someone know your needs and get help if drugs, violence, abuse or running away are impacting your family.

Remember, God is all about salvation, healing, restoration and redemption. It is never too late to turn to Him and His people for help to get through this very painful time with your child. He does not blame us for our ignorance and He forgives us for our sins (or the sins of our ancestors) that may have contributed to the child's pain. Keep in mind that all is not your fault; that young people have a will of their own, and pray for them to come to their senses. Take in all you can of God's ways from this day forth, preparing for your young person's return and someday for your grandchildren. Be sure to humbly admit to your son or daughter, and ask forgiveness for your lacks and failures as you allow yourself the grace to believe that your child is just "working on his or her testimony," and that "The Lord will heal the land that the locusts have eaten." (Joel 2:25)

TIPS FOR TEENS

HOW DO THE RULES CHANGE?

The three basic rules we've had "posted" for years—obey, be kind, respect others—will never change, but during the teen years, we may interpret and enforce them a bit differently. We will no longer be able to use physical force to pick that kid up and move him to another activity. They will be impossible to control. The consequences for acting unkindly or disrespectfully will be different. Again, know the coin of the realm that is important to your teen. But be very certain that you can pull off what you give as a consequence. Look at your own schedule, your own capabilities and what is involved in giving that consequence. Make sure that the keeping of it is on the teen's shoulders and not yours. They can get very sneaky and skirt the edge of the law you might want to lay down. Do you have to be present to enforce the consequence? Better not use that one.

As your teen grows and stretches for that coming independence, remember that she may act out for various reasons, but rules and boundaries are part of life. It will be good if you can distinguish between rules and boundaries. As long as the teen is "under your roof" there will be a place for both. Rules are something you give in hopes they will follow them with logical consequences if they don't; boundaries are something you decide that you will keep for yourself and what you will do if the teen decides to be a rule or boundary buster. You cannot control another person's behavior (rules) but you can control what your limit (boundary) will be concerning another's behavior. There will be consequences for breaking rules and boundaries, but the consequences may be a lot tougher for the teen if he or she persists in acting out.

As all children do, teens want some kind of fair and understandable guidelines in order to feel secure and know what to expect. All rules and boundaries should be very clear and consistently followed by appropriate and predetermined consequences, but keep them to a grace-filled minimum.

As the teen approaches the end of high school, if he or she is somewhat mature and responsible, the rules can become increasingly more minimal. When your student goes off to college or the military, he or she can do anything they want and you will not know about it. So begin to turn loose that last year they are home. Continue to put more and more responsibility upon their shoulders and allow them to pay the logical consequences of their choices. It will do them no good for you to bail them out of consequences just because it hurts you to watch.

If you haven't already, as part of shouldering more responsibility, the senior year is a good year to teach your teen how to do laundry and some cooking. When they leave, they will have to do these kinds of things for themselves.

MONEY

Hopefully, your young person has already learned many lessons about money. They have probably earned money by babysitting, mowing grass or even from having a "real" job. If you have instilled the three divisions of money (giving, saving and spending) in your teen, he may or may not stick to it. At this age, it should be totally up to the teen what she does with her money. Does he want to go to college? He will have to choose to save along the way. During the high school years, let her make mistakes while still at home and learn for herself how to manage a larger amount.

Through the years, I have been amazed at the number of adults who do not know how to handle a checkbook. It is a good life skill to teach your teen before they leave home. They should know how to balance the checkbook each month and why it is important. Perhaps in the future, checking will all be done electronically, but at least make certain that your child knows how it all works.

Here is another caution I'd like to give you—know that credit card companies flood the colleges and give kids a card. They want to hook them early on buying by credit so the card company can have their interest for the rest of life. If you have modeled not living by credit, the student may not fall into the trap. But it is good to have a talk about it before the temptation comes. Retail stores also love to give credit cards to young people. They don't even have to have a job first.

DRIVING, DATING, AND CURFEWS

When your young person begins to date and go out with friends in cars, your relationship with the Lord will take a big leap. You will learn to let go even more of things you cannot control. Try to rely on Jesus instead of worrying up into the night. The enemy loves to give us what I heard a teacher long ago call "vain imaginations." This Bible teacher took the words from Romans 1:21 (KJV) and described vain imaginations as allowing one's thoughts to race out of control, imagining the worst. I really understood this teacher's interpretation of vain imaginations the first time I watched my oldest son Jim, who had just gotten his license, drive out of the driveway, his little sister, Jodi in the front seat. Before they got to the stop sign, I had their funeral planned. Those kinds of thoughts are vain imaginations and will take us to unnecessary worry.

In some states now, a new driver cannot take anyone under eighteen in a car with them until they have been driving for six months. Talk to your teen about the seriousness of driving a car and having others' lives in their hands. Assess your teen's maturity and sensibility before allowing a license. It does not have to be automatic. Let it be known early on that having the license is a privilege.

I don't have lots of set tips and rules for dating. You will have to determine much of this as a family. I would encourage you to extend the age as long as you can and to encourage lots of group dating. And as I said before, you can require a guy to ask Dad for dates with your daughter. Jim asked Elizabeth's father if he could take her to the prom. Bob asked Amy's father if he could take her to Homecoming. It can be very helpful to have boys (girls) that want to go out with your daughter (son) spend time with your family in order for you as parents to get to know them. It is helpful all along to have your children's friends to your house, no matter the age, so that you have your kids at <u>your</u> house. If that has been a habit, it can carry over into the teen years if your family is joyful, fun, grace-filled, and accepting. This is one way to keep a little "control" in a very uncontrollable season of your child's life.

If your teen struggles with peer pressure during this season of his life, give him the option of making you the "bad guy." He can tell friends that you don't allow any activity that he really does not want to participate in. That will make it easier to say, "No."

My views on curfews were a bit different than most parents that I knew when my teens were growing up. It seemed that curfew was an issue that caused much conflict. Parents obsessed over minutes and punishments. Students argued and obsessed over being late.

In our family, the emphasis was not on getting home at an exact minute. The time was general and the kids had a say so according to the event. I do not remember one single hassle over curfew from the high school years of our four teens. They did not abuse the trust. It was part of letting go. Our emphasis was on courtesy to always tell us where they were going, about what time they would return, and most importantly that they were leaving. I know of families where the family members leave without telling anyone.

ATTENDANCE AT ACTIVITIES

A great way to encourage your teen and keep the relationship with him or her as they grow up is to attend as many of their activities as you can. Show interest in what they are interested in, even if it is not your cup of tea. Be careful not to embarrass your teen when around her friends and classmates. You are not the pal; you are the parent. Teens appreciate it more if a parent acts like an adult and stays sensitive to his or her feelings than that the parent is "cool." Schedule your time so that you can attend functions that mean something to your child. If you live nearby after they leave home, this will be an on going privilege that you will have even after they are grown.

PERSONAL STYLE AND PREFERENCE

As much as possible, allow your teen to express him or herself, while guiding them towards that personal style that reflects his or her heart. Developing that personal style is one of the Adult Stage tasks. The young person needs to know who he is, what he wants and where he is going. He needs a sense of purpose that fits his heart. But he must know his heart in order to know how it fits. She must know herself the way God sees her and move towards following Him, if not already. Marriage and a family of their own will bring new challenges to the young adult and they need a solid, steady foundation to meet those challenges. We will look more at that in the next chapter.

Jim and Jake

FAILURES AND CONSEQUENCES

If your family has walked in grace through the years, failures will be easier to deal with. If not, failures will bring shame and grief. Part of letting go is not getting in the way of failures and consequences. All of us learn best from failures if allowed to go through them. It does not help anyone to get "bailed out" of a logical consequence. Here are some examples of logical consequences: Not doing homework brings bad grades, which might hinder entrance into a preferred college. Not helping with laundry might leave one without favorite clothes. Not saving money might prevent a desired purchase. As parents, we do better to be supportive and accepting without bailing out. Too many people today feel that they are victims and have no responsibility for their problems. Don't try to prevent every failure. Let your young person learn as much as possible *before* he or she leaves home.

DRUGS, ALCOHOL AND PARTIES

I do not know what to say about these common vices other than that avoiding them is something that any teen has to do him or herself. Hopefully what you have taught and modeled will strengthen your child to say "no" on his own. Being in a good, non-legalistic youth group at a church can help your child's battle against these temptations. But other than forbidding parties (that you know about) these choices will ultimately be up to the young person. Though it feels like we have some control when they are young, we really never have true control of another person. The teen and future years will prove this lack of control to us over and over. The best we can do is cling to God and leave the children in His hands. We are powerless to control them and we must learn to trust Him and believe that He has their best interest at heart and loves them more than we do. And, where there are difficult issues to bear, that God will bring them through to a better place.

SEX EDUCATION

I know sex education begins very young these days whether it is formal or in the locker room. I earlier mentioned Pastor Kevin Meyers (PK) who is the senior pastor of the church I have been attending for the last six years. PK, as he is lovingly called, not only models humility and transparency, he models what it means to mentor one's children. I want to paraphrase a message he gave last year about how he explained dating and pre-engagement relationships to his daughter, Julesa (16). It fits well under this topic. My version will be brief, but I hope that it will at least strike some thoughts for you to ponder.

As Kevin was talking with his daughter one day, she asked about dating. PK drew a diagram to help explain how relationships could be broken down into five categories and what they would mean as she began to "date" and eventually find a mate. The five categories were: acquaintances, friend, boyfriend/girlfriend, engagement and marriage.

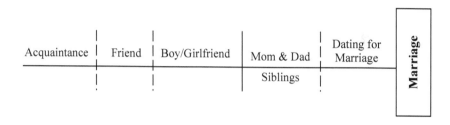

Acquaintance	Friend	Boy/Girlfriend	Mom & Dad	Dating for Marriage	Marriage
			Siblings		

"As you look at having a 'boyfriend'" Daddy told his daughter, "remember that at this point you do not give your heart away. I own your heart. Daddy owns your heart (as does your Heavenly Father). At this point you only give affection, not your heart. As you honor your father and your mother, we will be looking out for your best interest. When you get ready for dating, Mom and I and your siblings will be evaluating boys who cross over our "solid line." If we don't like what we see, he will be sent back to the friend category. As you begin dating for engagement, the family will still be checking things out, and as you will then begin to give your heart away, I'll agree to it if I see God is in it."

Dad went on to say with great passion, "As you begin to give your heart away, you never give your body away. You do not give your body until he has given you his heart and hand in marriage. That is the only condition for giving your body." PK then talked about how nothing works unless God has all of one's heart. Then he finished the diagram talking about how the "marriage box" represents that she will leave her parents and cling to her husband.

Another point that I heard in this message relates to what we talked about in Chapter One—that good parenting begins with a good marriage. PK reminded us that when a marriage is unstable, that makes it very difficult for children to honor their fathers and mothers. And that makes it more difficult to follow God's ways concerning dating and sex before marriage. You can find this message on www.12Stone.com or order a copy of it from 12Stone Church, Lawrenceville, GA. The date of the teaching was January 15, 2006.

COLLEGE, MILITARY, OR JOB

If your teen is college bound, likely he or she has been traveling that direction for a while. Help her remember the importance of grades through the high school years. Keep moving him towards self-discipline about homework and the balance of outside activities. Trust God to provide in various ways for the costs of college. Prepare your student to shoulder the responsibility of doing well in college, especially if you are paying. If he has to help pay, it will encourage him to do better. All four of my children found ways to get through college with very little to no help from us. They valued what they worked hard for and had tangible stories about God's faithfulness.

Your student may want to go into the military. Listen to his or her ideas and desires. The principle thing to move towards at this age is "independence" from you and "dependence" upon God. Be careful not to enable a young person to "veg" too long on your couch and not move towards that independence. When he reaches eighteen, he should be taking care of himself or contributing to the household if not in college or the military.

By the time a young person goes away to college or the military (or has a full time job) the principle rules when at home should be those that pertain to any adult living in the household. I personally think that within reason a college student should have complete freedom to come and go, but with that freedom they would have a respectful attitude towards others' needs and share responsibilities pertaining to the household when there on weekends or summers.

If you see grades dropping in high school or college, first determine if there is some problem going on with your teen. Check like you did when younger for an empty Joy Bucket or upsetting incident. If the teen is simply goofing off, let him pay his own consequences. If she starts to flunk out of college and it is not something you can help with, you might have to let it happen. But he or she can't then "veg" on the couch while you foot the bill.

Should your student go to college for a while and then decide that is not what he wants to do, consider this. I know a young man who was a straight A student in high school who went to college for a year and then wanted to stop and work for a while. His wise parents allowed him to make that decision. He worked for about a year and then returned to college and finished his degree. Another young lady I know went to college for a while and did not do well. She grew very discouraged and wanted to quit and become a cosmetician. Her parents were disappointed, but after some counsel decided to let her go to cosmetology school. She finished her courses there and worked for a while before returning to college and completing her degree. These are examples of supporting and encouraging your young person as they branch out to find their unique way in life. The years immediately after high school are a very short period of time in relation to the rest of life. There is plenty of time to get a degree if a person wants one.

ACCEPTANCE AND LISTENING

Remember back in the chapters about brain development where we talked about an infant becoming like the faces he beholds? That has remained an important part of our children's development throughout their growing years. It remains important during the teen and adult years as well. None of us ever get over needing to be seen "through Heaven's eyes." Children of all ages thrive on acceptance. Now your teen needs unconditional acceptance even more than ever, as he or she moves towards becoming an independent person.

Our ability to unconditionally accept our children gets fine-tuned as our teens grow up, because how and what they choose and how they change may not line up exactly as we had hoped. Some differences may be mild and some may bring us grief. Whatever the case, regardless of our feelings, it is imperative to accept and love the person no matter the behavior, the characteristics or the beliefs. We may not agree with the person and their choices, but our love does not change.

Listening and not lecturing are vital to accepting the person in spite of behavior and beliefs. We continue to synchronize throughout life, regardless of age. People want to be with people who synchronize and try to understand them. Nagging and lecturing do not help anyone. Treat your young person the way you would a good friend. As he grows and matures, you will have to "get to know him" in different ways at different ages. Keep the relationship going through every phase, as you respect the person she is becoming, and show interest in whatever you can.

You may be asking yourself, "Well, does this mean I never speak to anything that I disagree with?" Of course not. What makes the difference is how, when, and how many times you speak to an issue. Do you speak with condemnation? Do you erupt in anger out of frustration? Do you attack in front of other people? Do you bring it up over and over? None of these methods will help the relationship. Believe me; your young adult knows exactly what you think about most everything. His brain developed that at about five months of age. He does not need another lecture; he needs love. We can love without condoning behavior.

TOUGH LOVE

Sometimes love is tough, especially during waywardness or rebellion. Tough love allows logical consequences. Tough love draws a line, or a boundary, that says, "My <u>love</u> for you will not change, but what I <u>do</u>, (or allow to go on in our home) for you can change." This kind of love stands back and watches (and grieves) while strong, logical consequences occur. It does not enable or bail out the person nor keep them from learning a lesson. As I said before, the consequences of boundary busting can be more severe than some logical consequences.

Tough lovers hold on to God while they watch, pray and hurt. They trust that God is bigger than the circumstance. They believe that somewhere in the mess will blossom a testimony for His glory. Tough loving parents walk in the fact that God is in control while they refuse to look at appearances. I know this because I had to walk it myself. With permission, I will share three stories--two stories about tough love, one involving an incident where Greg paid some life-changing logical consequences, the other a story from Jodi's teen years. The third story will illustrate unconditional love and God's faithfulness in spite of appearances.

GREG'S STORY

"In my early teens, I began my "criminal" career. While it was confined to occasional shoplifting during those first years, by the time I turned 16, I was on my way to becoming a full-blown crook (or so I thought). This proclivity towards unlawful behavior could not be attributed to my parents, siblings, or upbringing. It was not because I was a "poor" kid, a "dumb" kid, or a "bad" kid either. Rather it was something that developed within me independent of all external sources.

My parents taught me right from wrong, ensured my attendance at church whenever the doors opened, and provided a moral compass for me to follow with their behavior. I was a nearly straight-A student with plenty to eat, fairly decent clothes, and a roof over my head. Yet none of this was enough to deter me. I simply had a talent and a desire for stealing, and enjoyed the rush of getting away with it.

Looking back, I really have no good reason for taking things that didn't belong to me. My best excuse was that, because of growing up without a lot of extras (needs were provided), I felt I was owed a better life, so to speak. When I saw something I wanted, but couldn't have due to my parents' very practical budget limitations, I did not accept that as my lot in life. Several years of practice led me to my biggest caper in the summer of 1987 prior to my sophomore year of college.

While working at a national grocery chain, I easily discovered a "foolproof" method for stealing money directly from the till. By logging on as an employee that had already left for the day (whose till had thus already been counted down), I was able to perform an undetected transaction and pocket the cash. After nearly three months of milking my employer, I got lazy and was caught, arrested and taken to jail.

Parents, I must tell you that your suspicions that jail is not a safe place are well founded. However, imprisonment (for a very short time comparative to others) was the only possible outcome that could hope to teach me the skills I had somehow grown up ignoring. If your teen is heading down this path, it may be the only way for him to understand that the consequences of his actions will catch up with him. As I sat in stir, I recall with absolute clarity when I finally understood that my behavior would lead to my eventual downfall if I did not mend my ways. The holding tank was also the place that the "real" felons would come to make phone calls, and one particular prisoner marked me for life.

The enormous man sat down directly beside me and began a series of phone calls. As he talked to first his mother, then his girlfriend, and finally his lawyer, I supposed that this gentleman was moving toward redemption. However, when his lawyer began to contradict his assertions of innocence, the convict simply replied (in a loud, booming voice), that he was certain he had not killed the man in question and that his lawyer better get that through his head lest he (the prisoner) feel obligated to "kill him too."

Now, people – you just can't give your child this kind of self-evaluating perspective in a loving Christian home! I decided then and there not to continue my illicit behaviors lest I end up bunkies with a gorilla like the one screaming at his lawyer in the chair next to mine. No matter of nagging, cajoling, threatening, or persuasion by my parents, teachers, or clergy could have ever made such a profound impact as this prisoner did. You simply lack, as a "good" parent, a believable framework for your criminally minded teen to relate to. Sometimes only another criminal can provide the lesson your child needs. It was the case with me, and I can happily say with honesty that I have never been tempted to steal since that day.

While your story may differ, remember that your teen decided very early on whether you would have input into his character. Be consistent, and prepare for the eventuality of county-sponsored discipline (if need be). You can beg, shout, and wave your hands all you want, but it may be something that has to happen in order for your child to become an adult.

JODI'S STORY

Well, that story warms a mother's heart, doesn't it? It's not so hard to hear now that twenty years have passed and her son is grown and quite stable. And I have to add--that in spite of some trials along the way-- I dearly love boys. I enjoyed (and still do) all the stuff that goes with having boys. I loved their wrestling and roughhousing. I love their humor and hugs. I love the men, husbands, fathers and leaders my boys and my son-in-law, Rick, have become. What a blessing! I without prejudice say that I have a most awesome family.

Having three boys was great fun and through the years we also wanted a girl very much. We decided to apply for adoption and thus be certain of getting a girl. After several weeks of paperwork and interviews, the call came from our agency—we have a baby for you; we will be in touch soon. A few days later, when I entered the door of a shoe repair shop to pick up my husband's shoes and nearly threw up at the smell, a nagging suspicion I'd had was confirmed—I was pregnant again. What I deeply wanted was to go ahead with the adoption and have five kids instead of four, but that was not to be. So I tearfully prayed to God, "If you don't want me to have a girl that is okay. I want what you want for my life."

A few months later, we got our precious daughter and she was (and is) all that I ever dreamed for. We brought her up in the ways of the Lord, and she was courageous enough to individuate and internalize during her junior year of high school. During this time, I learned more than I have time to write here. I had to walk what I'd talked many times and cling to God for about a year as Jodi tried and tested and grew. Not all of it was just individuation, because unrecognized marriage problems were causing her pain as well. But as issues escalated concerning a boy we did not want her to be with, a day came when we had to ask her to leave our house. We had arranged for her to be with close friends for a month.

With that friend's guidance and help we worked through a plan. Jodi would live with them as an adult, paying "rent" and letting them know how she would be coming and going, mostly being her own boss. With those privileges would come the same responsibilities that an adult carries such as car upkeep, gas, school activity schedules, etc. She already had a good relationship with Scott and Laurel and they encountered no problems during that time. Dad and I did not handle everything well, but with continual sessions with Scott we adjusted our mistakes and stayed in the "tough love" mode. (I was surprised how often I forgot to be tough.)

Towards the end of the month, Jodi asked if she could come back home. When we met with Scott to discuss a new plan, we decided that we would give her the choice to come back as an "adult" with all the privileges, but with the financial responsibilities involved there, or as our "child" and all that involved. She tearfully told us that she wanted to be our "child," that she had broken up with the boy. She returned to finish her teen years with very few hassles and lots of delight for us. God continued to work on her testimony through college and teach her many things as she continued to grow. I would not change anything about my lovely daughter today. She is a true blessing, a good friend, a wonderful wife and a great Mommy. And she truly loves, obeys, serves and shares God. What a blessing!

A YOUNG ADULT STORY

As you may have picked up by now, living with Greg and Chris has also been one of my biggest blessings. Knowing both of their stories from their early years just adds to the blessing. Chris has been part of my life since she was in the eighth grade and of course I've known Greg all of his life. When the two were in college, they went through a very difficult lesson. I have their permission to share it.

When Chris came into our lives, she was in the eighth grade and a strong follower of Jesus Christ. Greg was in his first year of college after skipping his senior year and entering college early. You've heard his story. He was back and forth at home and Chris secretly had a crush on him. Chris kept her secret all through high school while Greg saw her as his little sister's friend. Things changed the summer after he graduated and came home for good. Chris had finished her first year of college and was no longer a child.

As the two began to spend time together, they fell in love. Time passed, Greg moved into an apartment and Chris was living at our house. One evening Chris came to tell me that she was going to go over to Greg's but she was not coming home that night. I said to both of them, "You know how we feel about this, but it is not our business." Greg vehemently agreed.

A few months later, Chris again sat down with me and told me that she and Greg were going to move in together. I was not happy about it, as she knew I would not be, but all I did was entreat her to please be careful about getting pregnant.

What happened next appeared to many to be quite "crazy." I helped Greg and Chris to furnish their apartment. I gave them things we didn't need and we checked out garage sales. I accepted my children without condoning their behavior. I had to practice what I'd preached on an even deeper level than before. Some friends disagreed with my stand to love and accept regardless of behavior and I received a lot of flak.

A few months went by and I could see that Chris was a very unhappy young woman. In fact she was miserable. Finally one day she came to tell me that she was no longer going to live with Greg because God had told her to move out. After much pain from realizing that if she obeyed God, she would very likely lose this young man whom she had dreamed of having for so long, Chris moved back with her mother.

Greg was furious-- but in a day or two he realized what he was losing. Together they made an appointment with Scott (the man who had helped us with Jodi) and went to talk to him about what they should do. With Scott's help they dealt with God and each other, receiving and giving forgiveness. Scott led them in a prayer where God gave them a beautiful picture of Him cutting the soulical ties they had formed. God took the ends of the "strings" and held them in His hand and told Greg and Chris that on their wedding night He would restore the connection as He intends it to be when done properly in marriage. With God's grace, Greg and Chris remained pure until their marriage a year later, when God kept all His promises.

I tell these stories here to bring hope to those of you whose teens or young adults appear to be straying from the fold. I think the stories sum up what I have been trying to say in this chapter about wayward teens and how important it is to accept them even if their behavior is not so great. By this time in my journey, I'd had to rely on God to bring me through just about everything I'd learned about teens. I had to trust that letting someone go their own path was the best thing to do even if it tore out my heart. I had to hold on to God working things out in His way and time. Most of all I did not want to lose the relationships and that reality is my reward. Of course retrospect makes it easier to see that God was faithful, but don't let that keep you from hope and reliance on Him.

So, you might be wondering why there are no juicy stories about my other two. All I can say is that the older two did not stray from God as they went through their teens. What they had with God was real and viable to them from a very young age. There are probably several other reasons, one of which had to do with our church situations being different with each pair of teens as they came along. But what I usually tell others is this, "If I had only had the first two, you would not like me very much, because I would be full of pride that I had done such a great job." Nothing like a wayward teen to keep one humble.

Today I am glad that I have been on both sides and can relate with hope to other parents. The younger two were more "normal" in a lot of ways and God used the hard things I went through with them to teach me deeper trust and dependence on Him. I thank God every day for my wonderful children and for the path that each trekked through the years and how God used each one's journey to make them who they are today. Knowing that God was there in each one's trek is part of seeing them as individuals and loving them the way they are. I would not change anything about them. Their individuality makes each one a unique, obedient, loving servant of God and I am grateful to God every day for His grace and faithfulness to all of us.

SUMMARY

I hope that you were able to glean something from this chapter that will lighten your load through the teenage years and that you found something that will encourage you wherever you are in the journey of parenting a teen or young adult. God is in control and not surprised by anything. The difficulties can be extreme, but the blessings will outnumber them if you hang on to God and keep walking. They *will* *l*eave home and start their own. You *can* hope for a good relationship if all involved are willing to work through problems.

We are almost finished with our look at joy-filled parenting, and I want to end with a very important aspect of parenting--that of Spiritual mentoring and training. Our walk with God is the very foundation of life and is the only way to truly live. Knowing and trusting Him makes it easier to suffer well through the trials and hurts that are part of life. I hope that you will take this next section to heart as highly important— important enough to have it as part of your life in such a way that you can pass it on.

CHAPTER TEN: MENTORING AND SPIRITUAL TRAINING

Goal: For our children to love, serve, obey and share God

INTRODUCTION

I remember to this day the awe and excitement I felt when I first heard someone teach about mentoring (then called discipling) one's children. In 1976, my husband I had joined Campus Crusade for Christ after meeting some awesome people with teenagers like we wanted to have some day. As I listened to speakers, teachers and mentors, I soaked up everything I heard and wanted to learn more. I received great teaching about the family through Campus Crusade for Christ, as well as training for ministry, sharing my faith and living the Spirit-filled life. It was a privilege to be part of that organization and I know it also had a great impact on our two oldest boys.

As I studied the Scriptures for God's truth about living life, it felt like I knew very little, but I longed to do whatever it would take to one day see my children love and serve God. I wanted them to know His ways and how He says to live. I also came to the realization that I as a parent was a major part of the process, because "more is caught than taught." That realization increased my motivation.

This venture into full-time ministry is a large part of my testimony and how God brought me along my journey. I am so thankful for all I learned during those years that I sat under good teaching and diligently sought God with all my heart. He brought many changes in my life and I would like to share a few of them with you.

MY TESTIMONY

I grew up in a home where I was taken to church from the cradle. I asked Jesus Christ to be my Savior when I was nine years old. During my childhood and teen years, I never strayed away from God. I can't remember a time when I did not love Him and want to follow Him. Before I got married at the age of eighteen, I committed my life to be a good Christian wife and mother. When I was about thirty, not too long before we joined Campus Crusade staff, I understood total surrender to Jesus Christ in a broader sense than wife and mother, and thus made a deeper commitment that encompassed all of my life. After that surrender, I began to grow more as my relationship with Jesus grew deeper.

I have always been an avid reader and once I began to follow Jesus, I read everything I could find on prayer, the saints of old, and what some call the "deeper life." Many of these books were written, or took place, in the nineteenth century. I read these books and my Bible, over and over and over. In late 1979, God began another new work in my life. He took me down some difficult paths of brokenness in order to teach me that, not only is Jesus my Savior and my Lord, but He is also my very Life.

The mentors I had for this difficult path were Bill and Anabel Gillham, Dr. Charles Solomon, Dan Stone, Norman Grubb and Laurie Hills, and later Dr. Wilder. I have written extensively about this time of my life in *Jewels for My Journey*. For now I want to briefly describe what I learned from these mentors, because my journey is part of my parenting and what I want to say to you. I will condense about ten years of study into three topics: The Difference in the Old Man and the Flesh (who we are vs. what we do), Acceptance vs. Performance (Law vs. grace), and How to Walk Victoriously in the Spirit (truth vs. appearances.)

THE DIFFERENCE IN THE OLD MAN (OLD NATURE) AND THE FLESH—WHO WE ARE VS. WHAT WE DO:

In 1979, I met a couple who sat with me at my kitchen table and told me deep things of God that I had never heard before. They shared with me that, after receiving Christ, a Christian no longer has the *old man*, sometimes called the *old self* or *old nature* in some Bible translations. They said that *old man* and *flesh*, two words I had heard interchanged, were not the same Greek word. The next day I began a search to discover for myself if this were true. It was quite easy, as I soon found that there were two different words in the Greek. I looked at all the passages containing those words and decided to believe it was true, even though I had never heard anyone else teach it. The problem was that I had no idea what difference it made. That understanding would come almost a year later.

The two Greek words I found were *anthropos* (old man*)* and *sark* *(*flesh*)*. It is very important to distinguish these two words when reading the passages that contain them. While we no longer have the *anthropos*, we do still have the *sark*. *Anthropos* has to do with who we are; the *sark* has to do with behavior, lies that we believe about ourselves and old ways we try to get our needs met. As I have said many times in this book, we must separate the personhood and behavior when dealing with ourselves, with others and with our children. When I finally realized what a difference it made to know the words were different, it turned my life upside down. I no longer based my personhood and acceptance on my performance. I based it on what it means to be "in Christ."

ACCEPTANCE VS. PERFORMANCE—GRACE VS. LAW:

I lived most of my life by performance-based acceptance, looking at and accepting myself based on my behavior, on what I did rather than who I was. As a Christian I lived mostly under the Law, though I'd been saved by grace. I accepted myself and others based on how we performed. Just like Adam and Eve, I lived under the tree that carried the fruit of the knowledge of good and evil—the tree that said, "Man (I) will decide what is good and bad; I will decide the standards." And, wow, does it ever get confusing when Man makes the standards-- they change over and over! When Man makes the standards they are different in each family, each country, each church and each culture. God and His words can be the only standard.

Living under the Law, or performance-based acceptance, did not help me see myself or others "through Heaven's eyes." I did not love myself when I didn't perform perfectly. I knew nothing about living free in Christ. As I studied what it meant to be "in Christ," (I already knew He was in me), I came to realize that what happened to Christ happened to me and what is true of Him is true of me. Knowing this changed my view of myself as well as how I accepted others. Acceptance and personhood were no longer based on performance, but rather on who I now am as a born-again believer "in Christ." I quit hating myself when I messed up, I stopped beating up on myself when I couldn't do things perfectly and I learned to take every thought captive so that I could walk in victory.

WALKING VICTORIOUSLY IN THE SPIRIT—TRUTH VS. APPEARANCES:

Galatians 5:16 commands us to "Walk in the Spirit and you will not fulfill the lusts of the flesh." 2 Corinthians 4:18 says, ". . . look not at the things which are seen, but at the things which are not seen, for the things which are seen are temporal and the things which are not seen are eternal." Paul continues in 2 Corinthians 5: 7, "for we walk by faith, not by sight." What these verses have in common is the admonition to believe what God says in spite of how circumstances look, how we feel or how we behave. I learned to say the truth to myself about God's view, regardless of appearances. If God says many times over that I am accepted, loved, righteous, blameless, His child, then I must choose to believe that against any evidence (feelings, behavior and appearances) to the contrary.

My old self (*anthropos*) was crucified with Christ and a new creation rose from the grave with Him and is now seated in the Heavenly places with Him. My flesh (*sark*) has been programmed by experiences to react in certain ways (many of them lies) in order to get

320   © 2007 Barbara Moon

my love and acceptance from others besides Christ. I can decide which one to put my faith in--the Spirit or the flesh. And I also decide--will I listen and follow my heart (where Jesus lives) or will I listen to the *sark* (based on lies)? Teaching our children the Immanuel Lifestyle of going to Jesus for healing and freedom from lies will bring all of us to more consistent victory. **(See Appendix A for more on the Immanuel Process.)**

THE HEART AND THE SARK

The Life Model sums up what I learned as I studied and applied these three truths to my life, as I learned to follow my heart (my spirit joined to the Holy Spirit) and not the old fleshly ways that I had used in the past to get love and acceptance. The *Life Model* speaks of the *sark* as "the mortal enemy of our heart," meaning the new heart (spirit) that Jesus gives us when we receive Him. This heart is the real us, the place where we hear God and know what He wants, even when we can't explain it with words. On the other hand, the *sark*, the flesh, tells us nothing but lies. The flesh tells us that we can figure out if something is good or bad, but when we try to go that route, we are *always* wrong. We cannot see what God sees. (p. 72-73 TLM)

The *sark's* lies are connected to our pain. When we "hear" the lies in our thoughts they make sense to our experiences. Here is an example: Your child is not behaving well. There are problems at school and at home. Your flesh will tell you (in first person singular), "*I* am a bad parent." That lie lands on your pain and is easy to take as true. But what is God saying? Deep inside, you might hear Him say any number of things that would fit the situation, such as, "I am in control. I am teaching everyone something here." Or, "Find out why the child is acting out. What can you do to help instead of beating up on yourself?" Or perhaps, "Help is needed here. Find someone to help all of you work through this time in the family."

The *Life Model* tells us more. Living from the heart does not mean we throw away rules and live by feelings. The heart (knowing) is deeper than feelings. (p. 77) "Living from the heart Jesus gave you means you are being the person you were designed to be, acting like yourself in all situations." (p. 76) I think we've heard about acting like ourselves somewhere else in an earlier chapter.

So before we mentor our children and guide them to know the heart Jesus gave them, let us as parents turn our hearts to Him with all our strength. Our pain will show us what really matters to us if we face it and listen to it, because what causes us (and our child) pain is a signal of a characteristic of our heart. Only what is important to us causes us pain. For example if you feel pain (hurt) when someone accuses you unjustly, then one of your characteristics is honesty. If you feel pain when someone is not loyal, then you have the characteristic of loyalty.

Other people can help us (and our child) know our heart by telling us what they see in us. It goes deeply into us when another person says something like, "That shows me you are a very loving person." Or, "What you just did shows how dependable you are." We will know our heart when we resist the lies from the flesh and act like our true selves. We will know our heart as we give and receive life to and from others. (p. 76 TLM)

Verses For This Section and/or further study: Romans 6-8, Books of Ephesians and Galatians, Ezekiel 36:26, Hebrews 11:6b, Hebrews 6:20 to 7:10, Hebrews 4:12, Colossians 2:6, Colossians 3:4, 1 Thessalonians 5:23, 1 Corinthians 5:17, John 16:8, Genesis 3 and Matthew 6:22-23, Romans 8:28. At the end of the book is a list of books that will give the reader more details on the victorious, grace-filled life.

TIPS FOR MENTORING

TALK *ABOUT* JESUS, ALL DAY IN EVERYDAY CIRCUMSTANCES

We have already looked at Proverbs 6:26 which says, "Train up a child in the way he should go and when he is old he will not depart from it." Another verse that helped me focus on the task of mentoring was Deuteronomy 6:7: "And you shall teach them (My words) diligently to your sons and shall talk of them when you sit in your house and when you walk by the way and when you lie down and when you rise up." To me, that verse means that we talk about God and His ways all the time, taking every opportunity during a regular day to bring God into our conscious awareness of what is going on in life. Jesus is real and He is everywhere. He is inside us and is one with those of us who have received Him. So we don't wait on the church or Christian school to teach our children about Jesus. We thank Him out loud in front of the children for a parking space at the mall, we read stories to the kids about Him, we tell them how He provides materially, and we reinforce lessons taught at church. Whatever comes up as we're living life can be taken to what God says about it and that He is in it.

I have a memory that illustrates how one day I had an interaction about Jesus with Jodi when she was about four. It still makes me smile. I had just recently learned to take some time each day to read my Bible and pray. As I sat in my bedroom that morning, rocking in my chair with my head bowed and eyes closed, Jodi came into the room. She said, "Mommy, what are you doing?" I answered, "I'm talking to Jesus." She asked so innocently, "Where is He?" I answered while pointing to my heart, "He's in here." She looked at me in puzzlement and asked, "Did you eat Him?" I don't remember how I got out of that one, but I trusted that she would internalize that talking to Jesus was a very important part of my day.

TALK *TO* JESUS AND FOLLOW HIS WAYS

Not only do we want to talk *about* Jesus and God as we go through our day, we want to talk *to* Him with our children. We can pray aloud before bed, at meals, and when troubles or blessings come. We can play praise music in the car and home. Our family knows that we go to church without question—it is part of the week. We allow God to work on us so that "more will be caught than taught." As best we can in God's power, our actions and speech are loving, patient and accepting. When the actions don't look like Jesus, we admit fault and ask forgiveness.

I remember one of the first times I asked forgiveness from Jodi. She was about six or seven. The only kind of spanking she had ever had was the kind that I described in Chapter Six. On that day, I was reading in the living room and she was sitting in the floor. She kept kicking the swivel rocker around and around. I asked her to stop a couple of times and when she did it again, I smacked her on the leg. She burst into tears and I immediately got up and took her into my lap. I asked her forgiveness for not spanking her correctly and then we talked about obeying. She forgave me. I could write another book on all the times I have had to ask forgiveness, but I will just give one more story about how I had to ask forgiveness last week.

About three weeks ago, Kori (6 ½) came downstairs to my place to get a back for her earring. She went into my bedroom and got the back and then went upstairs. The next day I noticed that one of the baggies was missing that I keep earrings in. I asked Kori what she had done with the bag. She said she left it there. Fast-forward two weeks. Off and on, I had looked all over the place for that baggie and even asked Chris to look upstairs and ask Kori again if she remembered anything differently. No bag of earrings.

Finally this past week, I searched again, looking behind the dressers and under the bed. I decided to look in all my jewelry boxes. When I opened one of the small ones, there were all the earring backs and extra earrings that I had been searching for. I had put them into a new box a few months ago.

A day or two later, Kori was sitting on my lap as we were discussing her day at school and I said, "By the way, I owe you an apology." She looked at me with questions in her eyes. "Do you remember how I kept asking you about that bag of earrings?" She nodded her head. "Well," I said, "I found the contents of that bag in one of my jewelry boxes. You didn't even use that bag. I was wrong to doubt you. Will you forgive me?" I share this example for you to know her response—she threw her arms around my neck and said, "Yes." This is quite often the response we get around here when we ask forgiveness. What a great message asking forgiveness sends to our children.

BRING GOD INTO FAMILY DECISIONS

When possible, we let the kids in on family issues and decisions. We talk about not being able to live without God. We let the kids see and hear us seeking God's will and guidance. When age appropriate, we talk about things that are wrong in our culture, ideas in movies or television, or public school, that don't line up with God's words. We share the "whys" of some of our family rules and values. We keep Christ in Christmas and Easter.

SHARE YOUR POWER

I learned about sharing power from Dr. Wilder, though I feel that I already knew the principle without knowing the words to describe it. He writes extensively about power in *The Red Dragon Cast Down*. He says that children notice in their family who has the power, how it is used, and what the results are of having power. They notice that the one with power does not suffer (feel pain). This is usually Dad. If power is not shared properly, children learn to believe, *if I have power, I will not have pain.* This creates a desire to have power in order to control and get their way, to overpower others in order to feel powerful. The result is a person filled with fear and anger. (pp. 169, 176)

Dr. Wilder continues, "Providing your children with power and teaching them how to use it well, is a major form of Satan-proofing your children. Powerful children can do hard things. Building powerful love bonds is how we build powerful children." (p. 168) We parents can use three very good questions to evaluate our use of power and what we are communicating to our children about power: "What kind of power did our dad have? What got him to use it? And what induced him to share his power?" Parents must share their power lovingly. (p. 133, 134)

So comes the obvious question—how do parents share their power? Dr. Wilder gives a few suggestions: Help your children achieve their goals. Teach them to think wisely, to solve problems on their own and to plan things. Give them some power over their environment—their room, appropriate choices, their personal style. Help them learn to live with limitations. Make love bonds and not fear bonds. The strength of love bonds not only builds strength to do hard things, love bonds affect how people hear the Gospel. They are more likely to want to know Jesus when they see that our love for the Lord is greater than our fear. (pp. 172, 155)

It seems to me that we also share power with our children when we stay relational and act like ourselves when upset. Angry power is not blasted onto the child. And again when we do fail, we seek forgiveness.

We send a strong message about sharing power when we can allow the children to speak the truth in love to us when needed. I had such an opportunity with my oldest son, Jim, when he was about eleven years old.

Around this time, Jim (11) and I both were learning to walk in the Spirit and have an intimate relationship with Jesus. I wanted Jesus to change me in any way He wanted to. And I had my list ready. At the top of my list was--Stop yelling at my kids. So one day I sat down with Jim and we made a pact. We would help each other stop losing our tempers. If he heard me yell, he would scratch the top of his head. If I heard him yell, I would scratch the top of my head. No one else had to know what was going on. We would remind one another.

I want to tell you, it did not take very long before I stopped yelling and growling at my kids. It was wonderful! It was great! It was easy, because I had an instant, non-condemning reminder. The blessing from sharing power with my son was mostly mine, though he benefited as well.

And now I want to share a story from last year when I did not share my power very well and one of the twins called my hand on it. Chris and Greg wanted to go on a date and they asked if I would put the girls to bed (9, 6, 6, and 5). I agreed. Daddy gave instructions that no one should give Nana any trouble or they would not get to go to their cousin's party the next day. We watched a little TV and then it was time for bed. Tyler told me she wanted to stay up longer, that Mommy allowed it. I said, "No, not tonight." She pouted. I went into the twins' room and Kayli said, "I need a drink," and took off for the bathroom. Kori, on the top bunk, said, "My toe hurts." Brenna, who is always easy to put to bed, was fussing in the hall. I told Kori, "Your toe has not hurt while watching TV. Go to sleep." I left the room to put Brenna into her bed. When I returned to the twins' room, Kayli was still in the bathroom and Kori was downstairs getting a band-aid. Tyler had reluctantly gone to her room.

When Kori returned, I said nothing about her unscheduled trip to the first aid kit, and told her to get in bed while I went to speed Kayli along. As I turned to leave the room, I heard Kori say, "I'm stupid." I do not allow the kids to call themselves bad names, so I went over to the top bunk and tried to talk to her. She opened her mouth and began to squall very loudly. I began to lose it! Kayli returned to her bottom bunk as I was trying to find out why Kori was bawling. She finally sobbed, "I'm not gonna get to go to the party!"

I had said nothing at all about telling Daddy that they "gave me trouble," but I suppose she was quite concerned about it. My voice tone got tougher and tougher; I was feeling angry and frustrated and just wanted them to go to sleep. The battle in my mind was going back and forth between, "Act like yourself, synchronize, stay relational" and "I can't stand this squalling." I was feeling very grumpy and not sure exactly why. This intense impatience was not my usual way of handling things.

At the same time I am fussing at Kori and praying for myself to get control, I am taking her off the top bunk. I sat down on their beanbag with Kori in my lap. She was beginning to calm, but I was intent on making my point about the squalling and I imitated her. About the time Kori's cries turned to sobs, I heard a little voice from across the room say, "Nana, you are making fun of Kori." I answered with about the same tone that I'd been using with Kori, "Yes I am!" The Holy Spirit was about to break through my grouch.

In the next second I got it between the eyes. Kayli stood up from her bottom bunk, put her hands on her hips and declared quite royally, "That makes me want to hit you right in the nose!" I knew she was right as soon as she said it. I had begun the bedtime process with a wrong attitude. I had to take the blame. I began to melt and the Lord began to bring my brain back on line.

As I gathered both girls onto my lap, the next question I asked was, "What does Daddy mean by, 'don't give Nana any trouble?'" Kayli raised her hand and said, "I know what it means. It means, 'Don't give Nana any trouble.'" I kinda smiled inside as we explored the meaning a little further. By then both girls were in my lap and I was cooled down. I asked their forgiveness and said, "Can we start a new clean slate?" They gave me hugs and kisses and then climbed into their beds. I did not hear another peep from either one.

Later that night I was talking to the Lord Jesus about this yucky incident and how grumpy and short I was. He told me that the next morning I was to talk to all four girls again and tell them why I was so grumpy and to talk about the incident some more. I did not want to excuse my actions, but this was not my normal behavior and there was another factor besides plain old selfishness. So the next morning I went upstairs and called a little family meeting with the girls. I confessed again how grumpy I was to Kori. She nodded. I explained that I had been taking some medicine that I'd recently stopped taking and that was part of the reason I was so grumpy. I told them that I did not want to act that way with them and if I thought I was going to act like that again, I would get away from them. "And," I said, "If you notice I'm starting to get that grumpy, I want you to say something like, 'Nana, you're about to lose it.'" They heartily agreed. (Don't they love that kind of power?) I then said again, "Will you forgive me?" and they all gave me great big hugs. I love getting those kinds of hugs!

Another place I like to share my power is with the toddlers and preschoolers. We all let the tiny toddlers take us by the finger and lead us to the playroom or toys they want to share. Connor learned to say, "Sit, play, Nana," before he was two. With all the various ages, we can take a moment here and there to stop and play, or listen to a tale from school, a new rhyme, or a little story. And we do it lovingly, because we want them to be creatures of joy and love, not of fear. Sharing power builds loving and joyful bonds.

MODEL GIVING AND SERVING OTHERS

I've already shared about taking the girls to the Wal-Mart to buy supplies for the soldiers when the war in Iraq began. I mentioned taking them to buy gifts for the Christmas shoeboxes for needy children. Now I want to share a story that happened with Tyler (9). My best friend, Margie, and I took Tyler with us to a Waffle House that we go to frequently. We chat with the waitresses and are slightly acquainted with two or three of them. A while back we had noticed that one of the ladies was missing a front tooth and we had asked her about it. She told us that she was saving her money to get it fixed. On this day that Tyler was with us, Margie leaned over to me and said that the Lord was telling her to give the waitress a lump sum of money to help with her tooth. I was all for it and Margie left to go to the ATM to get the money. While she was gone Tyler asked me what was going on and I told her. When Margie returned with the money and gave it to the waitress, Tyler reached into her little purple purse and took out a dollar. She handed it to the waitress and said, "I want to help you, too." Neither Margie nor I had mentioned anything like that to Tyler. Watching young ones give spontaneously to others brings tears of joy and pride to all involved.

LEAD TO CHRIST WITH UNDERSTANDING

Many years ago I heard a wise pastor talk about child evangelism. He cautioned us to be certain that a child knows he or she is a sinner before encouraging them to receive Christ. He told us, "Never nod your head and say, 'You'd like to accept Christ, wouldn't you?'" I took this to heart and saw it proven when Jodi was about five. We were on staff with Campus Crusade for Christ and our business, our job, was evangelism and discipleship. It was normal to talk about these things around the house. One night Jodi asked us, "Can I ask Jesus into my heart?" We quizzed her a bit and asked, "Have you ever done anything wrong?" She sweetly answered, "N-o-o-o." Daddy told her that she could wait a while and we would talk some more about it later. About a year or so later, she asked again, "Can I ask Jesus into my heart?" We talked some more and this time the answer to, "Have you ever done anything wrong?" was an embarrassed, "Yes." Daddy led her in a prayer that went something like this: "Jesus, I know I have sinned. I know you died on the Cross for me. I thank you for forgiving me and I now ask You to come into my heart and teach me to follow You. Thank You for being my Savior. Amen.

I tell this story to illustrate how important it is to take your child seriously, but prayerfully do your best to be certain the child somewhat understands what he or she is doing. We want receiving Christ to be real on whatever level they are. We want to continue to talk about what they did so they will have assurance of their salvation. When it comes to communion and baptism, again we want to talk through on their level what the significance and symbolic nature of the events are.

SCHEDULED MENTORING

As your child reaches the age of ten or twelve to fourteen, beginning a scheduled time for Spiritual mentoring can be very significant. The age you do scheduled mentoring doesn't matter as much as does spending time together over the things of God. If Dad can do this, it will be even more powerful, especially as the child gets into the teen years.

Scheduled mentoring is my term for setting aside a particular time and place to meet with your child to talk about Spiritual things. My pastor takes his children when they are about eleven, one at a time, to a McDonald's before school one day a week. Chris spends special time with Tyler (age 9) on Tuesday nights before she goes to bed. Greg will begin taking her to breakfast in the 6th grade. At these kinds of get-togethers you can look at something in the Bible or use books that are designed for this kind of study with young people, or just be relational and talk. These kinds of devotional or instructional books come in many varieties.

You may already have some kind of ministry with adults, or you may feel petrified of talking to anyone, even your child, about the Bible and Jesus. Either way, it is worth the hard work and time to push through your fear to spend this kind of time with each child. If what you talk about matches how you walk, you will most likely see great results. Even if you don't immediately see great results, the time is not wasted when you spend time with your children in this way.

A PASTOR'S MESSAGE

Again I would like to share some ideas from a message that our pastor, Kevin Meyers (PK), gave on May 21, 2006. As I mentioned, PK does scheduled mentoring with his children and part of this teaching was based on what he is teaching his eleven-year old son through Jake's love of sports and playing football. The following is another of my rough paraphrases, but you can listen to the entire message on www.12Stone.com.

The Scriptural focus of the teaching was 1 Corinthians 9:24-27 where Paul compares the discipline and training required in sports and winning trophies with how we walk in our Spiritual journey. PK talked about three areas of discipline and how he wants to instill them in his son as he plays and watches sports.

The Discipline of Delayed Gratification

Athletes do not win trophies and championships overnight. They experience great pain in the present in order to win an award way into the future. Being able to delay gratification is important everywhere in life. Not delaying gratification causes losses in all areas of life— marriage, education, or any kind of reward we desire.

Pastor Kevin talked about a conversation he'd had with a friend, Jay Feely, who used to be a professional kicker with the Atlanta

Falcons. Feely told PK that he spent six months practicing and training in order to extend his kicking distance one to two yards further. He spent over 1000 hours practicing in order to have the privilege of 39 seconds on the field. PK reminded us that no one disciplines himself or delays gratification like that unless he or she wants something very badly. This is the kind of passion for loving God that we want to build into our children.

The Discipline of 'Now'

In PK's second point about discipline, he talked about how during a game, a good athlete has to shut out distractions and focus on the moment, the now. Fans at a basketball game try to take advantage of this when the opposing team is making a free-throw shot. Everyone yells and stomps and tries to distract the opponent's focus. Great athletes shut out everything else and fully engage in now. They take full responsibility for managing their focus. We can apply this focus on the now to how we walk with God and how we parent.

The Discipline of Voices

After making his points about delayed gratification and focusing on now, PK talked about two other lessons he wants his son to learn from playing sports. He frequently tells Jake to remember, "Who you listen to matters. You will hear many voices during a game. Listen to the coach. Know which coach to listen to. Know his voice." This applies to how we listen for God's voice to guide us rather than listening to what our culture, our flesh or the enemy tells us.

PK also reminds Jake to ask himself before and after a game, *who ought I to be pleasing?* He reminds Jake that there is an order for the ones that he must be pleasing: PK told the audience what he tells Jake:

> Number one, please your Heavenly Father. He is the most important. Second, please me, your Earthly Father. I am your first coach. I am not going to hand you over to another for his philosophy to become yours. That's why I am here at every practice and every game. Third, please yourself. Ask yourself after every practice and every game: *Did I do my best? Did I stand against my fear? Did I focus? Did I make good use of what God has put in me?* Fourth, *Did I please my coach?* Fifth, *Did I please my teammates?*" And Last, *Did I please the crowd?* Fans are fickle. They are the least important. At the end of it all, ask yourself, *did I get my rewards from the top three?* They are the ones who matter? The others will only give you worldly rewards.

I trust that not only will these points about self-discipline give you a good example of some things to teach your children, but will at the same time encourage you to walk your life the same way that PK is teaching Jake to live.

GRACE VERSUS LEGALISM

And what if you do "everything right" within your power and strive to follow God while rearing your children and the results in your child's life are not what you'd hoped? I encourage you again to stay away from shame and condemnation when you talk with your child about disappointments or failures, or even when you talk *about* him or her to others. I encourage you to avoid using any kind of verbal threats concerning God and how He may be evaluating behavior. Legalistic threats do not work or help and painting a distorted view of God can bring very detrimental results to someone's heart. Mentors do speak to behavior, but they speak to it in love without condemning the person. Love and acceptance of the person, without condoning the behavior, will go much further in keeping that relationship that is vital to you and your child, in spite of failure and disappointments that happen along the way. And don't beat up on yourself.

As we are going through life, Deuteronomy 6:7 is not telling us to bash our children over the head with God's wrath, but rather to speak of His love and acceptance. And when speaking of His ways to live, to speak of them without condemnation, to speak about why it is better to follow God's ways--and then leave the young person in God's hands.

SUMMARY: OUR LIMITATIONS

As we come to the end of our time here, I again remind you that, "More is caught than taught." It is vital that we parents grow in maturity, recover from our wounds and move forward in faith so as to be the best models possible.

Joy is the way we thrive best, and I am thankful that building joy is such a rewarding activity that benefits us all, making it easier for us to thrive. As we spread joy smiles and come alongside of one another, we will find the strength to suffer well. Synchronizing with one another will put us on the same page, build trust and understanding, and enable us to reconnect after conflict. In addition, we must share with others in authentic relationships the load of parenting, the pain of recovery, and the tasks for maturity.

If we desire a strong healthy family filled with mature people, we will have to walk on our "knees" some of the time, ask for help and set aside pride that will cause us to stumble. None of us can parent perfectly and no child will turn out without a flaw. So wherever you are in your journey, when you find yourself in a mess, don't dismay—find God in the mess—He is there and deeply desires to meet you. Seek help from others who have gone before you. Don't try to parent alone. Even if you feel alone, remember God is there.

I look back on what I did not know and I grieve. I look back on God's grace in spite of what I didn't know and I gratefully thank Him. I look back and thank my children for their forgiveness and love. But most of all, I want to encourage you readers to hold on to the fact that God's grace and faithfulness are greater than our limitations and failures. He is not surprised by anything in our lives. He has made a way for help and He truly desires that we thrive.

APPENDICES

APPENDIX A: BRAIN CALMING TECHNIQUES AND HEALING PRAYER

"SHALOM MY BODY"[4]

1) With your fingers or fists, lightly tap on each side of your chest (like Tarzan, but not so hard). Do it rhythmically to match your heartbeat while taking a deep breath. As you exhale, rub the same place on your chest as you say aloud, "Whenever I am afraid I will trust in You, Oh, Lord." (Psalm 56:3)

You can even insert different words into the verse such as "angry," "sad," "I want to run out the door," or "I want to scream at my children." The vagus nerve runs from the brain to the abdomen on both sides of the chest there and it is closest to the surface at that point. This will reset the RC's.

2) Just as newborn babies do the startle reflex, you can throw your hands up and backwards, head backwards at the same time, and loudly gasp a deep breath. Slowly bring hands and head back down while repeating the verse.

---

[4] "Shalom My Body" from www.thrivingrecovery.org pastor Ed Khouri's Belonging Module of Thriving Recovery.

3) Take a deep breath while "yawning" to the left, release and look ahead, take a deep breath while "yawning" to the right," release and repeat the verse. Any of these three will help calm the brain, reset RC's. Number one seems to be most people's favorite.

There is a fourth method for calming the brain and resetting relational circuits. When we think about something that we appreciate, it physically helps the brain. Appreciation is anything that makes us feel like saying, "Ahhhh." Thinking of the beach, children laughing, having a campfire or beautiful parts of nature bring a smile to our faces and calm our brains. Here is the way to incorporate this into your family's arsenal for calming:

Together with the children who are old enough, everyone closes their eyes and thinks of something that makes them feel good and want to say, "Ahhh." Then each person gives their memory a name of one or two words. We open our eyes and each tells their name. If desired, everyone can also describe their appreciation picture. Explain that when anyone gets upset, this will be one of the ways we can help each other calm. We will want to be kind and not pushy about it. When it is appropriate, we can use the "appreciation name" to help someone calm. Children can also know our appreciation memories' names and remind us when we are upset. Again, they will like this use of power. It is helpful to have two or three of these for each person.

THE IMMANUEL PROCESS (CONDENSED)[5]

When you know that someone has encountered a painful moment or has an unresolved trauma, first ask if they are willing to ask Jesus about it. If so, make sure the relational circuits are on by doing one of the "Shalom My Body" exercises from above. Then ask them to look for a memory when they sensed and knew Jesus was with them (or an appreciation memory).

Upon connecting with Jesus in a spirit of prayer, age appropriately, talk to Jesus about the painful event. You can ask Him to show the child where He was when it happened. He will show them. You can ask Him, "What do you want (name) to know about this?" Sit quietly and help the child, but do not give them suggestions.

If it is appropriate, you can ask Jesus to show the child, "What did (name) believe about himself/herself when this happened?" After Jesus shows them this, you can ask Him, "Please show (name) what You think about that, Jesus." This will uncover any lies believed and replace them with God's truth.

When you feel the person has found peace about the painful memory, thank Jesus and close the prayer. Process a little with them after they open their eyes. We want to develop an Immanuel Lifestyle that will keep both us and our children healed and free.

---

[5] For more information on this prayer process, see www.kclehman.com and www.lifemodel.org Books: *Outsmarting Yourself,* by Dr. Karl Lehman, *Share Immanuel* booklet, by Dr. James Wilder and Chris Coursey.

APPENDIX B: CHILDREN LEARN WHAT THEY LIVE

IF a child lives with Criticism, He learns to Condemn

IF a child lives with Hostility, He learns to Fight

IF a child lives with Ridicule, He learns to be Shy

IF a child lives with Shame, He learns to feel Guilty

IF a child lives with Tolerance, He learns to be Patient

IF a child lives with Encouragement, He learns Confidence

IF a child lives with Praise, He learns to Appreciate

IF a child lives with Fairness, He learns Justice

IF a child lives with Security, He learns to have Faith

IF a child lives with Approval, He learns to Like himself

IF a child lives with Acceptance and Friendship, He learns to find Love in the world.

Dorothy Law Nolte

BIBLIOGRAPHY AND RECOMMENDED READING

Living With Men; The Life Model; Red Dragon Cast Down; Between Father and Sons --Dr. E. James Wilder—available from www.lifemodel.org

How to Really Love Your Child—Dr. Ross Campbell, Victor Books, 1979

How To Really Love Your Teenager-- Dr. Ross Campbell, Victor Books, 1981

The Transformation of the Inner Man-- John and Paula Sandford, Bridge Publishing, 1982

Families Where Grace is in Place, Jeff VanVonderen, Bethany House Publishers, 1992

Six Point Plan for Raising Happy and Healthy Children—John Rosemond, Andrews and McMeel, 1989

The Developing Mind, Daniel J. Siegel, The Guilford Press, 1999

Parenting From the Inside Out, Daniel J. Siegel, Penguin Group, 2003

Healing the Hardware of the Soul, Dr. Daniel Amen, The Free Press, 2002

Toilet Training in Less than a Day, Nathan Azrin, Pocket Books, 1989

FOR SPIRITUAL GROWTH AND VICTORY

The Rest of the Gospel, Dan Stone, One Press, 2000

Lifetime Guarantee, Bill Gillham Harvest House Publishers, 1993

The Confident Woman, Anabel Gillham, Harvest House Publishers, 1993

Hinds Feet on High Places, Hannah Hurnurd, Tyndale House Publishers, 1975

Hudson Taylor's Spiritual Secret, Dr. and Mrs. Howard Taylor, Moody Press, 1932

Defeating Dark Angels, Dr. Charles Kraft, Servant Publications, 1992

Jewels for My Journey, Barbara Moon, lulu.com/barbaramoon, 2006

The Lost Dome of Atron, (fiction) Barbara Moon, lulu.com 2006

Leader's Guide and Workbook for Hinds' Feet on High Places (Hurnard), Barbara Moon, lulu.com 2007

FOR FUN: *The Craziosity Twins*, Barbara Moon, lulu.com, 2006

Made in the USA
Lexington, KY
07 April 2017